ATLANTIS
BENEATH THE
ICE

Praise for the previous edition:

"Rose and Rand Flem-Ath were the first authors to develop the idea that the earth's surface area may at times shift on its mantle, causing radical changes in the geography of the planet that result in the almost total destruction of civilization."

WHITLEY STRIEBER, AUTHOR OF *COMMUNION*
AND RADIO HOST OF THE SHOW *DREAMLAND*

"Rand and Rose Flem-Ath have assembled a daring and extremely convincing argument that the location of the lost civilization of Atlantis is the Antarctic continent. . . . Combining mythology with a wealth of scientific and historical information, the Flem-Aths' research will shake a few foundations."

NEXUS

ATLANTIS
BENEATH THE
ICE

THE FATE OF THE
LOST CONTINENT

RAND and ROSE FLEM-ATH

Bear & Company
Rochester, Vermont • Toronto, Canada

Bear & Company
One Park Street
Rochester, Vermont 05767
www.BearandCompanyBooks.com

Text stock is SFI certified

Bear & Company is a division of Inner Traditions International

Originally published in 1995 by Stoddart Publishing Co. Limited under the title
When the Sky Fell: In Search of Atlantis
Revised and expanded edition published by Bear and Company in 2012

Library of Congress Cataloging-in-Publication Data
Flem-Ath, Rand.
    Atlantis beneath the ice / Rand Flem-Ath and Rose Flem-Ath. — Rev. and
expanded ed.
        p. cm.
    "Originally published in 1995 by Stoddart Publishing Co. Limited under the
title When the Sky Fell: In Search of Atlantis."
    Includes bibliographical references and index.
    ISBN 978-1-59143-137-4 (pbk.) — ISBN 978-1-59143-895-3 (e-book)
    1. Atlantis (Legendary place) 2. Antarctica. 3. Lost continents. I. Flem-Ath,
Rose. II. Title.
    GN751.F54 2012
    998.9—dc23

2011040156

Printed and bound in the United States by Lake Book Manufacturing
The text stock is SFI certified. The Sustainable Forestry Initiative® program
promotes sustainable forest management.

10   9   8   7   6   5   4   3   2   1

Text design by Priscilla H. Baker
Text layout by Virginia Scott Bowman
This book was typeset in Garamond Premier Pro with Swiss and Copperplate used
as display typefaces

To send correspondence to the authors of this book, mail a first-class letter to the
authors c/o Inner Traditions • Bear & Company, One Park Street, Rochester, VT
05767, and we will forward the communication or visit the authors' website at
www.flem-ath.com.

In memory of Charles Hapgood,
a generous mentor who urged us to carry the work further.

CONTENTS

ACKNOWLEDGMENTS

As we wrote this Acknowledgements page we marvelled at how lucky we have been in the people we have met as a result of the original publication of this book. Those listed below have been either generous with their wise advice, encouragement, mentorship, patient art of listening or professional help; or helped with access to original research material or media exposure for our work. Sometimes all of the above! And so without further ado (listed here in alphabetical order since we could think of no other way to fairly distribute our heartfelt gratitude) are those who balanced the harsh lessons we learned with their fine professionalism or their friendship and generosity of spirit.

Mindy Branstetter for her patience, Barbara Hand Clow for her early enthusiasm, Steve Detwiler, Adrian Gilbert for wise counsel about a difficult subject, Jon Graham for opening the door, Ray Grasse for always 'getting it', Gwaai who shared his deep knowledge of his people's past, Bill Hamilton who gave support when it mattered the most, Beth Hapgood, Fred Hapgood, Doug Kenyon, Laura Lee, Jeffery Lindholm for his excellent eye on the manuscript, John Michell, Caroline North for seeing the big picture but never missing the nuances, Stel Pavlou for giving credit where it was due and for his sense of humor, Paul Roberts, Alan Samson who captained a listing ship through very dangerous waters and understood the source of the damage, Martin Schnell, Whitley Strieber, Greg Taylor, Jay Weidner, John Anthony West for an early invitation to join the quest, Tony and Carol Wharrie who have patiently heard it all.

Also, the staff at the Yale/Beinecke Rare Book and Manuscript Library were very helpful in facilitating our access to Charles Hapgood's archives. Likewise, the staff at the Jewish National and University Library in Jerusalem allowed us the privilege of viewing the Einstein-Hapgood correspondence. G. Thomas Tanselle of the John Simon Guggenheim Memorial Foundation generously sent us copies of Albert Einstein's writings about Charles Hapgood. Our thanks also go to the staff at the Dwight D. Eisenhower Presidential Library who provided copies of Charles Hapgood's correspondence with the President.

INTRODUCTION
TO THE NEW EDITION

It is good to see the word *Atlantis* prominently strutting its stuff in the title of this new and expanded edition of *When the Sky Fell*. This tarnished word has been maligned, misinterpreted, and tossed back and forth between timid suitors unsure whether to embrace or disdain it.

That is understandable, if a tad fainthearted. Bias is never easy to fight. But bias against a word that denigrates no one? Seems absurd. Nevertheless, after the first edition of *When the Sky Fell* was published in January 1995, we soon learned that there are those who lose their senses so completely when the "A-word" (as author John Anthony West so succinctly labeled it) is mentioned that they stumble about blind and deaf to anything else, devoid of the resources to grasp any other concept that happens to be in the same room—or more precisely, in the same book.

For example, the theory of earth crust displacement, which proposes that the earth's outer shell catastrophically shifts over the planet's subterranean layers, forms the scaffolding of our quest for the lost civilization. It receives what can only be described as a hysterical reception in some quarters, even though it has hung out with some rather respectable types in the past. Was Albert Einstein silly? Most of us can probably put our hand up to a resounding no on that one. Nevertheless, his support and his active guidance of Professor Charles Hapgood, who developed the theory and who, in turn, wrote that ours was "the *first* truly scientific exploration of my work that has ever been done," makes our critics break out in hives. Their answer to this conundrum? Ignore this uncomfortable fact. Or actually lie to their students about what the great physicist said about the theory. (Yes, it happened.) Or better yet, let's just claim that poor old Albert was growing senile or was out-of-date. Any or all of the above choices will do to whitewash this inconvenient truth.

Never did we imagine in 1977, when we started exchanging letters with Hapgood, that decades later we would find ourselves writing an introduction to a new edition of the controversial book that had gradually evolved as a result of that encouraging relationship.

In this new, expanded edition we detail our fresh research gleaned from three weeks of study at Hapgood's long-neglected Yale archives. We delve into his correspondence with President Dwight D. Eisenhower and visit the president's archives in Abilene, Kansas. These forgotten documents reveal how Christopher Columbus may have possessed a world map drawn by the survivors of Atlantis. Fragments of the map incorporate astronomical clues pointing to the date it was originally drafted, a date—3800 BCE—that coincides with the dawn of Egyptian civilization.

We learn how Einstein urged that Hapgood be awarded a Guggenheim Foundation Grant because his earth crust displacement theory was "fascinating and important."

You'll discover that a rare, debilitating genetic disease common to the Haida of British Columbia, on Canada's west coast, was also suffered by the pharaohs of ancient Egypt, suggesting that the two vastly separated peoples may have had a common ancestor.

We follow the career of the seventeenth-century Jesuit priest Athanasius Kircher as he skates across the fragile ice of a frozen river and watch as he survives that danger to rise to become the Einstein of his century. And we marvel at the lost Egyptian map of Atlantis that Kircher rediscovered.

You will be introduced to a new generation of international scientists who are challenging the fixations of their predecessors and independently studying the past with a fresh perspective.

Evidence is uncovered that demonstrates that intricate, advanced water-management systems were developed in the highlands of New Guinea immediately after the fall of Atlantis.

We reveal the existence of a shadowy cave where DNA samples taken from a young man's remains point to the astonishing fact that he had traveled thousands of miles from the southern tip of South America to his death in Alaska. Nobody knows how or why.

And we celebrate a new generation of Latin American archaeologists who have come to the radical conclusion that South America was populated *before* North America.

Science is exploding, and the blast is providing more and more energy to drive the theory of earth crust displacement and the search for the lost continent.

A lot has changed since 1981, when we quit our jobs in Canada and packed up a trunk with all our worldly belongings, enough money to survive for three months, and enough naïveté to believe we could manage on love and luck and presented ourselves at that mecca for librarians everywhere, the Reading Room of London's British Museum. Under its robin-egg-blue dome, shutting out the great city's roar, we devoured book after book. Some of them, like Charles Lyell's 1830 *Principles of Geology* or James Hutton's 1795 *Theory of the Earth with Proofs and Illustrations,* could only be accessed from the Rare Book Room. Books that took months to receive back home were presented to us in the Reading Room within hours. We're lucky enough to be able to say that even though, longing for the wilderness you can only find in this part of the world, we returned home five years later, our London adventure resulted in more rich experiences than we could have imagined and plenty of raw material for our own contributions to the library.

It's no longer necessary for any writer to go to such lengths to find the intellectual spring of his or her subject matter. The Internet delivers any text we want to our eager eyes within seconds. Has to be a good thing, right? You'd think so. And for most of us it probably is. But don't hold your breath thinking it will result in any paradigm-busting breakthroughs in the places where ideas are supposed to rule. Yes, in the years since *When the Sky Fell* was published a lot has changed. But a lot hasn't.

The Internet offers a potential gold mine of knowledge, bringing together more material than any individual could possibly explore in a lifetime. But it's not well known that the search engines used to access this wealth of information direct researchers primarily to articles that espouse the conventional streams of current thought. Good enough, perhaps, to access the latest trend in scientific pronouncements but far less effective for challenging hallowed assumptions and developing alternative theories. In fact, contrary to expectations, between 1945 and 2005, as millions of scholarly articles went online, researchers increasingly began to cite fewer and fewer articles. Rather than expanding the parameters within their fields of research, online access has unexpectedly resulted in a troubling narrowing of science and scholarship.[1]

In contrast with how the Internet has narrowed the world of some researchers, it has also opened the door for Atlantis to shine again. Brushed up and polished to be presented to a new audience—whether skeptical or keen, inspired artist or naysayer, geographer or psychologist—Atlantis can step out and be judged in the light of a new age of information.

The remnants of the lost continent surface in intriguing places. In these pages we delve into the records of people from around the globe who fled the rising ocean and scrambled to safety in the mountains where, in a bid to survive, they began the sophisticated task of domesticating native plants. This sudden, global rise of the finely tuned art and science of agriculture in the highlands starts mysteriously at the precise time that Atlantis fell, suggesting a forgotten past unexplored by traditional archaeology.

The chronicle of Atlantis is properly called a legend, not a myth. A legend tells of events that took place in the real world at a specific time involving human beings. A myth, in contrast, is enacted on a supernatural stage where events are controlled by all-powerful gods and goddesses. Plato, the source of the Atlantis legend, tells us that the island continent perished at a specific time, some 11,600 years ago. He says that the vast island was located in a "real ocean" and was destroyed by earthquakes and floods of extraordinary violence. Gods don't determine the unfolding events in this legend. Instead, it is the palpable forces of nature that prevail against Atlantis and end its rule. Atlantis is a legendary, but real, place that can be found.

For decades we have enthusiastically perused world mythology (which is implicitly denigrated by conventional scholars), examining its invaluable details about the lost continent's tragedy and its possible location that have been passed down from generation to generation by oral tradition. Every corner of the globe has generated a lost island paradise myth. Again and again similar events transpire: An island home is destroyed by a geological catastrophe. Often, a dramatic deviation in the sun's course immediately precedes a Great Flood. Each myth adds new particulars. In the Vedic literature the great destructive Flood is followed by a "dire winter" that encapsulates the island homeland in snow and ice. And the Cherokee story of a lost land talks of a place that experiences a climate opposite to that of North America, suggesting that their vanished paradise thrived in the Southern Hemisphere. But as much as mythology might enrich the legend of Atlantis, it is still Plato's account that provides the fullest and most complete record.

What is often forgotten is that Plato's account of Atlantis—passed to him from Solon, *the lawmaker of Athens,* who in turn had received it from one of the most learned of Egyptian priests—includes facts unknown to the ancient Greeks. It details the exact size, location, and fate of an actual island continent that lay in a vast body of water known as the real ocean, located beyond their known world. This description, as we show, is an accurate depiction of the world as a citizen of Atlantis would have seen it *from* the shores of Antarctica.

The word *Atlantis* has come to have many meanings. Some choose to interpret Plato's depiction as an allegory used to elucidate moral lessons about human history. Others see it as the key to a spiritual quest that might unlock mysteries of the human soul. We've often been asked about the spiritual aspects of the Atlantis legend. It is our deep belief that such explorations are private affairs for each individual to address in his or her own lifetime. In an age of uncertainty and manic change, we've seen that many of those who blithely offer spiritual advice to strangers are enticing vulnerable people to enter the superficial company of a pseudoguru.

The only message we see in the legend of Atlantis is one that is obvious to many of us living in the twenty-first century. Its fate provides an abject lesson in the reality that our planet is fragile and its existence can be finite. It can be destroyed by natural forces and, increasingly, human greed. The suffocation of overpopulation, the source of virtually every environmental problem we face, and our profound disrespect for the land will bring an end long before the next earth crust displacement. The good news being that we don't need to rely on gods or any other supernatural force to heal the earth. It's up to us.

Over the years we have consistently maintained that the word *Atlantis* signifies nothing less, and nothing more, than the name of earth's first advanced civilization. A civilization whose accomplishments even outshone those that followed thousands of years later, including those of Egypt, China, Mexico, or the ancient cultures of the Middle East. Plato's account describes engineering feats that far exceed the spectacular pyramids of Egypt or Mexico. The Atlanteans amassed considerable astronomical data and through their imperial navy accurately mapped the entire globe before they were felled by a worldwide geological disaster. Yet it is a disaster not due to devastate us again anytime soon but one that swept human history back to square one and tore page after page from the record, leaving gaping holes in the archive that remain as tantalizing, unsolved mysteries that many of us continue to try and solve, convinced that the answers are just within our reach.

Our own quest for Atlantis has always focused on the hunt for a technologically advanced civilization hidden from view by the ravages of time. On the way we've learned invaluable lessons about prejudice, duplicity, and the dangers of "group think"—from whatever direction it comes. But we've also been privileged to meet readers who bring fresh eyes and the gift of curiosity to the adventure. Hand in hand with them are artists from around the world, working in all mediums, who have favored our work with their imaginations. It's been a bumpy but fascinating ride. We invite you to jump in, fasten your seatbelts, and join us for the next leg of the journey.

ONE

MEMORANDUM
FOR THE PRESIDENT

KEENE TEACHERS COLLEGE

KEENE, NEW HAMPSHIRE

To: President Dwight D. Eisenhower

From: Charles H. Hapgood,   August 3, 1960

     Professor of History

Re: **THE PIRI REIS WORLD MAP OF 1513 AND THE LOST MAP OF
COLUMBUS**

Memorandum

For several centuries scholars have been searching
for the lost map of Christopher Columbus. The map is
referred to by Columbus' contemporaries and by the
historian Las Cada, as one he used to navigate to the New
World.

In 1929, a map was discovered in the former Imperial
Palace (The Seraglio) in Constantinople, authored by a
Turkish admiral of the sixteenth century, Piri Reis. In
the inscriptions written on this map the author states that
the western part, showing the American coasts, was copied
from a map that had been in the possession of Christopher
Columbus, but which had fallen into the hands of Piri Reis

with the booty seized from eight Spanish ships captured by him in a battle off the coast of Valencia in 1501 or 1508.

The Piri Reis map (a copy of which accompanies this memorandum) attracted the attention of President Kemal Ataturk, and of the American Secretary of State, Henry Stimson, who, in 1932, asked the Turkish Government for a color facsimile of the map, and for a search of Turkish archives and collections to see if the lost map of Columbus might not be found. The facsimile of the map now hangs in the Map Division of the Library of Congress, but the original Piri Reis worked from—Columbus own map (or a copy of it)—was never found.

We now have excellent reason to believe that the original map still exists, and in the Spanish archives! The reason that this map has remained so long undiscovered appears to be, simply, that it is very different from the other contemporary maps and is not at all what scholars would expect to find in a map of Columbus'. It is not a map Columbus himself made, but one he found in the Old World. It should resemble the western side of the Piri Reis map, if it can be found.

Evidence of its present whereabouts came to me through my old friend and scientific collaborator, James H. Campbell, who, together with his father, a professional geographer, actually saw this map in 1893. I am enclosing a separate account of this incident in Mr. Campbell's own words. It seems that in 1893, at the time of the Columbian Exposition in Chicago, the Spanish Government built and sent to America replicas of Columbus' three ships. The caravels were sailed across the Atlantic and through the Great Lakes to Chicago. It was there that Mr. Campbell and his father were invited, as he describes in detail, to see Columbus' own map in the chart room of the *Santa*

Maria. In addition to the important purpose of clearing up many mysteries relating to the Discovery of America, we have another purpose in asking that a search be made for the map now. Studies of the map by various scholars have shown that it contains many details that were not known to the geographers in 1513. These indicate that the map must descend from maps made in very ancient times, and that navigators (possibly of Phoenician origin) discovered and explored the coasts of America, perhaps a millennium before the Christian era. This, of course, tends to give support to the tradition that Columbus brought a map from the Old World. It seems that Columbus left the Old World with quite a good map of America in his pocket!

The most remarkable detail of the Piri Reis map indicating its enormous age was pointed out by Captain Arlington Mallery some years ago. He stated that the lower part of the map showed the sub-glacial topography of Queen Maud Land, Antarctica, and the Palmer Peninsula. After four years of study of the map we came to recognize that Captain Mallery's statement was correct, but, desiring the most authoritative checking of our conclusions, we submitted the data to the cartographic staff of the Strategic Air Command. I attach a letter from Col. Harold Z. Ohlmeyer, Commander of the 8th Reconnaissance Technical Squadron, SAC, in confirmation. Needless to say this is a matter of enormous importance for cartography and for history. The Antarctic ice cap is at present one mile thick over the areas shown on the Piri Reis Map. Consultations with geological specialists have indicated beyond question the truth that the data on the map is many thousands of years old. It seems that the Antarctic ice cap covered the Queen Maud Land coast not later than 6,000 years ago. The map information must have been obtained

earlier by the Phoenicians or by some earlier (and
unknown) people.

If the Columbus map can now be found we shall learn
whether it contained the Antarctic data, or whether Piri
Reis used another source map. If the Columbus map did contain
the data, then we will know he found the map in Europe, and
that therefore he had a good idea of where he was going.

The most important step at the present time is to push
the search in Spain for the map that was on the replica of
the *Santa Maria* during the summer of 1893. Success in this
search will make it possible to rewrite, in a fundamental
way, the history of the Discovery of America.

Very sincerely yours,
Charles H. Hapgood
Keene Teachers College[1]

Professor Charles Hapgood's memo got the president's attention. Eisenhower authorized the search for the ancient map that Columbus had on board during his historic 1492 voyage across the Atlantic. The American ambassador to Spain was instructed to use his influence to find the map.

Hapgood was seeking the holy grail of ancient maps, the so-called *mappa mundus,* thought to be the original map of the world. He believed the Piri Reis map was but a fragment of this much older, complete, and accurate document that predated the European age of discovery.

We'll follow Charles Hapgood's attempt to locate a surviving copy of the mappa mundus and reveal why his quest was frustrated.

THE ROE DEER SKIN

In November 1929, Halil Edhem, the director of Turkey's National Museum, was hunched over his solitary task of classifying documents.

He pulled toward him a map drawn on roe deer skin. As Halil opened the chart to its full dimensions (about two feet by three feet wide, or sixty by ninety centimeters), he was surprised by how much of the New World was depicted on a map dated 1513.

The document was the legacy of a pirate turned Turkish admiral, Piri Reis (ca. 1470–1554). He was born in Gallipoli, a naval base on the Marmara Sea, and was the nephew of Kemal Reis, a pirate who had reinvented himself as a Turkish admiral adventurer who had made his name in naval warfare. At the time, the distinction between pirate and admiral was more flexible than might be expected looking back through the lens of Hollywood.

Piri Reis began his career as a pirate sailing with his famous uncle from 1487 to 1493. It was during these voyages that he was introduced to the lucrative spoils of piracy. The fleet fought other pirates and captured and plundered enemy ships. In 1495, Kemal Reis's skill in the art of battle earned him an invitation to join the Imperial Turkish Fleet. His nephew accompanied him to his new assignment.

The pirates had become respectable admirals.

After Kemal Reis was killed during a naval battle in 1502, Piri Reis turned his back on the seafaring life and began a second career as a mapmaker. A perfectionist, Piri Reis would not tolerate the slightest error in his drawings. He authored a careful and detailed study of the Mediterranean titled *Kitabi Bahriye*.

Professor Afet Inan's *Life and Works of the Turkish Admiral: Piri Reis,* with its bold subtitle, *THE OLDEST MAP OF AMERICA, DRAWN BY PIRI REIS,* was translated into English in 1954. Its pages contain a hint of Piri Reis, the man.

> The first official acknowledgment of Piri's deeds is an account of the sea fights in the years 1499–1502. The actual commander-in-chief of the fleet belonging to the Supreme Admiral of all Sea-Forces was Kemal Reis. In his fleet Piri was given official command of some of the vessels. His service in the battles (1500–1502)

against the Venetians was remarkable. The great advantages that the Ottoman Empire acquired by the Treaty of Venice in 1502 were made possible mainly by the brave deeds of these seamen.[2]

Piri Reis created his famous map in 1513 using older source maps, including charts captured from Christopher Columbus. The Turks had boarded one of Columbus's ships before the crew had a chance to throw the charts into the sea, which was standard practice in a time when the contours of the planet remained veiled in mystery and maps held precious secrets.

A COLUMBUS CONTROVERSY

The general public first learned of the map's existence in the February 23, 1932, issue of the *Illustrated London News*. Titled "A Columbus Controversy: America—And Two Atlantic Charts," the article noted, "Columbus got little further than the mouth of the Orinoco, in Venezuela, in his voyage along the coast of South America in 1498, so that the stretches of the South American coast given in the Piri Reis's chart must have been copied from other sources."[3]

In the July 23 edition of the same magazine, Akcura Yusuf, president of the Turkish Historical Research Society, wrote a more detailed account:

Piri Reis himself explains, in one of the marginal notes on his map, how he prepared it:

This section explains the way the map was prepared. It is the only chart of its kind existing now. I, personally, drew and prepared it. In preparing the map I used about twenty old charts and eight "Mappa Monde" (i.e., the charts called "Jaferiye" by the Arabs, and prepared at the time of Alexander the Great, in which the whole inhabited world is shown); the charts of the West Indies; and the new maps made by four Portuguese, showing the Sind, Indian, and

HAPGOOD—
THE U.S. AIR FORCE CARTOGRAPHIC OFFICE

One of Charles Hapgood's students told him about the radio broadcast. Hapgood was immediately fascinated and decided to "investigate the map as thoroughly as I could."[6]

Since Mallery had used the U.S. Navy for his investigations, Hapgood decided to get a second opinion from the cartographic staff of the Strategic Air Command (SAC). The U.S. Air Force investigators came to the same conclusions as those of the U.S. Navy. They determined that the southern part of the map did in fact depict portions of *subglacial* Antarctica. However, conventional wisdom dictated that the island continent hadn't been discovered until 1818.

U.S. Air Force Lt. Col. Harold Z. Ohlmeyer wrote to Hapgood on July 6, 1960.

COPY

RECONNAISSANCE TECHNICAL SQUADRON (SAC)*

UNITED STATES AIR FORCE

WESTOVER AIR FORCE BASE

MASSACHUSETTS

                                        6 July 1960

Subject: Admiral Piri Reis World Map

To: Professor Charles H. Hapgood

Keene Teachers College

Keene, New Hampshire

Dear Professor Hapgood:

     Your request for evaluating certain unusual features of the Piri Reis World Map of 1513 by this organization has been reviewed.

     The claim that the lower part of the map portrays the

---

*SAC stands for Strategic Air Command

Princess Martha coast of Queen Maud Land, Antarctica, and the Palmer Peninsula is reasonable. We find this the most logical and in all probability the correct interpretation of the map.

The geographic detail shown in the lower part of the map agrees very remarkably with the results of the seismic profile made across the top of the ice cap by the Swedish-British-Norwegian Expedition of 1949.

This indicates the coastline had been mapped before it was covered by the ice cap.

The ice cap in this region is now about a mile thick. We have no idea how the data on this map can be reconciled with the supposed state of geographic knowledge in 1513.

(signed)

HAROLD Z. OHLMEYER

Lt. Colonel, USA

Commander[7]

This letter from Lt. Col. Ohlmeyer was included in Hapgood's 1960 memo to President Eisenhower. Not included, however, were the salient remarks of U.S. Air Force Capt. Lorenzo W. Burroughs (chief of the Cartographic Section that worked on the Piri Reis map). He wrote, "The agreement of the Piri Reis Map with the seismic profile of this area made by the Norwegian-British-Swedish Expedition of 1949, supported by your solution of the grid, places beyond a reasonable doubt the conclusion that the original source maps must have been made before the present Antarctic ice cap covered the Queen Maud Land coasts."[8]

CORRESPONDING WITH HAPGOOD

Our adventure with the study of ancient maps began in the summer of 1977 when Charles Hapgood replied to an article we wrote outlining our belief that Antarctica was once the site of Atlantis. We'd concluded that Hapgood's theory of earth crust displacement was the missing link that could unravel the mystery of the lost island continent. Hapgood sent the following letter.

CHARLES H. HAPGOOD

R.F.D. 3

WINCHESTER, NEW HAMPSHIRE 03470

August 3rd, 1977

Dear Rose and Rand,

I am astonished and delighted by your article, which arrived here today. Believe it or not, it is the <u>first</u> truly scientific exploration of my work that has ever been done. You have found evidence for crust displacement that I did not find.

However, it would seem that you are not aware of a book I published in 1966 entitled *Maps of the Ancient Sea Kings.* Since you are considering presenting your article to the Royal Geographical Society (of which I was a member until I stopped paying my dues), you should examine this book, and I am mailing a copy of it to you.

What I found, after long research, was that many maps considered of medieval or Renaissance origin are in fact copies of copies of maps drawn in very remote antiquity, and among them is one showing a deglacial Antarctica. I was able to solve the projections of these maps with the help of a mathematician, and have them confirmed by the Cartographic staff of the Strategic Air Command at Westover Air Force Base in Massachusetts. . . . It may be that after examining this book you may decide to reduce somewhat your emphasis on Atlantis, that is on the myths, for the book contains enough hard evidence to stand by itself.

Let me congratulate you on the work you have done!

Sincerely,

(signed)

Charles H. Hapgood.[9]

A week later a copy of *Maps of the Ancient Sea Kings* arrived. Far from dampening our enthusiasm for the idea that Antarctica may have once been Atlantis, the book had the opposite effect. We concluded that the ancient maps of subglacial Antarctica provided stunning evidence in support of our theory.

After the publication of the first edition of *When the Sky Fell* in January 1995, we returned to the Piri Reis map with two purposes in mind. First, to determine if there were grounds to support Mallery and Hapgood's claim that the source maps used in the construction of the Piri Reis map were hundreds of years older than the 1513 date of its construction. And, second, to discover where these source maps, if they still existed, might be today.

SOURCES FOR THE PIRI REIS MAP: HOW OLD?

Hapgood and his students found to their surprise that this ancient map, which should have been full of errors, was remarkably accurate. It possessed a standard of technical excellence beyond what Europeans could have achieved in 1513.

It wasn't until the 1730s, when John Harrison invented and perfected the marine chronometer, a highly sophisticated mechanical clock, that determining longitude at sea was even possible. The incredible mechanical obstacles that the chronometer's inventor had to overcome are documented in Dava Sobel's *Longitude*.[10]

One of the oddities about the Piri Reis map was that it had been drawn using an extremely sophisticated projection. An "equidistant projection" depicts the features of the earth from a single point on its

Figure 1.1. Twenty-four points on the 1513 Piri Reis map are accurate within one-half of a degree of longitude. This level of longitudinal accuracy wasn't achieved by Europeans for more than two centuries after the time of Piri Reis.

surface. This projection can be calculated from any spot on the globe. Perhaps the most familiar equidistant projection is the blue and white flag of the United Nations, centered on the North Pole. To draft a map using this method requires advanced mathematics, instrumentation, and knowledge unrealized by the Europeans of 1513.

The equidistant projection was one that was very familiar to the cartographic staff of the Strategic Air Command at Westover Air Force Base in Massachusetts. It was used to target Soviet military and economic assets. For example, a map drawn using Moscow as its center allowed the military to calculate the quickest delivery time for a missile to travel from any NATO base to the Soviet capital. In November 1962, when Soviet missiles were introduced to Cuba, an equidistant projection map centered on Castro's island revealed in terrifying detail how much United States territory could be targeted. Hence, the Cuban missile crisis.

Charles Hapgood explained to Arch C. Gerlach (chief of the Map Division at the Library of Congress) that the Piri Reis map "required more astronomy than was known in the Renaissance. The mathematics require that whoever constructed it had to know the linear distance from Syene to the North Pole to within a degree of accuracy. Piri Reis did not know that, neither did Columbus."[11]

Mallery and Hapgood, as well as the U.S. Navy and Air Force experts, had become convinced by their exhaustive studies that the Piri Reis map offered compelling evidence that an unknown ancient civilization possessed advanced astronomical and geodesic knowledge.

SYENE OR THE TROPIC OF CANCER?

Hapgood and his students (notably Frank Ryan) spent months trying to determine the exact center of the Piri Reis Map. At first, Hapgood was convinced that it was the city of Syene, where Eratosthenes, the librarian and father of geography, had made his famous calculations about the size of the earth. Hapgood submitted this suggestion to the cartographic crew at Westover Air Force Base. Captain Burroughs concurred. He wrote, "Piri Reis' use of the portolano projection* (centered on Syene, Egypt) was an excellent choice."[12]

We see in figure 1.2 on page 22 how the complete map must have looked, based on the same projection used by Piri Reis in 1513. The chart Christopher Columbus carried on his voyage would have resembled this projection.

Despite the fact that professionals had verified Syene as the center of the map, Hapgood remained skeptical. He thought that the ancients would have been more likely to use the Tropic of Cancer, which divides the tropical from the temperate climatic zones. Hapgood was certain that such an important global marker would have been highly significant to the ancient navigators.

---

*Portolono projections were used in "port-to-port" maps familiar to Europeans in the sixteenth century.

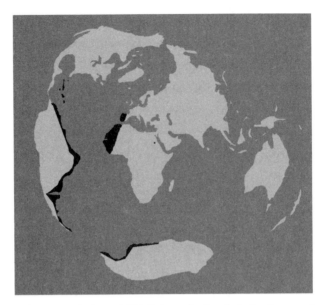

Figure 1.2. The 1513 Piri Reis projection is but a fragment of the secret map that Columbus may have possessed. If the lost map is ever found, it should depict the entire globe using an equidistant projection centered on the ancient Egyptian city of Syene. Drawing by Rand Flem-Ath and Rose Flem-Ath.

Today, the Tropic of Cancer lies near Syene but not precisely over it. The difference in distance is small, but Hapgood and his students wanted to be exact in their calculations. There was considerable debate whether to use the measurement from the ancient city or from the climatic marker. Hapgood mistakenly assumed that it had to be an either/or choice between Syene or the Tropic of Cancer. It was a false choice. There was a time when the Tropic of Cancer lay directly over Syene. We believe that a clue to that synchronicity of time and place lies within the very projection of the Piri Reis Map.[13]

When did the Tropic of Cancer and Syene share exactly the same latitude? Astronomers have concluded that it takes a century for the Tropic of Cancer to drift 40 seconds of latitude. This gives us a formula for our calculations and enables us to bull's-eye the date when the original mapmakers were at work. By calculating the difference in distance from the latitude of today's Tropic of Cancer (23°27' N) to that of Syene (24°05'30" N), we discover the answer: about 5,775 years ago, that is, circa 3763 BCE.

Syene is 38 minutes and 30 seconds from today's Tropic of Cancer. This is 2,280 seconds (multiplying 38 times 60 to convert minutes to seconds) plus the 30 seconds to give us a total of 2,310 seconds difference. We then divide these seconds by 40 to find that Syene was last on the Tropic of Cancer some 57.75 centuries ago.

The projection of the Piri Reis map points like an arrow at a pivotal turning point in human history. Archaeology teaches that Egyptian civilization dawned circa 3800 BCE.*

THE SECOND *SANTA MARIA*

Hapgood feared that the Spanish authorities would not take up the president's challenge to locate the source maps that Columbus had used to chart his trip to the New World. After all, they had no motive to rewrite history since they were content with its outcome—Spain had discovered America. To overcome this problem Hapgood drafted a letter for President Eisenhower to send to General Francisco Franco, Spain's fascist leader.

DRAFT PROPOSAL

A Letter from the President to General Franco

Dear General,

I have the honor to request your kind cooperation in securing an item of information of equal importance to the peoples and historians of Spain and the United States, relating to the discovery of America.

It is a question of a map, said to be the map of Columbus, which was seen by an American geographer on board the flagship of the Spanish fleet that visited the Columbian Exposition in the year 1893.

---

*It's perhaps just a fascinating coincidence that the Jewish calendar begins at 3760 BCE.

The Spanish fleet consisted of three ships, which were exact replicas of Columbus' ships. The flagship was, therefore, named *The Santa Maria*. I enclose a copy of a memorandum from one of our historians explaining in detail why we think it important to find the "Columbus map" that was on board the replica of the Santa Maria that summer (in 1893). I also enclose a statement by the gentleman (now 89 years old) who saw the map on the Santa Maria and some related documents.

If it would not be a matter of inconvenience, we would greatly appreciate a facsimile copy of the map, which, we presume, must now be found in your archives.

Professor Hapgood's memorandum and the supporting statement from our Col. Ohlmeyer will make clear, I am sure, the very remarkable importance that may be attached to this map.

With all personal good wishes,
(signed)
DWIGHT D. EISENHOWER

Enclosures:
1. Mr. Hapgood's Memorandum
2. Mr. Campbell's Statement
3. Col. Ohlmeyer's Statement
4. Photograph of the Piri Reis Map

Included with the letter was James Hunter Campbell's (1873–1962) account of his sighting of the elusive map. Campbell was only nineteen years old in the summer of 1893 when he accompanied his father to see the replica of the *Santa Maria* while it was docked in Toronto on its way to the World's Columbian Exposition (the Chicago World's Fair), held to celebrate the four hundredth anniversary of Christopher Columbus's arrival in America.

STATEMENT OF JAMES H. CAMPBELL OF OCEAN BLUFF,
MASSACHUSETTS, REGARDING THE COLUMBUS MAP HE SAW ON THE
REPLICA OF THE *SANTA MARIA,* IN 1893:

The Spanish Government built and sent over to this
country for exhibition at the Columbian Exhibition at
Chicago, three replicas of Columbus' vessels. There was
the Santa Maria, which was the largest of the three; then
there was the Pinta, and I think the third one was the
Nina. They came to Chicago by way of the St. Lawrence
River and the Great Lakes, and as they were passing
through Lake Ontario they stopped at Toronto. My brother,
who was on the reception committee of the Royal Canadian
Yacht Club, met the officers and they made him promise
that when he went to Chicago to see the Fair that he would
call on them. The Fair was open for six months, and as
near as I can remember my brother came to Chicago about
the end of July or the first of August. My father was
living in Chicago at the time, and was employed by one of
the publishing houses.

When my brother came to Chicago to visit the
Exhibition my father and I went along with him, as he was
going to pay a visit to the officers of the caravels.

The caravels were tied up alongside of the
Agricultural Building and right next to the boathouse of
the Electrical Launch and Navigation Co. Since I was in
charge of the electrical launches I was able to guide them
directly to the caravels.

We went aboard the *Santa Maria,* and my brother
introduced my father and me to the officers. When the
officers learned that my father was a geographer and the
author and publisher of geographies and other school books
in Canada, they became much interested, and asked my dad if
he would like to see Columbus's map. Up to this time my dad

had left the conversation to my brother and me, but after that the conversation was carried on between the officers and my dad, and what made it worse when the Spaniards were at a loss to find words in English to express their thoughts, my dad invited them to speak in French, and to their surprise they found out a little later that my dad could also speak Spanish, so that cut out both my brother and me out of the conversation for the remainder of the visit.

The officers invited us into the Chart Room, and took out a large map. As I remember it now it was about four feet square. It covered most of the table that was situated in the center of the Chart Room. My dad was very short sighted, so he pored over the chart with his nose almost touching the paper. He was tremendously pleased, but he didn't say much, until we got home again, and then he said he had difficulty in reading the map, not in understanding the language as he was a Spanish scholar and had at one time published a Spanish journal, and he also understood navigation, but he said he didn't have enough time to study the map. Nevertheless he was overjoyed at having seen it. I might add that my father was an enthusiastic yachtsman, and at one time contemplated making a trip around the world in his yacht, the *Oriole*. . . . I am sorry I don't remember the names of the officers who showed us the map, but it is most likely that they signed the log at the Clubhouse, and this has probably been preserved.[14]

The mention of the chart being "four feet square" intrigued Hapgood since the Piri Reis map was about two by three feet. Might the map that Campbell saw actually depict the entire world and not just the Piri Reis fragment?

Hapgood was also curious about the senior Campbell's reaction to the map. Campbell's father had written geography texts, and the fact that he "pored over the chart with his nose almost touching the paper" was suggestive. We know that the senior Campbell was not puzzled by the inscriptions since he was a "'Spanish scholar.'" So what was it that fascinated him? We suggest it was the unusual equidistant projection—uncommon in 1893.

THE WHITE HOUSE ACTS

When we reviewed Hapgood's correspondence contained in President Eisenhower's archives, we discovered that the White House did in fact follow through on the memorandum. The U.S. State Department, on orders from Eisenhower, directed the American ambassador in Spain, John David Lodge, to pursue the matter.

Ambassador Lodge's younger brother, Henry Cabot Lodge (1902–1985), was Richard Nixon's vice presidential running mate during the 1960 campaign. Despite the obvious distractions, Lodge followed through on the presidential order. Unfortunately, the Spanish authorities came up empty-handed.

With the election of President John Kennedy in 1960, the dynamics in Washington changed. The new administration never found time to pursue Hapgood's quest. Hapgood never knew what happened. Instead he devoted a decade to writing *Maps of the Ancient Sea Kings: Evidence of Advanced Civilization in the Ice Age*. The preface begins:

This book contains the story of the discovery of the first hard evidence that advanced peoples preceded all the peoples now known to history. In one field, ancient sea charts, it appears that accurate information has been passed down from people to people. . . . It becomes clear that the ancient voyagers traveled from pole to pole. Unbelievable as it may appear, the evidence nevertheless indicates that some ancient people explored the coasts of Antarctica when its coasts were free of ice.[15]

WE TAKE UP THE HUNT

As librarians, we were challenged by the problem of finding this most important of documents. We began by contacting a friend in Toronto, Shawn Montgomery, to see if he could follow up on Campbell's suggestion that the Royal Canadian Yacht Club might have log entries concerning the visit of the *Santa Maria* replica. Unfortunately the logs from 1893 no longer existed.

We then turned to the Chicago side of the mystery and contacted Ray Grasse, an author and friend living in Chicago. He suggested that we contact the Chicago Historical Society. The librarian at the society, Emily Clark, told us that the captain who sailed the replica of the *Santa Maria* in 1893 was named V. M. Concas. Clark turned our request over to an assistant working in the archives department named Cynthia Mathews. She hit on the mother lode and sent us an account of the trip written by the captain himself.

From this account we discovered that Hapgood's logical assumption that the "lost map of Columbus" was housed in the Spanish archives was incorrect. In fact, according to Captain Concas, the Columbus maps were kept in an entirely different location. He wrote, "She (Spain) has sent also the original charts of America, but the difficulties attending the proper custody in the Convent of Rabida of this valuable collection of charts, where are also the original documents connected with the discovery of America (also belonging to Spain), has resulted in their being examined by a very limited number of persons."[16]

It was within the sand-colored walls of the modest La Rábida Monastery that the "lost map of Columbus" could be found. The monastery was originally built by the Knights Templar in 1261. After they fell from power in 1307, the Franciscans chose the monastery as one of their Spanish bases.

In 1485, Christopher Columbus began lobbying European royalty to finance an unprecedented voyage to India and China. He would sail west across the Atlantic, something that had never been done before. Until then all voyages to India and China had sailed south, hugged the coast of Africa, and then traveled east.

Frustrated in his attempts to enlist a patron to support his "westward" route to Asia, Columbus decided to join the rich pilgrims who regularly journeyed across Europe. His hope was that one of them would finance his venture or use his or her influence to obtain an audience for Columbus with one of the royal families.

In 1490, he arrived at La Rábida. Fortunately for Columbus, the prior of La Rábida took a liking to him and intervened on Columbus's behalf with King Ferdinand and Queen Isabella. The great explorer was at the monastery when he received the exciting news that his ambitious voyage had been approved. It is not surprising that he left his most valuable maps to the prior who made his dream possible.

Is the lost map still lying in the shadows on some dusty shelf in a quiet Spanish monastery? What could we discover from it if we could see its ancient face? How would our concept of history be changed if Hapgood and Campbell were right about the mappa mundus?

The path that the two men took together in their quest for the source map of the 1513 Piri Reis map was not the first adventure they had shared. Starting in the late 1940s, the Hapgood/Campbell team had explored an idea central to *Atlantis beneath the Ice*—the theory of earth crust displacement.

Like their quest for ancient maps, the exploration of this idea would involve many others, most notably, Albert Einstein.

TWO

ADAPT, MIGRATE, OR DIE

On May 8, 1953, an elderly professor with a fondness for the violin sat down at his desk in Princeton, New Jersey, and wrote a letter to Charles Hapgood, an obscure instructor at a small New England college. The professor was Albert Einstein, and the topic of the letter was a theory of Hapgood's that had "electrified" the great physicist. Einstein wrote, "I find your arguments very impressive and have the impression that your hypothesis is correct. One can hardly doubt that significant shifts of the crust of the earth have taken place repeatedly and within a short time."[1]

Charles Hutchins Hapgood (1904–1982), a graduate of Harvard College and the Harvard Graduate School of Arts and Sciences, was born in New York City. After graduating, Hapgood traveled to Germany, where his studies at the University of Freiburg coincided with Adolf Hitler's rise to power. When World War II erupted, he returned to the United States and joined the Office of Strategic Studies (OSS, the forerunner of the CIA) as a civilian with inside knowledge of Nazi Germany. After the war, Hapgood became a professor of anthropology and the history of science at Keene State College in New Hampshire. In the early 1950s, he began formulating his theory of earth crust displacement, a project that would occupy him for nearly twenty years.

Einstein's correspondence with Hapgood began in November 1952 and lasted until Einstein's death in April 1955.[2] Einstein wrote at least ten letters to Hapgood and conducted scientific correspondence with other interested parties about Hapgood's theory. In 1954, Einstein approached the Guggenheim Memorial Foundation in support of Hapgood's application. Einstein wrote that Hapgood's idea of earth crust displacement was: "fascinating, justified, promising, and important."[3]

Einstein recommended Hapgood as one who had the "energy and patience" to pursue the theory. However, despite the support of one of the greatest minds of the twentieth century, Hapgood did not receive a fellowship.

One of Hapgood's most rewarding experiences came in January 1955 when he and his friend and co-theorist James Hunter Campbell met with Einstein. Hapgood explained that his own contribution lay mainly in the fields of geology and paleontology. He left to Campbell the issues of mechanics and geophysics. The conversation ranged over a number of topics, from the "elastic limit of the crustal rocks" to the value of the new tool of radiocarbon dating. As the men were about to leave, Einstein offered two pieces of advice.

1. He said that it was not "necessary to take the present state of knowledge very seriously," adding that "what we regard as knowledge today may someday be regarded as error."
2. He added that the "gradualist notions common in geology were . . . merely a habit of mind, and were not necessarily justified by the empirical data."[4]

Earlier, in May 1954, Einstein had written a foreword to Hapgood's book, *The Earth's Shifting Crust: A Key to Some Basic Problems of Earth Science*.[5] Part of that foreword reads, "A great many empirical data indicates that at each point of the earth's surface that has been carefully studied, many climatic changes have taken place, apparently quite suddenly. This, according to Mr. Hapgood, is explicable if the virtually rigid outer crust of the earth undergoes, from time to time, extensive displacement."[6]

Einstein's enthusiasm was tempered by one concern: "The only

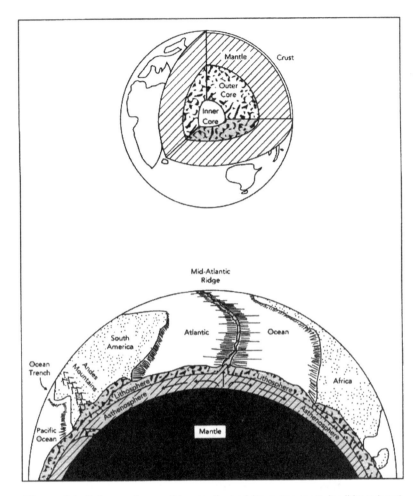

Figure 2.1. Between the earth's mantle and its outer crust (or lithosphere) lies a semiliquid layer known as the asthenosphere. Charles Hapgood believed that the asthenosphere allowed the outer crust of the earth to shift. Such a displacement includes continents and the ocean basins.

doubtful assumption is that the earth's crust can be moved easily enough over the inner layers."[7]

The bulk of the earth's mass lies at its center and is believed to consist of an iron-nickel alloy core surrounded by an outer liquid core. The outer core is encircled by the thickest part of the earth, a lower and upper mantle of solid rock. Above the upper mantle lies the asthenosphere, or "weak zone" (see figure 2.1). It is the mobility of the asthenosphere that makes it possible for the earth's lithosphere (crust) to shift.

This crust of lithosphere, which cradles the continents and ocean basins, is the thinnest layer and is the one upon which all life depends. It is divided into a series of plates that shift periodically, provoking earthquakes and volcanoes. Over millions of years, the inch-by-inch movement of these plates, explained by a theory known as "plate tectonics," can separate continents and create mountain ranges.

Plate tectonics and earth crust displacement both share the assumption of a mobile crust. The ideas are not mutually exclusive but rather complementary. Plate tectonics explains long-term, slow changes like mountain building, volcanic activity, and local earthquakes. Earth crust displacement accepts that these processes are gradual but posits a much more dramatic and abrupt movement of the crust that can explain different problems such as mass extinctions, glaciation patterns, and the sudden rise of agriculture. In stark contrast to plate tectonics' slow motion of individual plates, an "earth crust displacement," as postulated by Hapgood, abruptly shifts all the plates *as a single unit*. During this motion the core (the heavy bull's eye of the planet) doesn't change, leaving the earth's axis unaltered.

The consequences of a crustal displacement are monumental. As the earth's crust ripples over its interior, the world is shaken by incredible earthquakes and floods. The sky appears to fall. Of course, the sky remains in place. It was the crust that shifted. We still speak of sunrises and sunsets even though it is the earth's spin that creates the illusion of movement. During a displacement the sun appears to rise and set over an altered horizon until finally the crust grinds to a halt. Beneath the ocean, earthquakes generate massive tidal waves that crash against the coastlines, flooding them. Some lands are shifted to warmer climates. Others, propelled into the polar zones, suffer the direst of winters. Melting ice caps, released from the polar areas, raise the ocean's level ever higher. All living creatures must adapt, migrate, or die.

Roughly 11,600 years ago (9600 BCE), vast climatic changes are known to have swept over our planet. Massive ice sheets melted, forcing

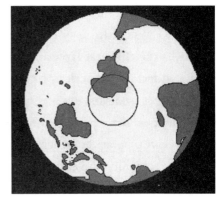

Figure 2.2. The Arctic Circle 11,600 years ago.

Figure 2.3. The Antarctic Circle 11,600 years ago.

the ocean level to rise. Huge mammals perished in enormous numbers. There was a sudden influx of people to the Americas, and throughout the world men and women began to experiment with agriculture. Each of these critical events has become a subject of intense scientific scrutiny.

Because Hapgood's idea can be applied to so many different problems, it constitutes a "scientific revolution." In *The Structure of Scientific Revolutions,* a work commonly called "the most influential treatise ever written on how science does (and does not) proceed,"[8] philosopher and sociologist Thomas S. Kuhn traces the characteristics of the great changes in scientific thought. Kuhn shows how a dynamic new idea can initiate a scientific revolution by solving a set of persistent, unanswered problems. When the dust settles, intellectual territory has been expanded and scientists are presented with a fresh set of problems to explore. But, ironically, the new idea that originally sparked the scientific revolution is often met with either violent controversy or smothering silence.

New theories are more often resisted than welcomed and indeed are often ignored, only to be recognized as scientific revolutions by a new generation. The sociology of science explores this paradox. For instance, Darwin's theory of evolution was met with great outrage, not only by the church, but by scientists as well. Copernicus was wise enough to have his theory published at the end of his life. He appreciated the dangers of his radical idea that the earth was not the center of the universe.

Kuhn distinguishes between what he calls "normal science" and science in "crisis." Normal science includes activities that we commonly associate with scientific achievement, such as building a bridge, launching a space shuttle, or searching for a cure for cancer. Scientists are trained to solve problems by using well-established theories. In normal science, they make a "devoted attempt to force nature into the conceptual boxes supplied by professional education."[9] Each discipline surrounds itself with a layer of insulation from problems not perceived to be within its domain. Kuhn calls these assumptions about what are "real problems" a "paradigm," a framework for approaching any scientific enigma.

Kuhn argues that the acceptance of a new framework by any scientific discipline is similar to the retooling of a factory. Initially, the costs of retooling often seem to outweigh the rewards of the improved design: *If it ain't broke don't fix it.* But if the competition across town is solving more problems using the new design (the new paradigm), then all manufacturers are eventually compelled to adopt the improvements.

However, the force of competition has a less immediate impact on science than it does in the world of commerce. Only when an old paradigm's blind spots are dissolved by a new idea do scientists begin to consider retooling their theories. Until this crisis occurs the old tools are wielded relentlessly, dull or outmoded as they are, even as they steadily lose their grip on the problem.

We will explore several long-standing, unsolved, and ignored problems by looking at them through the fresh lens provided by the theory of earth crust displacement. We consider the unsolved problem to be the most fundamental unit of science. Theories are the nets that scientists use to capture problems and solve them. Earth crust displacement is a significant new theory because of its wide scope. It can solve a range of unsolved problems that are currently considered the isolated domain of different disciplines. For example, an odd geological mystery surrounds today's ice sheets on Greenland and Antarctica.

It is a fact that the land that holds the thickest ice sheets now receives the least annual snowfall. At the same time, the areas of thinnest ice receive the most annual snowfall. Current geological assumptions can't explain this puzzle. And, more significantly, geologists have yet to come up with a single theory that can solve this long-standing unsolved problem. We will show that Hapgood's theory can explain the distribution of ice sheets on a global scale. No other theory can come close to the scope of explanation offered by the idea of a shifting crust.

Likewise, several competing theories have been advanced to explain the sudden mass extinctions that punctuate our planet's history. However, when it comes to an explanation of the extinctions that happened 11,600 years ago, Hapgood's concept can explain why mammoths became extinct in North America while elephants survived in Africa. It can account for the rates of death, continent by continent, on a global scale.

Two other long-standing problems are seen in a new light when viewed through the lens of the earth crust displacement theory. The origins of agriculture remain a mystery and the full story behind the peopling of the Americas continues to elude the existing archaeological paradigm—and again, earth crust displacement offers answers.

Funding also heavily influences attitudes toward new ideas. The choice of which scientific problems to pursue is seldom left to scientists themselves. They are more often than not chosen by industrial, governmental, and educational institutions. Most scientists are *assigned* to problems that seem solvable. Other problems simply receive no funding.

Moreover, the scientific community shares an implicit covenant within its ranks. Separated as it is from society, it eagerly celebrates science's success stories. Unveiling long-awaited solutions to scientific problems is a noble act. But if the general public is invited to examine a set of unsolved problems, then the scientific community becomes indignant. And indignation can rapidly lead to bitter controversy. Often a new idea is met with stony silence. That, despite the enthusiastic support of Albert Einstein is the fate that greeted Hapgood's theory of earth crust displacement.

With one simple idea (a shifting crust), Hapgood's theory can simultaneously solve long-standing problems in geology, archaeology, anthropology, and paleontology. By opening new frontiers, this theory clears a whole new intellectual territory for scientists to explore.

The quest for Atlantis has been treated as either a scientific curiosity or with great skepticism as belonging to the murky realm of fantasy. It was inevitable that a scientific revolution would be required to find the lost continent.

We will show that there is reason to believe that we are not the first advanced civilization to inhabit our world. This recognition provides the key to unlocking one of the most compelling mysteries of all. Using the theory of earth crust displacement, we will travel across the planet as it was in 9600 BCE., watch the incredible results as the surface of the earth buckles, and share the survivors' memories of the great flood.

THREE

THE WAYWARD SUN

The sky fell. The land was not. For a very great distance there was no land. The waters of the ocean came together. Animals of all kinds drowned.

THE CAHTO OF CALIFORNIA

It is sunset at the camp of the tribe known as the Ute. Preparations for the annual sun dance have begun. Men and women draped in rabbit-skin robes are drawn to the fire's glow. Dishes of simmering turtle, lizard, and insects, and generous servings of berries and seed are shared around the circle.

It is time.

An elder rises and passes a lined hand over his buffalo-skin cloak. The children are immediately alert, their eyes wide with anticipation. Listen now, on this feast of the sun dance, to the Ute's myth of the taming of the sun god.

Once upon a time Ta-wats, the hare-god, was sitting with his family by the camp-fire in the solemn woods, anxiously waiting for the return of Ta-va (the wayward sun-god). Wearied with long watching, the hare-god fell asleep, and the sun-god came so near that he scorched the naked shoulder of Ta-wats. Foreseeing the vengeance, which would be thus provoked, he fled back to his cave beneath the earth.

Ta-wats awoke in great anger, and speedily determined to go and fight the sun-god. After a long journey of many adventures the hare-god came to the brink of the earth, and there watched long and patiently, till at last the sun-god came out, and he shot an arrow at his face, but the fierce heat consumed the arrow ere it had finished its intended course; then another was sped, but that also was consumed; and another, and another, till only one remained in his quiver, but this was the magical arrow that had never failed its mark.

Ta-wats, holding it in his hand, lifted the barb to his eye and baptized it in a divine tear; then the arrow was sped and struck the sun-god full in the face, and the sun was shivered into a thousand fragments, which fell to the earth, causing a general conflagration.

Then Ta-wats, the hare-god, fled before the destruction he had wrought, and as he fled the burning earth consumed his feet, consumed his legs, consumed his body, consumed his hands and his arms—all were consumed but the head alone—which bowled across valleys and over mountains, fleeing the destruction from the burning earth, until at last, swollen with heat, the eyes of the god burst, and the tears gushed forth in a flood, which spread over the earth, and extinguished the fire.

The sun-god was now conquered, and he appeared before a council of the gods to await sentence. In that long council were established the days and the nights, the seasons and the years, with the length thereof and the sun was condemned to travel across the firmament by the same trail day after day till the end of time.[1]

The Ute, after whom Utah was named, were among the most warlike tribes in the American West. They fought with the Comanche, Arapaho, Kiowa, and Cheyenne for domination over hunting grounds. Young braves were taught when to attack, when to retreat, and when to find honor in vengeance. These challenges were interwoven with forceful lessons about the humbling power of nature. Tales of the hare god's antics and the sun god's power were much more than exciting children's stories. The myths illustrated the critical factors a warrior must weigh in times of battle, how the seasons came to be, and why the sun follows its predictable path across the sky. This cohesive view of the world was strong glue binding the tribe together.

This particular myth was also a reflection of the human need to create order out of nature's chaos. The social problems of war and peace were mirrored in nature's forces of chaos and order. Ta-wats, the hare god, is sleeping in the woods when the wayward sun provokes him by scorching his shoulder. He rises and seeks revenge on the fleeing sun god. Eventually the sun god is attacked with a magic arrow, and the explosive forces of nature are released. The sun erupts, and then a Great Flood engulfs the world. Order is restored only when a council of the gods creates predictable seasons and condemns the sun to follow an unalterable path across the heavens until "the end of time."

The myth of the wayward sun can also be seen as a distant echo of the last earth crust displacement. As the ground shuddered beneath them, it would have seemed to the earth's shocked inhabitants that the sky, sun, and stars were tumbling from their place in the heavens. The violent earthquakes caused by the displacement generated great tidal waves that rolled across the ocean, smashing vulnerable coastlines. Ice caps melted, forcing the ocean level higher and higher. For many it was the end of the world. But for the survivors, it became the first day of a brand-new era.

The German-American anthropologist Franz Boas (1858–1942) traced the mythology of the Ute to the Canadian province of British Columbia,[2] where the mythological trail connected the Utes with the Kutenai and in turn the Okanagan. The Kutenai occupy territory encompassing parts of British Columbia, Alberta, Washington, Idaho, and Montana. Like the Ute, the Kutenai speak of a great fire that erupted over the earth when the sun was struck by an arrow. "Coyote is envious, and shoots the sun at sunrise. His arrows catch fire, fall down, and set fire to the grass."[3] And the Kutenai speak of the fear they have that the world will come to an end when the sky loses its stability. "The

Kutenai look for Polaris (the North Star) every night. Should it not be in place, the end of the world is imminent."[4]

Little is known of the origin of the Kutenai.[5] They often have wavy hair, light brown skin, and slight beards.[6] Their neighbors in the plains, the Blackfoot, gave them the name Kutenai, Blackfoot for "white men."[7] Boas believed that the Kutenai's mythology linked them with their neighbors to the west, the Okanagan.[8] The Okanagan called the Kutenai *skelsa'ulk,* meaning "water people."[9]

In 1886, the American historian Hubert Howe Bancroft (1832– 1918) related the Okanagan myth of their lost island paradise of Samah-tumi-whoo-lah.

> Long, long ago, when the sun was young and no bigger than a star, there was an island far off in the middle of the ocean. It was called Samah-tumi-whoo-lah, meaning White Man's Island. On it lived a race of giants—white giants. Their ruler was a tall white woman called Scomalt. . . . She could create whatever she wished.
>
> For many years the white giants lived at peace, but at last they quarreled amongst themselves. Quarreling grew into war. The noise of battle was heard, and many people were killed. Scomalt was made very, very angry . . . she drove the wicked giants to one end of the White Man's Island. When they were gathered together in one place, she broke off the piece of land and pushed it into the sea. For many days the floating island drifted on the water, tossed by waves and wind. All the people on it died except one man and one woman.
>
> Seeing that their island was about to sink they built a canoe [and] . . . after paddling for many days and nights, they came to some islands. They steered their way through them and at last reached the mainland.[10]

The Okanagan and the Ute feared any dramatic change in the heavens as an ominous portent of another great flood. The fear that the sun might once again wander or the sky might fall became an obsession.

The Ute related, "Some think the sky is supported by one big cotton-wood tree in the west and another in the east; if either get rotten, it may break and the sky would fall down, killing everybody."[11]

And the Okanagan believed that in a time to come the "lakes will melt the foundations of the world, and the rivers will cut the world loose. Then it will float as the island did many suns and snows ago. That will be the end of the world."[12]

We can barely imagine the power of the tsunamis that rolled across the earth at this time. Shipboard survivors who had escaped the doomed continent could not escape the sight of successive tidal waves destroying their homeland. It would seem to them that Atlantis had vanished beneath the ocean. This misperception distorted the fact that it was the ocean rising—not the land sinking. Atlantis never actually sank beneath the ocean. The survivors were long gone when the tidal waves subsided and the land was once again visible. But their traumatic memory of a sinking island was passed from generation to generation.

As we move south we encounter the Washo of western Nevada, who are famous for their decorative basketry. They live on the eastern flank of the Sierra Nevada Mountains. The tribe was always small, never over-hunting the earth. They ranged from a population of 900 in 1859 to just over 800 in 1980. In earlier times, their numbers may have reached 1,500.[13] They are a solitary people who tell a tale of a time, long ago, when the mountains shook with volcanoes and "so great was the heat of the blazing mountains that the very stars melted and fell."[14]

Along the Gila and Salt River valleys of Arizona live the remnants of the A'a'tam tribe, who have been misnamed by outsiders not once, but twice. Because one Italian explorer sailing under the Spanish flag in 1492 didn't know where he was, the entire native population of the Americas was christened, wrongly, Indians. And when the early mission-aries demanded that the A'a'tam tribe identify themselves, they refused, answering in their native tongue with the single word *pima*, meaning "no." From this exchange a misunderstanding arose that remains to this day. The missionaries took the "pima" response as an answer to their question rather than a refusal to cooperate, and so the tribe came to be known as the Pima.[15]

In fact, A'a'tam means "people." Part of the A'a'tam history was carried across the centuries in an age-old myth of a Great Flood that had once overwhelmed the earth. Their tale of the Flood included an event absent from the frontiersmen's Bible. Using the symbolism of a magical baby created by an evil deity, the myth told how the screaming child "shook the earth," catapulting the world into the horrors of the Great Flood.[16]

The A'a'tam now feared that the sky was insecure. Corrective measures were called for, and the Earth Doctor created a gray spider that spun a huge web around the edges of the sky and the earth to hold them secure. Even with these protective measures the fear remained that the fragile web might break, releasing the sky and causing the earth to tremble.[17]

In 1849, the California gold rush brought fortune seekers streaming across the Rocky Mountains to the West Coast, home of the Cahto. Ten years later, the pioneers of Mendocino County in northwestern California killed thirty-two Cahto because they took some livestock belonging to the whites. These thirty-two men represented more than 6 percent of the Cahto's population. To put this tragedy in perspective, we can imagine the havoc wreaked today if the populations of New York, Chicago, and Los Angeles were suddenly murdered by some alien force. The Cahto never recovered. By 1910, 90 percent of the population was dead.

The mythology of the Cahto stretched back nearly twelve thousand years to the time of the last earth crust displacement. Through this legacy we learn of the catapulting events in California at the time of the Great Flood. "The sky fell. The land was not. For a very great distance there was no land. The waters of the ocean came together. Animals of all kinds drowned."[18] The original title of this book paid tribute to the Cahto, who poetically recalled the Flood as a time *when the sky fell.*

American native mythology identifies four westerly mountains tied to the aftermath of a Great Flood (see figure 3.1 on page 44). All four mountains are 1,800 meters or higher above sea level. At the time of

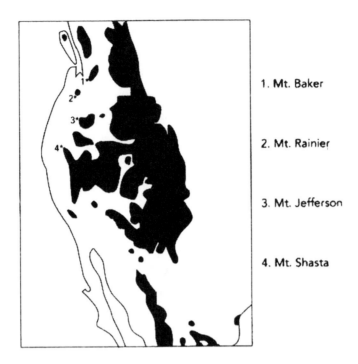

Figure 3.1. First Nations myths honor four mountains as sites of ancestral survival after the Great Flood. These sites suggest the ancestors arrived from the Pacific.

the Great Flood these mountains at the western extremity of North America would have been the first hope for those survivors of the lost island paradise who had traveled so far across an endless ocean.

The native people of Washington and Oregon claim that their ancestors arrived in great canoes and disembarked on Mount Baker[19] and Mount Jefferson.[20] They believed that Mount Rainier[21] was the refuge of those who were saved after the wicked of the earth were destroyed in a Great Flood. The Shasta of northern California tell of a time when the sun fell from its normal course.[22] A separate myth relates how Mount Shasta saved their ancestors from the Deluge.[23] On the opposite side of North America lies another great mountain chain, the Appalachians. There, also, tales were told of terrifying solar changes, massive floods, and the survivors of these catastrophes.

The lush green forests of the southern tip of the Appalachian Mountains were once the home of the Cherokee. In the early nineteenth century, a Cherokee named Sequoya created an alphabet for his language. He left a rich legacy of myths transcribed from his people's oral tradition. In one myth the Flood is attributed to the uncontrollable tears of the sun goddess. It was said that she hated people and cursed them with a great drought. In desperation the Cherokee elders consulted the "Little Men," whom they regarded as gods. The Little Men decreed that the Cherokees' only hope of survival was to *kill the sun*. Magical snakes were prepared to deal a deathblow to the sun goddess. But a tragic mistake was made, and her daughter, the moon, was struck instead.

> When the Sun found her daughter dead, she went into the house and grieved, and the people did not die any more, but now the world was dark all the time, because the Sun would not come out.
>
> They went again to the Little Men, and told them if they wanted the Sun to come out again they must bring back her daughter. . . . [Seven men went to the ghost country and retrieved the moon but on the return journey she died again. The sun-goddess cried and wept . . .] *until her tears made a flood upon the earth,* and the people were afraid the world would be drowned.[24] (italics added)

The Cherokee, like the Ute and Okanagan tribes, held a dark prophecy of how the world would end. "The earth is a great island floating in a sea of water, and suspended at each of the four cardinal points by a cord hanging down from the sky vault, which is of solid rock. When the world grows old and worn out, the people will die and the cords will break and let the earth sink into the ocean, and all will be water again."[25]

Despite the fact that they both lived in mountain ranges that lay far from the ocean, the Cherokee and Okanagan both associated the mythological Flood with *an island*. For the Okanagan this island lay "far off in the middle of the ocean." For the Cherokee the myth of the "great island floating in a sea" contains clues to the lost land. "There is another world under this, and it is like ours in everything—animals, plants, and people—save that the seasons are different."[26]

There is, in fact, just such an island in the middle of the ocean with a climate opposite to that of the northern hemisphere (see figure 3.2). The island continent of Antarctica was partially ice free before the last earth crust displacement. Was it the doomed island of Okanagan and Cherokee mythology?

The people of Central and South America also hold rich mythologies about the lost island paradise and its destruction in a Great Flood.

Figure 3.2. Antarctica is an island in the middle of the ocean, just like the lost land of Okanagan mythology. And like the floating disc of Cherokee mythology, Antarctica would have experienced seasons opposite to those of North America. The formerly temperate parts of Antarctica may have been, before the last earth crust displacement, the lost island paradise of Okanagan and Cherokee mythology.

The Ipurina of northwestern Brazil retain one of the most elegant depictions of the disaster. Their myth states, "Long ago the Earth was overwhelmed by a hot flood. This took place when the sun, a cauldron of boiling water, tipped over."[27]

Further south, the Spanish conquistadors assumed after their sweeping victories in Mexico and Peru that Chile would be another easy target. Santiago, the Spanish capital, was founded in February 1541 by Pedro de Valdiva, the first Spanish governor. Six months later the city was destroyed by the native people of Chile, the Araucanians, who launched a war that continued for four centuries. Here was a tribe so valiant that they would fight for generations rather than submit to slavery. But even these brave people trembled before a traumatic memory. "The Flood was the result of a volcanic eruption accompanied by a violent earthquake, and whenever there is an earthquake the natives rush to the high mountains. They are afraid that after the earthquake the sea may again drown the world."[28]

Like the Araucanians, the Inca were paralyzed by the fear that any change in the sun foretold doom. A 1555 Spanish chronicler recorded their terror, stating when "there is an eclipse of the sun or the moon the Indians cry and groan in great perturbation, thinking that the time has come in which the earth will perish."[29]

The Peruvian historian, Carcilasso de la Vega, the son of a Spanish conquistador and an Incan princess, asked his Incan uncle to relate the story of his people's origins. How had Lake Titicaca become the source of their civilization? The uncle explained, "In ancient times all this region which you see was covered with forests and thickets, and the people lived like brute beasts without religion nor government, nor towns, nor houses, without cultivating the land nor covering their bodies. . . . [The sun god sent a son and daughter to] give them precepts and laws by which to live as reasonable and civilized men, and to teach them to dwell in houses and towns, to cultivate maize and other crops, to breed flocks, and to use the fruits of the earth as rational beings."[30]

The supposed gods who brought agriculture to the vicinity of Lake

Titicaca were said to have come *"out of the regions of the south"*[31] immediately *"after the deluge."*[32] Those whom the Inca called gods may have been people who possessed precious skills and were forced to leave their southern home after it was destroyed by a flood.

The word *inca* means "son of the sun" and was a title originally granted only to the emperor. To preserve his culture from the ravages of the conquistadors, Inca Manco II left the great capital of Cuzco in 1536 and retreated into the daunting heights of the Andes. He took with him three sons, each of whom would, in turn, become inca and suffer a succession of bloody encounters with the Spanish. Manco II chose a mountain peak overlooking the Urubamba Valley to build his palace. Francisco Pizarro, leader of the Spanish invaders, was never able to find this secret base, and its existence intrigued those who followed him. But all who tried to discover the lost city failed.

Later, in the same century, two monks, Friar Marcos and Friar Diego, did come tantalizingly close to lifting the veil of the hidden city. Friar Marcos was fired with a "desire to seek souls where not a single preacher had entered, and where the gospel message had not been heard."[33] Traveling with him was a medical missionary, Friar Diego, who became popular with the local people and a favorite of the royal inca. The two monks had established a convent at Puquiura, near Vitcos, and were fascinated by Incan stories of the "Virgins of the Sun," who dwelled in a fabulous city known as "Vilcabamba the Old." This mountain city was said to house "wizards and masters of abomination."[34]

The two monks repeatedly tried to coax an Inca who sometimes emerged from the hidden city into revealing its location. Finally, he agreed to take them. Higher and higher they traveled, the air becoming thinner with every step. The Inca was carried in a litter and enjoyed the view, while the monks stumbled through the thick jungle, tripping over their long robes. After three days they arrived at the foot of yet another barrier of mountains that jutted even farther into the sky.

For three weeks the monks preached to and taught the natives who lived in a settlement just beyond sight and sound of the mystery city.

They were forbidden to enter its enclaves for fear they would learn something of its rites, ceremonies, and purpose. During the night the Incan priests high in the forbidden city conspired to corrupt the monks by sending beautiful women to tempt them from their vows of celibacy. Friars Marcos and Diego resisted to the end and finally concluded that they would never reach the sacred city. It was never found by the Spanish.

In 1911, four centuries later, the American historian and explorer Hiram Bingham (1875–1956) discovered the marvelous, haunting ruins of a lost Incan city cradled in the summit of a mountain called Machu Picchu.

Bingham believed that he had discovered the lost city of "Vilcabamba the Old," where the "Virgins of the Sun" catered to the wishes of their Incan master.[35] He recovered a number of skeletons from Machu Picchu, which he sent to Dr. George Eaton of Yale University. The professor concluded that among the skeletons, "there was not a single one of a robust male of the warrior type. There are a few effeminate males who might very well have been priests, but the large majority of the skeletons are female."[36]

Why did the Inca maintain a settlement of young women in their sanctuary, Machu Picchu? A clue might come from the U.S. Air Force and its bunker buried deep beneath Colorado Springs. It was built as a retreat in the event of nuclear war and a base from which civilization might be reestablished. For the Inca, the threat was not nuclear, but rather a Great Flood. To meet this danger, they created bases on mountains far from the ocean. If another deluge was unleashed, a base like Machu Picchu could repopulate a drowned world.

In his book *The Lost City of the Incas,*[37] Bingham described a ritual performed on the winter solstice by the priests of Machu Picchu. A mystical cord was secured by a great stone pillar to "guide" the sun across the sky, preventing it from losing course. This *intihuatana,* or hitching post of the sun, may have represented a symbolic attempt to prevent another earth crust displacement. If so, then the mysterious solar megaliths (known as sun stones) that are found around the globe may have represented ancient attempts to secure the sun in its new path across the sky after the Flood. A reined sun could not release another Great Flood. The earth would be safe for another year.

This obsession with the stability of the sun's path is also found in the American southwest among the ruins of the Anasazi (a Navajo word meaning "the ancient ones"). They are famed for their cliff dwellings, their circular architecture, and other artistic achievements. Chaco Mesa in New Mexico is the site of one of the most remarkable solar megaliths in the world. Three slabs of stone, each weighing two tons, have been arranged so that the light of the sun falls on a spiral petroglyph, marking the summer and winter solstices and the spring and fall equinoxes.

It was discovered in 1977 by artist and amateur archaeo-astronomer Anna Sofaer,[38] who called it a "sun dagger" because of the pattern the sunlight makes on the rock carvings during the summer solstice. Since its true purpose may have been the Anasazi's equivalent of the Inca's hitching post of the sun, it could be called a solar cord, designed to prevent a wayward sun or at least to monitor the sun's path to ensure that all was in order.

The fear of a wayward sun or falling sky became a global nightmare for the survivors of the last earth crust displacement. For example, from 400 to 1200 CE, the Celts occupied much of central and western Europe. They were known as fearless warriors who "did not dread earthquakes or high tides, which, indeed, they attacked with weapons; but they feared the fall of the sky and the day when fire and water must prevail."[39] And in 1643, a bishop in Ireland discovered an ancient manuscript containing the most detailed Germanic mythology ever found. These myths open with the haunting prophecy of an inspired seeress: "The sun turns black, earth sinks into the sea. The hot stars down from the heavens are whirled."[40]

The overwhelming anxiety that earthquakes might foreshadow a worldwide flood was suffered not just by those who dwelled on the lip of the ocean. The Mari, who still occupy the land west of the Volga

River in Russia, believed that the earth was supported on the remaining horn (the other had broken before the Great Flood) of a massive bull. The bull, in turn, balanced precariously on the back of a giant crab, which crouched on the ocean floor. Any movement of the bull's head was thought to cause earthquakes. The Mari lived in terror that the bull's remaining horn would snap, sending the earth tumbling once more into the ocean. As the beast's head tipped, throwing the earth forward, violent earthquakes would erupt. And then, as the earth was pitched from the bull's horn and hurtled through the air, the sky would seem to fall. Finally, the earth would tumble into the ocean, releasing a cataclysm of water that would drown the world.[41]

Throughout ancient Europe giant stones were erected to honor the sun. Stonehenge in Wiltshire, England, is one of the most famous of these sites. Like the structures in North and South America, Stonehenge may have been built as a magical device designed to prevent another earth crust displacement. People clung to the belief that by controlling the sun's movements, these massive stones might ensure the safety of the world.

The horseshoe mouth of the stones is open to receive the sun's rays on the summer solstice. The body of the horseshoe corresponds to the path of the sun from sunrise to sunset. Each day, as spring moves toward summer, the sun rises slightly farther north on the morning horizon. On the summer solstice this "migration" north seems to stall. On the day after the solstice the sun reverses its journey and begins to rise farther south each morning. To a people ever vigilant to the dangers of a wayward sun, any irregularity threatens catastrophe. To prevent this, the priests may have, like their counterparts on Machu Picchu, attempted to symbolically harness the sun by tying its rays to successive stones within the horseshoe. The world would be safe for another year.

The Greek's fear of a wayward sun involves their god, Helios, who was responsible for the passage of the sun across the sky. Helios drove a chariot drawn by winged horses that flew a regular route across the sky. The burning sun was dragged behind Helios's chariot. Helios had a son,

Phaethon, by a mortal woman. The boy traveled to the ends of the earth to find his father. After many adventures he arrived at the edge of the earth, where he saw Helios preparing to harness the winged horses. The son begged for his father's approval. Helios granted Phaethon one wish.

Phaethon asked to drive the winged chariot to impress on his doubting friends that he was truly born to a god. Helios was horrified and tried to dissuade his son. The boy would not relent and forced the issue. Locked into his promise, Helios reluctantly relinquished the reins.

Under Phaethon's inexperienced hand, the horses veered from their normal path, swinging the raging sun closer and closer to the earth. Fire erupted across the globe. Phaethon was powerless to bring the winged steeds under control. The world was ablaze. Desperately, the gods appealed to Zeus, who reluctantly cast a thunderbolt at Phaeton, killing him. A Great Flood was unleashed to drown the fire.

The story of the misguided son playing with powers beyond his control traces the sequence of events that would erupt during an earth crust displacement: a shocking change in the path of the sun, followed by a violent worldwide flood.

In Egypt, the pyramids were also precisely aligned with the rising sun on the summer solstice. In an ancient Egyptian writing, the sun god decrees, "I am the one who hath made the water which becomes the Great Flood."[42] The sun "is usually said to have been born on or by 'the great flood.'"[43]

In Egyptian mythology, the world was seen as a bubble within an endless "Primordial Abyss of Waters." "This was unlike any sea which has a surface, for here there was neither up nor down, no distinction of side, only a limitless deep—endless, dark, and infinite. . . . It was thought that the seas, the rivers, the rain from heaven, and the waters in the wells, and the torrents of the floods were parts of the Primeval Waters which enveloped the world on every side."[44]

The Egyptians feared that these primeval waters might eventually seep into the world, flooding it. The pyramids, artificial mountains aligned with the new path of the sun, may symbolize the mountain on which the survivors of the last Great Flood ultimately found refuge.[45] The builders of these ancient monuments may have been paying homage to the land that their ancestors clung to after the Flood.

From all corners of the earth, the same story is told. The sun deviates from its regular path. The sky falls. The earth is wrenched and torn by earthquakes. And finally a great wave of water engulfs the globe. The survivors of such a calamity would have gone to any length to prevent it from happening again, and they lived in an age of magic. It was natural and necessary to construct elaborate devices to pacify the sun god or goddess and control or monitor the sun's path.

Is it any wonder that so many ancient people called themselves children of the sun? It was perhaps only later that this label became one of pride. At first it may well have originated as a frantic appeasement to the violent sun god. The sun was feared, the sky untethered, and the ocean volatile. A wayward sun might initiate a chain of events that could brutally shatter our world.

FOUR

ATLANTIS
IN ANTARCTICA

It began on a morning like any other. Steam rose from the swamps and bogs of the tropics. Clouds of mist covered the quiet lakes of Africa. Only a faint rustle across the grasslands betrayed the presence of the morning's first breeze. But on this day the silence was broken by a sound and a trembling that filled the earth with alarm. A rumbling that slowly turned to a roar as the earth's foundations were uprooted.

The beat of hundreds of thousands of wings brushed the sky as flocks of birds rose from their nests to seek safety. Roaming herds raised their heads from their foraging, sniffed the air, and shuffled uneasily. As the terrifying roar began to deafen them and the undulations of the earth triggered a deep panic, the wild animals began to run, desperately seeking shelter from the coming catastrophe. Terror struck the hearts of men and women as they flung themselves to their knees, pleading with the gods to spare them. But no mercy was to be shown.

Earthquakes of extraordinary violence strained the very foundations of the earth. At the polar caps, mountains of ice began to crumble and dissolve. The din became unbearable as great shelves of ice were shaken loose from their precarious perches and slid into a relentlessly rising sea.

Unchained, the ocean spilled from the confines of its gigantic basin. Gathering its mighty force, it began a slow, inevitable roll to the shore.

Gaining speed and power, the unrestrained wave raced with the turning earth to overwhelm defenseless shores.

The earth itself was an active performer in the tragedy. The sliding crust was the unseen instigator of the ocean's rebellion. Beneath the sand and rock of the ocean floor, the earth's crust buckled like an angry horse ridding itself of a dreaded rider.

Tidal wave followed tidal wave as earthquakes broke new ground. Rivers overflowed as gales of rain relentlessly pounded the earth. A flood, a deluge, a storm, and a hell—the likes of which no living human had seen—plagued the planet as the world's ocean broke its boundaries.

Slowly the water began to die down, the roar of the earth subsided, and the sun once again rose on a silent world. But it was not a silence of peace. It carried with it the ominous quiet of the slow and deadly process of freezing. A third disaster was preparing to strike opposite sides of the globe.

In Siberia, the reign of the great ivory-tusked, shaggy-haired mammoths came to a sudden end. The lush grasslands that had provided them with a bountiful living disappeared as snow began to fall. When it was over, Siberia had been transformed from a country that could support the voracious appetites of mammoths to a land whose very name would come to be synonymous with desolation.

The deadly process was not confined to the animals of Siberia. On the other side of the globe, in Lesser Antarctica, a veil of snow and ice was drawn across the land. As each century added more snow, the history of the people who once lived there began to fade.

The Atlanteans perished in such an overwhelming catastrophe that the fruits of their long and profound history were torn to shreds by the upheaval of the earth. Locked in the Antarctic Circle; Atlantis was buried beneath the ice. But a great legend had begun.

The Greek philosopher Plato (ca. 427–347 BCE) launched the adventures of a thousand armchair and boots-to-the-ground explorers with an intriguing tale that he assured his listeners, "though passing strange, is yet wholly true, as Solon, the wisest of the Seven, once confirmed."[1]

Solon (ca. 638–559 BCE) was Plato's ancestor and one of the seven acknowledged wise men of ancient Greece. The Roman biographer Plutarch (ca. 46–124 CE) describes the dire situation that led to the appointment of Solon as Athens's ultimate judge.

> The city stood on the brink of revolution, and it seemed as if the only way to put a stop to its perpetual disorders and achieve stability was to set up a tyranny. . . . At this point the most level-headed of the Athenians began to look toward Solon. They saw that he, more than anyone else, stood apart from the injustices of the time and was involved neither in the exhortations of the rich nor the privations of the poor, and so finally they appealed to him to come forward and settle their differences.[2]

Solon is considered the father of democracy. His concern for freedom and his compassion for the underprivileged compelled him to overturn long-ingrained injustices. Serfdom and slavery as payment for debt was outlawed, and the exclusive power of the aristocrats was abolished. But soon Solon faced obstacles, as Plutarch explains.

> Once Solon's laws had been put into effect, people came to visit him every day, praising some of them and finding fault with others, or advising him to insert a certain provision here or take out another there. A great many wanted to ask questions and cross-examine him on points of detail, and they kept pressing him to explain what was the object of this or that regulation. Solon saw that it was out of the question to meet such demands, but also that he would earn great ill will if he turned them all down. He was anxious to disengage himself from these complications and thus escape the faultfinding and captious criticism of his fellow countrymen, for as he remarks himself, "In great affairs you cannot please all parties." So he made his commercial interests as a ship owner an excuse to travel and sailed away obtaining leave of absence for ten years from the Athenians, in

the hope that during this period they would become accustomed to his laws. He went first of all to Egypt.[3]

Solon and his compatriots considered Egypt the fountain of knowledge. To travel there, no matter the hardship, was a necessary pilgrimage for those seeking wisdom. Clustered around the searing sand at the base of the pyramids were not the looted vaults echoing the edicts of dead pharaohs that greet us now, but instead a thriving community, wise with age and possessing a wealth of information controlled by the esteemed priests, whose authority could challenge even that of the pharaoh.

A deep reverence for the past permeated the priests' every action, thought, and deed. The past was the key to the future. It determined the pattern and shaped the mold that the priests were honor bound to preserve. More than mere caretakers of ritual, they were astronomers, mathematicians, magicians, civic administrators, and guardians of the secret sciences of antiquity. Only the brightest children could enter the priesthood. If they were fortunate, after a long period of study and devotion, a handful were chosen to see the sacred texts.

These were the priests that the esteemed Solon sought out. "He spent some time studying and discussing philosophy with Psenophis of Heliopolis and Sonchis of Sais, who were the most learned of the Egyptian priests. According to Plato it was from them that he heard the legend of the lost continent of Atlantis."[4] What we do know of the location of Atlantis is voiced by the Egyptian priest whom Plutarch identifies as Sonchis.

Sonchis had tutored the philosopher Pythagoras (ca. 582–507 BCE), who was recognized as a genius in his time. (Rumors persisted that Plato owed more to Pythagoras than he revealed to his devoted followers. It was whispered that he had plagiarized a book written by Pythagoras.)*

Pythagoras was the first person to claim that the earth was spherical, that it was "inhabited round about and that there were places on

---

*Some ancient sources claimed Plato purchased (or otherwise illegally obtained) three books written by Pythagoras and used them to compose the *Timaeus* dialogue containing the legend of Atlantis.

the opposite side of the globe where: our 'down' is their 'up.'"[5] He also believed that a vast island continent lay in the southern hemisphere. Some regard him as the first to suggest that Antarctica and the other continents even existed.[6]

Pythagoras established a brotherhood in the Italian city of Croton. The community was eventually overthrown in a revolt that may have taken the teacher's life. The Roman poet Ovid (43–18 BCE) claimed to have the text of a speech the great philosopher gave to the citizens of Croton "For my part, considering how the generations of men have passed from the age of gold to that of iron, how often the fortunes of differing place have been reversed, I should believe that nothing lasts for long under the same form. I have seen what was once solid earth now changed into sea, and lands created out of what was ocean . . . ancient anchors have been found on mountain tops."[7]

Like Sonchis, Pythagoras shared the belief that what is most ancient is most perfect. This attitude is hard for those of us who live in the twenty-first century to grasp. For unlike the children of ancient Greece and Egypt who were raised with myths that spoke of perfect beings who thrived in ancient times, children now gaze at incredible science fiction projections of the future. Although our confidence is sometimes shaken, it is still to the future, rather than the past, that we look for perfection.

The idea of "progress" has penetrated current thinking so completely that it is vaguely disturbing, yet endlessly fascinating, to learn of the great achievements of ancient Egypt, Mexico, or Peru. Impressive ruins shake our sense of the inevitable march of progress and make us wonder about our own future. That an advanced civilization thrived and then perished in remote times is an uncomfortable realization for those who believe in the inevitability of progress.

Six centuries after the death of Pythagoras, the Roman geographer Pomponius Mela published a map of the world that included a depiction of the philosopher's southern island continent (see figure 4.1). Mela called this mysterious island Antichthones, meaning "land of the people of the other side of the earth."

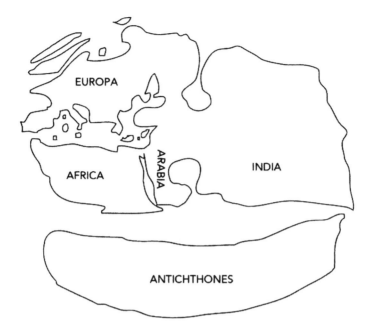

Figure 4.1. The Roman geographer Pomponius Mela adopted Pythagoras's idea of a great southern island continent.

Solon met Pythagoras's tutor, Sonchis, in the Egyptian city of Sais, where he tried to impress the priest with tales of Greek mythology about the Great Flood. But Sonchis interrupted his visitor, saying, "O Solon, Solon, you Greeks are always children: there is not such a thing as an old Greek. . . . You possess not a single belief that is ancient and derived from old tradition, nor yet one science that is hoary with age."[8]

Sonchis gave Solon a lesson in what ancient history *really* meant with his vivid description of events that had devastated the earth before the Flood wreaked its havoc.

Many and manifold are the destructions of mankind that have been and shall be; the greatest are by fire and water; but besides these there are lesser ones in countless other fashions. Your own story of how Phaethon, the child of the Sun, yoked his father's chariot, and because he was unable to drive it along his father's path, burnt up things on the earth and himself was smitten by a thunderbolt and slain is a mythical version of the truth that there is at long intervals a deviation of the bodies that move around the earth in the heavens and consequent widespread destruction by fire of things on earth.[9]

To save humankind, Zeus destroyed Phaethon with a thunderbolt and then unleashed the Flood to put out the fire. This "story" traces precisely the sequence of events that would erupt during an earth crust displacement. A shocking change in the path of the sun is followed by violent worldwide earthquakes and floods.

Sonchis possessed an extremely "modern" perspective about mythology. He treated the Greek myth of Phaethon and his careening horses dragging the uncontrollable sun behind them as a symbolic version of real physical events. Considering the literal mentality of his time*—six centuries before the birth of Christ—this is an amazing example of thinking outside the box. His sophistication extended to his geographic description of the world, a view radically different from what is taught even in the twenty-first century.

THE EUROPEAN WORLDVIEW

Our current geographic perspective originated with the European age of discovery and reflects the ethnocentric prejudices of those Europeans. Even the common divisions of east and west as presented on a typical map—the Middle East, the Far East, and so forth—are strictly relative to Europe. There is no *geographic* justification for placing Europe at the center of the world (see figure 4.2).

As the European explorers of the late fifteenth and early sixteenth centuries traveled around Africa and South America, charting unknown

---

*The perspective articulated by Sonchis is usually attributed to the fourth century BCE Sicilian philosopher Euhemerus, yet Sonchis lived in the sixth century BCE, some two hundred years before Euhemerus.

Figure 4.2. A world map centered on North America misleadingly makes the Atlantic Ocean and Pacific Ocean appear to be distinct bodies of water. Drawing by Rand Flem-Ath and Rose Flem-Ath.

seas and seeking routes to exotic treasures, they renamed sections of the ocean. The prospect of navigating an unknown and overwhelming sea became less terrifying if it was divided into manageable sections (no matter how artificial) that could be tidily plotted on the explorer's newly drawn maps. For example, after a dangerous voyage through the treacherous straits that now bear his name, Ferdinand Magellan (ca. 1480–1521) finally reached a calm and open stretch of water, which, in his relief, he christened the Pacific Ocean, meaning the "peaceful ocean." Similarly, Vasco da Gama (ca. 1460–1524) named the route that took him to India, the Indian Ocean.

The prospect of navigating an unknown and overwhelming ocean was made a little less terrifying by dividing it into manageable sections (no matter how artificial), which could then be plotted on the explorers' newly drawn maps. Soon the clamor for spices, silk, and other precious goods created a demand for even more detailed ocean charts. These maps reinforced the false concept of a divided sea and effectively erased the original

Greek meaning of the word *ocean*—a single body of water they called the Atlantic. Aristotle, Plato's contemporary, described the Atlantic, stating, "This sea, which is outside our inhabited earth, and washes our region all round is called both 'Atlantic' and 'the ocean.'"[10] To the Greeks the Atlantic lay to the north, south, east, and west of their world.

Our habitual view of the planet depicting north at the "top" of the globe reinforces the appearance of the ocean being separated into several bodies of water. However, oceanographers have long recognized that our planet has only one ocean—the "World Ocean."

"The concept of the World Ocean held by a marine scientist is somewhat different from that of the layman. All of us learn in grade school to identify the names and placement of the continents and oceans. This exercise reveals that the oceans completely surround the landmass, but it is slightly misleading because it suggests that the oceans are separated geographically. From an oceanographer's point of view, the emphasis should be on a world ocean that is completely intercommunicating."[11] The unity of the single world ocean is obvious when the planet is viewed from the southern hemisphere (see figure 4.3).

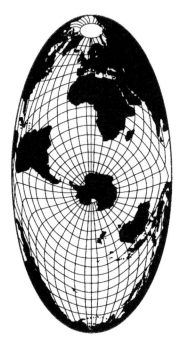

Figure 4.3. The world seen from the vantage of Antarctica as the center point highlights the unity of the earth's single ocean. This map also reinterprets our notion of what constitutes a continent. Seen from Antarctica, the earth's presumably separate continents can be seen to be parts of a single land mass. Source: U.S. Naval Support Force *Introduction to Antarctica* (Washington D.C.: U. S. Printing Office, 1969, centerpiece).

Sonchis described Atlantis as being beyond the known world of the Greeks in the "real ocean." This "ocean truly named" matches the single world ocean of modern oceanography. The European-centered view dictated that the earth consisted of seven continents and an ocean blocked into a series of individual, smaller bodies of water: classifications that are unrelated to the earth's actual geographic contours. The prejudices of European explorers became the world's prejudices. Even the common divisions of east and west are only relative to Europe. But there is no *geographic* reason to place Europe in the center of the world. Our planet is quite democratically round.

So there is really only one world ocean rather than five separate oceans. Now let us consider whether there are really seven continents. Twelve thousand years ago a land bridge, Beringia, connected America to Asia. It was theoretically possible to walk through what today we call Europe, Africa, Asia, North America, and South America and never touch water. For the people of Atlantis these five "continents" formed the outer rim of their world: a "whole opposite continent" that *encircled* the world ocean.

Unlike our ancestors, who were forced to sail their way around the globe in patchwork fashion, we can see the entire planet through the all-encompassing eye of a satellite. Photographs from space reveal Europe as merely a peninsula of the Afro-Euro-Asian continent and North and South America as one continuous land mass separated only by the man-made Panama Canal. Treating North and South America as separate continents served the colonial interests of the kings and queens of Portugal, Spain, and England, not the science of geography. This dated perspective has blinded us to the location of Atlantis.

Sonchis attempted to explain to Solon the nature and location of Atlantis, but in order to give an accurate account he had to reach beyond the Greek's limited notion of the globe. His description contains sixteen clues[12] to the site of the lost land.

1. 9560 BCE
2. Change in the path of the sun
3. Worldwide earthquakes of extraordinary violence
4. Overwhelming worldwide floods
5. Island
6. Continent (larger than Libya and Asia)
7. High above sea level
8. Numerous high mountains
9. Impressive cliffs rising sharply from the ocean
10. Other islands
11. Abundant mineral resources
12. Beyond the Pillars of Heracles (known world)
13. In a distant point in the "Atlantic" ocean
14. In the real ocean
15. The Mediterranean Sea is only a bay of the real ocean
16. The true continent completely surrounds the real ocean.

THE ANCIENT GREEK WORLDVIEW

The Greeks of Solon's time saw the world as an island in the middle of a vast ocean. This world-island was divided into three important cultural units: Europe, Libya, and Asia.

The Pillars of Heracles were a psychological barrier, a forbidden gateway beyond which none but the foolish would dare to venture (see figure 4.4). The Greek poet Pindar (518–438 BCE) wrote that the Pillars were considered "the farthest limits [of the Greek world]. . . . What lies beyond cannot be trodden by the wise or unwise."[13] This original concept of the phrase "Pillars of Heracles" is often forgotten or ignored by searchers for Atlantis, who assume only a literal interpretation of the phrase, thereby limiting the location of the lost continent to the North Atlantic.

What the Greeks called "Libya" described the area we know as North Africa. Their "Asia" was equivalent to the present-day Middle East. Only their "Europe" matched its contemporary area. In an

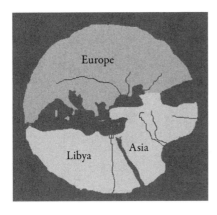

Figure 4.4. The Greek world-view at the time of Solon. The Straits of Gibraltar were then known to the ancient Greeks as the Pillars of Heracles.

encounter described by Plato 2,500 years ago, Sonchis told Solon that Atlantis was larger than Libya (North Africa) and Asia (the Middle East) combined—a match with the size of Antarctica.

Plato added that compared to the "real ocean," the Mediterranean Sea is "but a bay having a narrow entrance." In describing Atlantis, he stated, "To begin with the region as a whole was said to be high above the level of the sea, from which it rose precipitously . . . [and the mountains] were celebrated as being more numerous, higher, and more beautiful than any that exist today.[14]

A description of Antarctica, published in 1992 (*more than twenty-four centuries later*), offers a strikingly similar geographic account. "The most conspicuous physical features of the continent are its high inland plateau (much of it over 10,000 ft.), the Transantarctic Mountains . . . and the mountainous Antarctica Peninsula and off-lying island. The continental shelf averages 20 miles in width (half the global mean and in places it is non-existent)."[15] Like Atlantis, Antarctica rises high above sea level. Indeed, it is the highest continent in the world.

Average Elevation in Feet[16]

Antarctica	6,500	North America	1,900
Asia	3,200	Europe	940
South America	2,000	Australia	800
Africa	2,000		

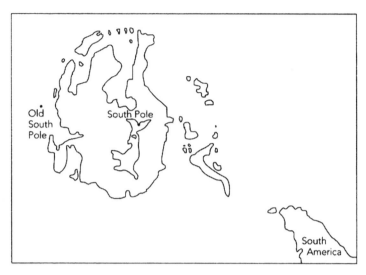

Figure 4.5. Antarctica has a set of islands that are obscured by today's ice sheet.

Geologists, using the theory of plate tectonics, have concluded that Antarctica was once joined to the mineral-rich lands of South Africa, Western Australia, and South America, and so they have reasoned that similar mineral resources must be locked beneath its frozen soil.

Two of the geological clues could only have been confirmed by modern science. In 1958 it was discovered that Antarctica, contrary to what we see on most modern maps, is not a monolithic landmass, but rather an island continent adjoined by a group of smaller islands not visible to the naked eye. Although these neighboring islands are covered by a fresh ice cap, seismic surveys have penetrated their blanket of snow to reveal the true shape of the island continent. An ice-free map of Antarctica unveils the "other islands" mentioned in Plato's account (see figure 4.5).

THE ATLANTEAN WORLDVIEW

Ultimately, every search for the lost continent must answer to Plato's detailed description of the island's geography. When we step outside the comfort zone of our distorted cultural perception, Antarctica passes Plato's test. Plato's account provides an accurate, global view of the world as described to a Greek with a limited view of the earth. Although different from our current perspective, it is accurate if we imagine ourselves residents of Antarctica. Atlantis is described to the Greek as being beyond his known world (Pillars of Heracles), and encircled by a vast body of water called the "real" ocean. Compared to the real ocean, the Mediterranean Sea is "but a bay having a narrow entrance." The real ocean was the world ocean. Plato's chronicle states that, when seen from Atlantis, the "real ocean" appeared to be framed by an unbroken mass of land that "may with the fullest truth and fitness be named a continent" (see figures 4.6 and 4.7).

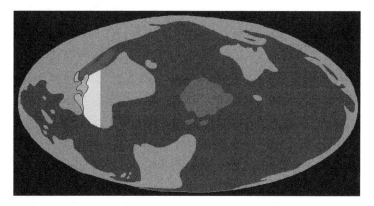

Figure 4.6. These features of Plato's Atlantis correspond directly with a worldview centered on Antarctica: a single world ocean, a surrounding whole opposite continent, some islands off Atlantis, the Mediterranean Sea is but a bay of the "real ocean," and the size of "Libya" (North Africa) and "Asia" (the Middle East) approximates the actual size of Antarctica. Drawing by Rand Flem-Ath and Rose Flem-Ath.

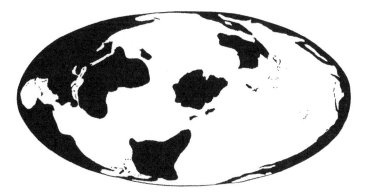

Figure 4.7. The Atlantean worldview. Drawing by Rand Flem-Ath and Rose Flem-Ath.

The map above reconstructs this ancient worldview. It shows the earth as seen from Antarctica before the last earth crust displacement and the catastrophic destruction of Atlantis. Due to the lower ocean levels at the time, England and Japan were not islands and Beringia joined the Americas with the Afro-Euro-Asia continent, forming the unbroken world continent.

Sonchis said that Atlantis was "larger than Libya and Asia combined; from it there was passage for the sea-farers of those times to reach the other islands, and from them the whole opposite continent which surrounds what can truly be called the ocean. For these regions that lie within the strait we were talking about seem to be but a bay having a narrow entrance; but the other ocean is the real ocean and the land which entirely surrounds it may with fullest truth and fitness be named a continent."[17]

Every search for Atlantis is built upon the foundation of these two sentences spoken by an Egyptian priest twenty-five centuries ago. The priest claimed the location of Atlantis was recorded in Egypt's most ancient records, presumably originally written by a survivor of the lost land. When compared to figure 4.7, this Atlantean account of the earth becomes exactly what Plato claims: an accurate depiction of a real place at a very specific time.

After the catastrophe, torn and shattered, abandoned to a freezing death, Atlantis lived on with a strange fascination in the memories of peoples scattered throughout the globe. Shreds of the past and wisps of recollection were woven together over the centuries.

Remnants of this delicate fabric of history eventually came into the hands of the learned Egyptian priest, Sonchis. Many rare documents had no doubt passed through the hands of this honored priest, but the story of Atlantis he carefully wrapped, sending it intact from generation to generation through the voice of Solon and, eventually, Plato.

These words were spoken around 600 BCE. As can be seen from the map in figure 4.7, they describe the earth as it would have been mapped by someone from Antarctica almost twelve thousand years ago as he or she looked out to the wider world.

From this perspective Plato's account is an accurate depiction of the *entire globe* as it would have appeared in 9600 BCE. Plato relates that this finely tuned geographic knowledge originated with the survivors of Atlantis, who passed their maps to the ancient Egyptians.[18] Only an advanced civilization could have achieved such a highly sophisticated conceptualization of our planet.

Despite the evidence before our eyes, we lost sight of Atlantis because we inherited the skewed worldview of the European explorers. But if we remove that prejudicial lens, the earth's contours fall into place like the final pieces of a puzzle to reveal a crystal-clear image of Atlantis in Antarctica.

FIVE

THE LOST ISLAND PARADISE

To this point, we have been exploring through words and ideas and images on maps that have been passed down to us through the ages, pointing us to Atlantis. But now we take a different approach, using the modern science of genetics to draw a link between the ancient pharaohs of Egypt and a native people of Canada, half a world away. But how could these distant people be connected? Perhaps, through Atlantis?

Off the northwest coast of Canada lie 150 islands known as the Queen Charlottes. Incongruously named after a long-dead, bewigged, British aristocrat, this exquisite place was more suitably christened Haida Gwaii, or Islands of the Surface People, by the Haida, who have occupied the land for at least ten thousand years.[1] They believe that they live in a special place suspended between the sky and the sea gods. The Haida's wood, shell, and bone carvings are world-famous. But their art reaches its fullest expression in the haunting features of the totem poles that still stand guard in some isolated inlets.

This fog-swept, rugged area of the 150 scattered islands cradles some of the oldest living forests in the New World. The great trees have thrived there because the western edge of the islands remained unglaciated during the last ice age.

The Haida celebrated elaborate traditions like the potlatch, a means of distributing wealth among all the people, until the practice was savagely repressed by the Canadian government. The ruthless new order was further enforced when Haida children were pressed into residential schools and forbidden from speaking their own language under pain of severe punishment. The scythe of tragedy continued to cut through the people when in the summer of 1862 a plague of smallpox, helped along its deadly path by government intervention, killed 83 percent of the population.[2]

Despite this painful recent history, the Haida are enjoying a renaissance. Their culture is intimately tied to the land and sea, and that bond is reflected in their magnificent art, which is among the most sought after First Nations' art in the world.

Like the Egyptians, Greeks, and other ancient peoples, the Haida feared for the safety of their home when earthquakes shook the land. They placed their faith in a god who restrained the buckling earth and secured the sky from falling. "Sacred-One-Standing-and-Moving . . . is the Earth Supporter; he himself rests upon a copper box, which . . . is conceived as a boat; from his breast rises the Pillar of the Heavens, extending to the sky; his movements are the cause of earthquakes."[3] If the Earth Supporter ever lost control of the Pillar of the Heavens, the ensuing catastrophic effects would mirror the events of an earth crust displacement: earthquakes, the illusion of a falling sky, and a disastrous worldwide flood.

A Haida legend tells of a time before the Great Flood when their ancestors lived in a magnificent city in a distant land.

> The great chief of the heavens . . . decided to punish this great village
> . . . he caused the river waters to rise. Soon the rivers and creeks all
> over the country began to swell. Some of the people escaped to the
> hills, while others embarked in their large canoes. Still the waters were
> rising higher and higher until only the high mountain peaks showed
> above the swollen water. . . . [The Haida ancestors landed on a moun-
> taintop.] When the Flood was over, the lost stone anchors were found
> there, at the place where they had anchored their canoes.[4]

The Haida language, which the people are making a heroic effort to preserve, has never satisfactorily been pigeonholed by linguists. It is usually grouped with the Na-Dene First Nations language.[5] The Na-Dene language may be related to the language of the Sumerians, who created the world's first known civilization in the vicinity of Iraq six thousand years ago.[6]

As we will see, the Haida and the people of the distant land of ancient Sumer share many things, from cultural traits to genetic traits, but before we can link them, let's examine Sumer a bit. The Sumerians domesticated rabbits, goats,* sheep, wheat, rye, and barley. In northern Syria, on a mound overlooking the Euphrates River, archaeologists have discovered one of the oldest remains of agriculture in the world.[7] For hundreds of thousands of years, people in this part of the world lived by hunting and gathering. Suddenly within the same century as the fall of Atlantis, they turned to agriculture.

Radiocarbon dating at Tell Abu Hureya revealed that by 9500 BC some early villagers had begun to practice farming alongside their hunting and gathering, domesticating wild rabbits, goats, sheep, wild wheat, rye, and barley. From these early developments arose what archaeologists believe was the first civilization after Atlantis—Sumeria—which began to flourish around 3300 BCE.

Three gods were held in high esteem by the Sumerians. The first, Enlil, was known as the lord of the air and the king of kings. He was the most worshipped and feared because he wielded the most destructive weapon: the power of the Flood. "The word of Enlil is a breath of wind, the eye sees it not. His word is a deluge which advances and has no rival."[8]

Enki, the second great god, was the lord of the earth and the god of waters. The Sumerians believed Enki saved them from the Flood. He overheard the birth of a conspiracy between the flood god, Enlil, and the third powerful god, the sky god, An, in which they planned to

---

*Goats were mentioned by Plato in *Laws* as one of the first animals to be domesticated.

destroy mankind. Enki determined that he would save one man and his family from the coming disaster. He chose Ziusudra, a king and priest living on the island of Dilmun. A Babylonian myth records Enki's words: "Destroy thy house, build a vessel. Leave thy riches, seek thy life. Store in thy vessel the seeds of all life."[9]

We learn the fate of Ziusudra's ark from the original Sumerian tale, which states, "When for seven days and seven nights, the Flood had raged over the land, and the huge boat had been tossed on the great water by the storms, the Sun-god arose shedding light in Heaven and Earth. Ziusudra made an opening in the side of the great ship. He let the light of the hero Sun-god enter into the great ship. Before the Sun-god he bowed his face to the ground."[10] The vessel comes to rest on the top of a mountain in the Middle East. Like Noah, Ziusudra and his family must begin life anew.

In 1899, the lost Sumerian culture offered up another legacy. A team of American archaeologists were excited when they unearthed thirty-five thousand tablets from a treasure trove that contained the written records of the world's oldest known civilization. They were from Nippur, the ancient Sumerian city dedicated to the flood god, Enlil.

Such a rich find could reveal the very roots of civilization.

According to the tablets, those roots were to be found in a place called Dilmun, a mountainous island in the ocean. Most of Dilmun's people had perished when the sky god conspired with Enlil to destroy humankind. The survivors escaped the Flood in a great ship (in which they stored "the seeds of all life"), sailing to a mountain near Nippur.[11] The tablets said that Dilmun, the island paradise from which they had fled, lay across the Indian Ocean[12] toward the south—toward Antarctica.

BASIC ELEMENTS OF
HAIDA AND SUMERIAN MYTHS

The Haida and the Sumerians share a remarkably similar story of their origins.

The basic elements of the Haida myth are: Long ago, our ancestors lived in the world's largest village. Life was carefree until the chief of the heavens decided to destroy humankind by changing the sky and bringing a worldwide flood. Survivors escaped in giant canoes, which took them to a new home, where they landed on a mountaintop. A new era began.

The basic elements of the Sumerian myth are strikingly similar: Long ago our ancestors lived on the island paradise of Dilmun. Life was carefree until the flood god Enlil decided to destroy humankind by changing the sky and bringing a worldwide flood. Survivors escaped in a large ship which took them to a new home, where they landed upon a mountaintop. A new era began.

The rain-drenched forests of Haida Gwaii lie half a world away from the sun-baked plains of Iraq, yet their mythologies and languages share critical elements. It is unlikely that they made contact even though they both have a long tradition of ocean voyages. But could it be that they shared a common motherland? It was this curiosity about the similarities between the Haida and the Sumerians—the possibility that they could be connected through memories of a lost island paradise to the south—that Rand Flem-Ath (coauthor of this book) took with him on his first visit to Haida Gwaii.

The Haida carver and master jeweler Gwaai* was intrigued by the similarities between his people and those of ancient Sumer and Greece. He shared his knowledge of the many Haida myths celebrating the plants and animals, the sea and earth that are so precious to the people who have occupied these beautiful islands since the time of the Great Flood.

Gwaai told Rand about Foam-Woman, the great goddess who emerged from the sea to establish a dry home for those who lived beneath the ocean. She became possessive of the newly discovered land and prevented the other beings, confined to their increasingly over-

---

*The name Gwaai means "first son" in Haida and is not to be confused with Gwaii, which means "islands."

crowded ocean, from joining her. The sea dwellers were too afraid to challenge Foam-Woman, even though they longed to rise from the water and become earthlings.

Gwaai also revealed a story of the Haida carving tradition that dates from these ancient times. It is a tale about one of the smallest, most humble of animals.

Only Mouse-Woman dared to challenge Foam-Woman. Mouse-Woman, who at this time was of normal size, rose from the ocean and scolded Foam-Woman for not sharing the new land with all the people. As she advanced on Foam-Woman the goddess cast a spell over her. With each step she took, Mouse-Woman shrank. Until finally, she was transformed into the tiny creature we know today.

But Foam-Woman was so impressed by Mouse-Woman's bravery that she yielded to the wishes of the sea people to join her on land.

To honor the courage of Mouse-Woman, Gwaai and other Haida artists often conceal an image of a mouse in their carvings.

Raven, one of the most significant creatures in Haida mythology,* is described as a serious-minded god rather than the trickster that he became. At that time, the myth says, "Hereabouts was all saltwater," which suggests a time right after the Flood. And the "first land" was a rock protruding from the ocean, where Raven landed.

Sumerian mythology tells of the time when a creature from the sea emerged as the first person. Both the Haida and Sumerians had a long love affair with the sea. The Sumerians' vocabulary contains hundreds of nautical terms. They also share with the Haida unique stories about amphibious god ancestors with tails. The god Oannes was half man and half fish. During the day Oannes taught the Sumerians how to write and the other arts of civilization before returning to the sea as night fell.

Then Gwaai volunteered that there is a genetic trait uniquely

---

*The Raven is a trickster. In Haida mythology, the Raven and the Eagle are the two most important creatures.

prevalent among the Haida that results in a high incidence of ankylosing spondylitis (AS), a form of inflammatory arthritis and a painful and potentially debilitating disease. AS attacks the skeleton, particularly the neck, pelvis, and spinal column. Scientists had tested the Haida for this trait by taking hair samples for DNA analysis.* Rand was reminded of Robert Brinchurst's description in *A Story as Sharp as a Knife: The Classical Haida Mythtellers and Their World* of Skaay, the blind Haida myth teller who was "an old man with a crippled back and a beautiful mind."[13] The crippled back could be the result of AS.

Ninety-three percent of people with AS carry the antigen HLA-B27, including half of the Haida—among the highest percentage of any group of people in the world. Thirty-six percent of the Navajo (also known as the Dine)—the largest tribe of First Nations people in North America—are also burdened with the antigen. As we've seen, the languages of the Haida and Dine are usually grouped together linguistically (although not all researchers agree with the grouping) into the Na-Dene language group

Surprisingly, these two North American peoples share their rare medical condition with a powerful dynasty from halfway around the world. "Among the pharaohs of the eighteenth and nineteenth dynasty of Old Egypt, at least three had ankylosing spondylitis: Amenhotep (Amenophis) II, Ramses II (Ramses the Great), and his son Merenptah."[14] Egypt's geographic proximity to Sumer is suggestive. Both civilizations were largely dependent on the same crops: wheat and barley. These founding crops came to Egypt via Sumer and helped launch Egyptian civilization.

Ramses the Great, one of the most famous of all the pharaohs, is often featured in the story of Moses and the Exodus. He suffered from AS and was so badly crippled that, gruesomely, before his corpse could

---

*The Haida Nation stopped the experiments when it was learned that the scientists had other than medical reasons for obtaining the samples. They had introduced an anthropological agenda. The Haida blood samples were to be DNA tested to compare them with other tribes. The Haida felt they had been tricked and withdrew their cooperation.

be lowered into the sarcophagus, the mummifiers were forced to break his neck so that his body would lie flat.

Merenptah was Ramses the Great's thirteenth son, and like his father, his remains exhibit all the hallmarks of ankylosing spondylitis. That father and son should bend beneath the same affliction is not unusual since AS is assumed to be primarily genetic. What *is* curious is the fact that the earliest of the three mummies that exhibit signs of AS was that of Amenhotep II, who was not a direct ancestor of either Ramses the Great or Merenptah. Ramses I (Ramses II's father) had ascended to the throne through a military coup.

So AS appeared in different Egyptian dynasties through different bloodlines. This suggests, as Gwaai pointed out to Rand, that the prevalence of AS must have been high within the royal family of the New Kingdom of Egypt. Gwaai's idea made sense. What didn't make sense was the fact that Egypt's closest neighbors, the Ethiopians to the south and the Berbers to the west, are among the populations that carry the lowest rates of HLA-B27. The Mediterranean Sea lies to the north, but there was no successful sea invasion of Egypt by which the genetic disease could have been introduced until the Roman period. This suggests that the AS that was so prevalent among the pharaohs probably came from the east—from the direction of ancient Sumer.

So how *did* HLA-B27 end up in ancient Egypt? The answer, it seems, might be found in the bloodlines of the foreign pharaohs who ruled immediately before the eighteenth and nineteenth dynasties.

For centuries no intruder dared invade Egypt. The Egyptians grew smug in their security and independence. This smugness offered a clear opportunity for imaginative invaders with a revolutionary new weapon. The Hyksos descended from the east in horse-drawn chariots that moved so swiftly that the Egyptians had no time to marshal a defense. The Hyksos, according to the ancient Egyptian historian Manetho, came from the Persian Gulf, the homeland of the Sumerians. They brought with their victory the seeds of a painful disease, ankylosing spondylitis.

Bryan Stykes, author of *The Seven Daughters of Eve*,[15] has developed a technique by which DNA can be extracted from ancient bones. This new science could prove the radical theory of an ancient link between the Haida and the Sumerians. The discovery of such a link would open the door to the idea that they could have originated as one people. A people who shared a common motherland—a lost island paradise that perished in a Great Flood.

SIX

AZTLAN AND THE POLAR PARADISE

From Egypt and the northwest coast of Canada, our attention again turns to Peru, where we last explored the ruins of the great mountain city, Machu Picchu. We look at the highest major lake in the world and its connection to the flooded and lost Atlantis.

Anyone who attempts the 4,350-meter climb up the rough and winding road to Lake Titicaca in the Peruvian Andes gasps as the thin mountain air evades his or her lungs. But the struggle is worth it, for at the summit lies a mysterious lake. Only the graceful reed boats of the native people who still fish its depths and the restless winds of the past disturb the surface of the lake.

The Inca claim that their ancestors came here in the remote past to construct the great city of Tiahuanaco and its amazing Temple of the Sun. The city was built from massive boulders, comparable to those of the Egyptian pyramids. But the construction is incomplete, as if it had been abruptly abandoned.

No one has spent more time or effort studying Tiahuanaco's ruins than Arthur Posnansky (1874–1946). He spent the better part of his life trying to unravel its mysteries. Posnansky concluded that the Temple of the Sun had been constructed more than ten thousand years ago, around the same time that Atlantis was destroyed. He was convinced that a Great Flood had drowned much of the earth. In one amazing passage he offers a prophetic conclusion. "The face of the earth has with the passage of time undergone great transformations. Where today we find the arctic region covered with a vast tunic of ice, there lies hidden, perhaps, in an impenetrable silence, the ground which in very remote epochs was the dwelling place of great concentrated masses of human beings.[1]

The same words could apply to Antarctica.

In the center of Tiahuanaco, the massive Temple of the Sun is aligned with the rising sun, as are the pyramids of Egypt and Mexico. However, there is a slight discrepancy in its angles. Posnansky reasoned that if the ancient builders were capable of constructing such elaborate monuments in the thin air of the high Andes, then surely they could accurately align their holy temple with the rising sun on the summer solstice.

It occurred to him that perhaps the boulders were correctly aligned when first erected, but gradual alterations of the earth's axis over a long period of time had resulted in what now, at first glance, appeared to be a misalignment. If the temple had been properly aligned when it was first built, then a construction date could be estimated based on the precession of the equinoxes. Posnansky concluded that the temple was correctly aligned to a date "somewhere beyond ten thousand years."[2]

Archaeologists have dismissed this notion as fantasy. It is simply not possible, in their view, for a civilization to have existed at such an early date. (This would be four thousand years before Sumer, the "first" civilization recognized by archaeologists.) Posnansky's research has consequently been ignored.

However, the Polish researcher's estimated date for the construction of the Temple of the Sun on Lake Titicaca has recently been given a boost with the unexpected discovery of the age of the Great Sphinx of ancient Egypt. Two methods have been used to date the construction of the Sphinx: one using evidence of erosion and the other using the gradual changes in the heavens as seen from Earth.

The idea that the Sphinx might be much older than Egyptian

civilization was first proposed in the late 1940s by the French scholar R. A. Schwaller de Lubicz. In *Le roi de la theocritie pharaonique (Sacred Science* in the English version), Schwaller claimed that the Great Sphinx had experienced extensive *water* erosion. We all know that the Sphinx lies in a vast desert where rain is rare. In 1972, John Anthony West focused on this insight of Schwaller's and included it in his book, *Serpent in the Sky: The High Wisdom of Ancient Egypt.*[3]

The revolutionary idea that the Sphinx might predate Egyptian civilization was too radical for Egyptologists to consider. They ignored it, preferring silence to debate.

West continued to explore the idea. Eventually, he interested a geologist from the University of Boston, Dr. Robert M. Schoch, in his work. Schoch was skeptical but curious. He went to Egypt with West to see for himself the weathering patterns on the Sphinx. It soon become clear to Schoch that the Sphinx had indeed been weathered by rain for thousands of years before the desert claimed the region. Wind erosion cuts sharp, straight patterns into sediment layers. But the Sphinx exhibits the round, furrowed contours typical of water erosion. This meant that the monument must have been constructed during a long rainy period sometime before 5000 BCE and very possibly much earlier. Since this predates the appearance of Egyptian civilization by thousands of years, the question was at once raised: who carved the Great Sphinx?

On October 23, 1991, Schoch presented his conclusions to the Geological Society of America. His data were accepted at once. Schoch and West had begun to turn back the clock of human history by thousands of years. In 1992, they took their argument to Chicago before the American Association for the Advancement of Science. Once again support was forthcoming from geologists, but Egyptologists simply could not accept such an ancient age for the Sphinx. It *must* be incorrect, so their reasoning went, for the alternative was to suggest a notion that, as one Egyptologist claimed, undermined "everything we know about ancient Egypt."[4]

In the fall of 1993 and again in the summer of 1994, West presented his documentary, *The Mystery of the Sphinx*, on U.S. television. The arguments were now too strong to be ignored. It was clear that the very existence of the Sphinx and the impressive temples standing in front of it, built with stones weighing more than 180 metric tons, was evidence for the existence of a long-lost ancient, yet advanced, civilization.

In 1994, Robert Bauval and Adrian Gilbert published *The Orion Mystery*.[5] They discovered that the layout of Egypt's great pyramids followed the pattern of the constellation Orion as it would have appeared in the year 10,450 BCE. Orion, representing a giant star-belted god striding across the heavens, appears near the Milky Way, which to the Egyptians seemed to flow in an immense stream across the heavens. Its counterpart on Earth was the Nile River. The three pyramids of Giza mirror the positions of the three stars of Orion's belt.

Bauval and Gilbert, using precessional astronomy, dated the actual construction of the Great Pyramid to 2450 BC. They concluded that this date corresponded to what the ancient Egyptians called the "First Time"—an age when the gods entrusted mortals, the first pharaohs, with the laws and wisdom that would enable them to rule Egypt.

The Great Sphinx, as part of the Giza pyramid complex, is also orientated to the "First Time" (10,450 BC) and may actually have been built then. It's possible that the Great Sphinx is a remnant of a much larger project constructed sometime after 10,450 BC. The discoveries of Bauval and Gilbert, when coupled with the research of West and Schoch, hints at the possibility that there are much older structures, physically connected to the Great Sphinx, hidden beneath the pyramids.

Now, two sciences, geology and astronomy, are pushing back humankind's achievements to a time well before any known civilization. Bauval and Gilbert's astronomical evidence followed the same measurements that had led Posnansky to conclude that an advanced civilization once existed. Geology and astronomy are working in tandem to provide evidence that our notion of the age of civilization is flawed. But archaeologists, the scientists most directly involved with the human past, have never discovered any physical evidence for the existence of any civilization as old as 9600 BCE. All that changed with the discovery of the world's oldest monumental buildings.

GÖBEKLI TEPE, THE WORLD'S OLDEST MONUMENTUAL ARCHITECTURE

It is one of the most sensational archaeological discoveries ever made. Known as Göbekli Tepe, this "temple" complex covers an area of twenty-two acres of Turkish territory just north of the Syrian border. Initially, archaeologists thought that the large limestone slabs rising out of the ground were Byzantine graves. But when Dr. Klaus Schmidt and his team from the German Archaeological Institute excavated deeper, they realized that this was a much more significant site than the initial examination of the slabs had indicated.

The Byzantine "grave stones" crowned a series of eighteen-foot-high T-shaped stone pillars, many of which weighed sixteen tons. Schmidt estimates that the strength of as many as five hundred people would have been needed to move the massive pillars, "the oldest known example of monumental architecture" in the world,[6] from their quarry half a kilometre away.

The exploration of Göbekli Tepe is still in its infancy with only about 10 percent of the site having been excavated. But one astonishing fact has already bewildered archaeologists. The most sophisticated and colossal pillars, which date to 11,600 years ago, were found at the oldest levels of the site. Archaeologists believe that humans had not yet domesticated animals or developed the wheel at this time. So how could primitive hunters and gatherers possibly transport such massive pillars? We just don't know. What we do know is that the building techniques at Göbekli Tepe degenerated from 11,600 years ago onwards. Pillars that were erected after that were smaller and less sophisticated.

Dr. Schmidt was aware that the earliest evidence of agriculture in the world is to be found at key archaeological sites that lie within a hundred mile radius of Göbekli Tepe. Curious about which came first, agriculture or the Göbekli Tepe site, he concluded that Göbekli Tepe was built *before* agriculture began. So what force was strong enough to motivate primitive foragers to suddenly build monuments of such astonishing size? Dr. Schmidt's answer to the mystery is religion. The powerful human impulse to create a holy place for ceremony, he suggests, anchored people to one place. Once it was constructed, Göbekli Tepe drew them like a magnet to its monuments. Agriculture was developed after its emergence as a holy location in order to feed temple workmen and the pilgrims who were increasingly attracted to the complex.

Dr. Schmidt audaciously argues that the very existence of the monuments implies that both priests and stone masons practiced their craft at the site. While we can imagine the rise of a priest class at this early stage in human cultural development, it is more difficult to imagine hunters and gatherers suddenly developing the technical skills to cut, shape, and transport immense limestone pillars. Where did their building knowledge come from? Where is the evidence of a gradual accumulation of engineering knowledge? Where are the failed attempts at monument building? And why did construction skills so dramatically decline over time?

These questions aren't answered by Dr. Schmidt's bold religion-based idea because his fixation focuses on which event came first: the construction of Göbekli Tepe or the rise of agriculture? But we ask the even bolder question: Is there a connection between Göbekli Tepe and Atlantis?

The earliest and most sophisticated sixteen-ton T-shaped pillars uncovered at Göbekli Tepe date to the same century that saw the end of Atlantis. The loss of an advanced civilization whose survivors re-emerged around the globe would explain why the oldest constructions at the site are the most sophisticated. The Atlanteans were formidable monument builders. Their engineers had the needed expertise, built up by trial and error over centuries, to conceive and design such an elaborate complex.

Plato relates that the fall of the great civilization brought with it a dark age during which the sum of knowledge declined dramatically. When the last Atlantean died their sophisticated building knowledge began to fade. While the Atlanteans undoubtedly tried to pass on their technical skills to succeeding generations, the highly developed civilization that allowed them to develop those skills in the first place was gone. Without the Atlantean civilization to back them, the succeeding generations eventually lost their knowledge of the craft of building.

Ultimately, Dr. Schmidt concludes that the construction of Göbekli Tepe as a religious center caused an unprecedented influx of people, which, in turn, led to the development of agriculture as a means to feed these workers and pilgrims. But there is no more actual evidence for this idea than the possibility that the sudden emergence of agriculture near Göbekli Tepe was the result of advanced skills practiced by the survivors of a lost civilization.

Monument building and the rebooting of agriculture were happening *simultaneously* 11,600 years ago as the Atlanteans desperately tried to rebuild their civilization. At Göbekli Tepe we find exactly the kind of construction projects that we would expect to be built by survivors of a devastated, advanced culture. The site tantalizes as it holds out one piece of the large puzzle that is our lost legacy. Like the megalithic structures at Tiahuanaco in the central Andes that so intrigued Arthur Posnansky and the colossal 180-metric-ton stones used to construct the Sphinx Temple that have fascinated John Anthony West, this evocative place offers one of the latest challenges to traditional assumptions about human existence at the close of the ice age.[7]

ANCIENT LANGUAGES AND COMPUTERS

But what became of the incredible architects of these remarkable temples in Bolivia, Egypt, and Turkey? How and why did they perish? We can find some clues in the central Andes, back at the site of the uncompleted city of Tiahuanaco.

The tale is told by the Aymara, who still live on the shores of Lake Titicaca. The Aymara are a very ancient and proud race. More than 2.5 million people speak the Aymara language, raise llamas, and grow potatoes along the lakeshore, just as their ancestors have for thousands of years. Even the renowned Incan Empire borrowed heavily from their ancient customs of sun worship, agriculture, and the use of llamas.[8]

The Aymara tell of strange events at Titicaca after the Great Flood. Strangers attempted to build a great city on the lake. An Aymara myth retold by an early Spanish visitor tells of how an ancestor crossed Lake Titicaca and with his warriors "waged such a war on the people of which I speak that he killed them all."[9]

After struggling so long and so hard to survive the ravages brought by the last earth crust displacement, these strangers perished, not by the hand of nature, but by the spears and arrows of their own species. Something drove the Aymara to rise in rebellion against the foreigners. Perhaps they were forced to labor on the great city of Tiahuanaco? Did they discover that the strangers were not, after all, gods? Were the Aymara outraged by the prospect of laboring for mere mortals?

The Aymara's contribution is not confined to a distant myth whispered by the waves lapping at the reeds of Lake Titicaca. When the twentieth-century's unique wand, the computer, passes over the Aymara language, it reveals an amazing secret. In 1984, Ivan Guzman de Rojas, a Bolivian mathematician, scored a notable first in the development of computer software by showing that Aymara could be used as an intermediate language for simultaneously translating English into several other languages. Guzman's Atamiri (the Aymara word for "interpreter") was used as a translator by the Panama Canal Commission in a commercial test with Wang Laboratories.

How did Guzman accomplish, using a simple personal computer, a task that experts at eleven European universities, using advanced computers, had failed to complete? "His system's secret, which solved a problem that had stumped machine translation experts around the world, is the rigid, logical and unambiguous structure of Aymara, ideal for transformation into a computer algorithm."[10] In addition, "Aymara is rigorous and simple—which means that its syntactical rules always apply, and can be written out concisely in the sort of algebraic shorthand that computers understand. Indeed, such is its purity that some historians think it did not just evolve, like other languages, but was actually constructed from scratch."[11]

The Aymara were productive farmers, but is it likely that they would spend their leisure time constructing a language? Such a development is more likely the product of an advanced civilization, one capable of constructing the Temple of the Sun and the Great Sphinx.

Could it have been the survivors of the lost island paradise who gave the Aymara a language so precise and grammatically pure that it would become a tool for the most advanced technology of our own century? What other advances in science might we glean from a language spoken by peasants on the highlands near Lake Titicaca?

MONTEZUMA

After studying the mythology of the Aymara and raking over the remains of their Temple of the Sun, Posnansky concluded that Tiahuanaco, the abandoned city of Lake Titicaca, was originally populated by people from Aztlan, the lost island paradise of the Aztecs.[12] The Aztecs ruled a vast empire that stretched the length and width of Central America. In the spring of 1519, they became terrified that their world was coming to an end.

Imagine the following scene from five centuries ago: It is almost sunset. Montezuma, priest, warrior, astronomer, and first lord of the Aztecs, methodically prepares for his evening salutation to the sun. For these few moments the tumultuous empire of the Aztecs is at peace. Darkness approaches quickly as the sun slants behind the mountains that crowd the city of Teotihuacan, in what is now Mexico. Montezuma drapes himself in the comfort of ancient ritual as he prepares to meet the night.[13]

Two humble fishermen are brought into the hall to be presented to their venerated leader. The shuffle of their feet disturbs the temple's silence as they move toward him, avoiding his gaze to look back at the creature they drag behind them.

Montezuma's eyes dart toward the awkward bundle they offer him so nervously. It is a large gray crane, its ashy wings pinned against the fishermen's mesh net. Montezuma recognizes this important Aztec symbol. It is traditional that on the tense morning of a battle two feathers from the long-legged crane be inserted in each warrior's hair as a symbol of readiness to fight to the death. A strange, smoky mirror protrudes from the bird's head. The fishermen quiver, prepared for the worst if Montezuma is angered by his interpretation of this sign.

A smile touches his lips, and the lord of the Aztecs leans back, gathering his ceremonial robes around him. He dismisses the fishermen, showering them with compliments and treasures to reward their capture of this wonderful bird. Montezuma hopes that this unexpected omen means that Blue Hummingbird, the god of war, has been transformed into a crane. Aztec legend dictates that on this day the Aztecs will conquer all their enemies.

As the last hot dust of the Mexican day sifts through the apertures in the temple's carved stone, Montezuma's shiver of anticipation is suddenly laced with fear. As he watches the magical obsidian mirror, the scene changes to daytime over the sea and a sandy beach. It is written of this vision, "Up from the waters came the strange bearded men on their hornless deer. They advanced and before them came fire and destruction."[14]

Montezuma gazes on a vision of the devastation of his world. The fear gnaws at him as he remembers other vile omens that have haunted the empire in recent years. In 1509, a great light appeared on the eastern horizon.[15] Later, three comets and three terrifying earthquakes brought chaos to the Aztecs. Nature's furies were followed by a strange vision visited on Montezuma's sister. She saw their precious capital destroyed by bearded men of gray stone who came from the sea.[16] Perhaps most ominous of all, for no apparent reason, the lake on which the Aztec capital rested began to flood.

Montezuma has not forgotten that in 1508, the year before the wondrous light appeared on the eastern ocean, the planet Venus, symbol of Quetzalcoatl, the Plumed Serpent, challenged the sun by crossing its path. Could this sign mean that Blue Hummingbird's hated enemies, the Toltecs, would be returning? Quetzalcoatl was the ancestral king and esteemed god of the ancient Toltecs, the former glorious rulers of Mexico before the Aztecs, and Montezuma's personal bloodline is traceable to the imperious Toltecs. He is torn by the implication of the omens. How can he welcome the enemies of Blue Hummingbird?

Montezuma's fear of disaster is tempered with his knowledge of the Plumed Serpent's reputation as a great god. It is his duty to correctly interpret and act on the omens. Everything depends on it. No battle, however fierce, has ever disturbed his soul like the whisper of doubt that this twilight has brought, when this crane, carrying a strange, dull mirror reflecting disaster, was placed at his feet. The people of the Aztec Empire are restless and nervous. Wild rumors are everywhere, rumors of floating mountains carrying odd strangers.

Montezuma is painfully aware that historical parallels are lining up against him. As ninth ruler of the Aztecs, he stands at the peak of their power and should be exulting in his honored position. Instead he is torn by doubts and fears. The Toltecs also had nine kings before the Plumed Serpent left them and they fell from power. Is he to be the ninth and final king of the Aztecs? The gods must be consulted.

He turns to the skies and the stars. From his astrological calculations and recollections of ancient myths, Montezuma calculates that the Plumed Serpent will return during the next one reed year, 1519.[17]

Montezuma waits, checking and rechecking his calculations. He now believes that he has narrowed the date of the Plumed Serpent's return to the very day. Surely, he reasons, the god will come back to his homeland on his name day, Nine Wind Day. On the European calendar that would be April 21, 1519. Montezuma sends spies to the eastern shores to watch for the coming of the god on this sacred day.

AZTLAN

On April 21, 1519, the silence of Mexico's Caribbean coast was broken by the clang of swords and the shuffle of marching boots across the white beach. From his ship stepped a bearded conquistador named Hernando Cortes, his helmet adorned with "a plume of feathers."[18] The Spaniard pounded a great cross into the soft sand to honor his faith, little realizing that the cross was also the symbol of the Plumed Serpent.[19]

The Aztec spies watched in amazement and horror before hurrying back to Montezuma to confirm his prediction. Never in the course of human history has there been a greater case of mistaken identity. On that day, Cortes, with blind luck on his side, began a bloody march that would ultimately end in the annihilation of the Aztec Empire.

The Spanish conquerors believed that Mexico was once an Egyptian colony. It is little wonder, since the Aztecs shared several common mythological themes with the Egyptians. The Egyptians believed that the world was surrounded on all sides, including the heavens, with water. In Aztec mythology, "The sea was thought to extend outward and upward until—like the walls of a cosmic house—it merged with the sky. . . . The sky, therefore, was known to contain waters which might in perilous times descend in deluges, annihilating man."[20]

This empire, like that of the Egyptians, had built great pyramids that symbolized the land that saved their ancestors from the Flood.[21] And like those of Egypt, the solar megaliths were aligned with the rising sun. It was atop the Temple of the Sun that Montezuma met Cortez. He recounted their conversation in a letter to the king of Spain. Montezuma told Cortes about the island homeland of the Aztecs' ancestors, saying, "Our fathers dwelt in that happy and prosperous place which they called Aztlan, which means whiteness."[22] Aztlan is described as "a bright land of shining light and whiteness, which contained seven cities surrounding a sacred mountain."[23] Perhaps the blazing lights of Aztlan were actually the southern lights of Antarctica before that land was thrust into the confines of the Antarctic Circle.

Aztlan was said to be "located beyond the waters, or as surrounded by waters; and the first stage of the migration is said to have been made by boat."[24] Once again we have the familiar story. "They believed that two persons survived the deluge, a man, named Coxcox, and his wife. Their heads are represented in ancient paintings, together with a boat floating on the waters, at the foot of a mountain."[25]

Throughout North and South America the myth of a lost island paradise haunts the memories of the native people. But they were not alone in their grief for the lost land. Across the ocean the tale was told in India, Iran, Iraq, and Japan, too.

POLAR PARADISE

In 1922, Mahatma Gandhi, about to be sentenced to six years in prison, said to the judge, "Since you have done me the honor of recalling the trial of the late Lokamaya Gangadhar Tilak, I just want to say that I consider it the proudest privilege and honor to be associated with his name."[26]

Bal Gangadhar Tilak forged the tactic of passive resistance as a means of overthrowing British rule in India. He was held in such esteem that Gandhi used the title Lokamaya (meaning "beloved leader of the people") when referring to him. Tilak earned his title while imprisoned in 1897 for seditious writings. The British hoped to curb his role in the rising tide of Indian nationalism by locking him up. The harsh conditions of his Bombay cell took their toll. Tilak's health waned. Fearing that his death in custody might spark a general uprising, the British moved the "beloved leader of the people" to a safer prison in Poona. Helped by donations of fruit and vegetables, Tilak partially recovered his health. But soon a new hunger overtook him—the need for intellectual stimulation. Relief came from an unlikely quarter: England.

Tilak had published a respected work on India's oldest texts, the Vedas, and Sanskrit scholars at the universities of Oxford and Cambridge were outraged by his imprisonment and treatment. Professor F. Max Muller, the world's leading authority on the Vedas, was successful in having Tilak's case reviewed by Queen Victoria. She shortened his sentence and granted him a reading light in his cell. Denied access to newspapers or any other current material, Tilak used this "privilege" to continue his studies of the Vedas.

Upon his release, Tilak retired to the mountains to rest at a favorite family retreat. In 1903, his great work, *The Arctic Home in the Vedas,* was published. In it he argued that the remains of an island paradise could be found beneath the Arctic Ocean. "It was the advent of the Ice Age that destroyed the mild climate of the original home and covered it into an ice-bound land unfit for the habitation of man."[27]

Tilak summarized a key passage in the oldest saga of Iran, the *Zend-Avesta.* "Ahura Mazda warns Yima, the first king of men, of the approach of a dire winter, which is to destroy every living creature by covering the land with a thick sheet of ice, and advises Yima to build a Vara, or an enclosure, to preserve the seeds of every kind of animal and plant. The meeting is said to have taken place in the Airyana Vaêjo, or Paradise of the Iranians."[28]

Tilak chose the Arctic Circle as the location of the lost continent of Airyana Vaêjo after reading *Paradise Found: The Cradle of the Human Race at the North Pole,* written in 1885 by the founder of Boston University, Dr. William Fairfield Warren. Warren had been impressed by how often the story of a falling sky and Great Flood was to be found intertwined with accounts of a lost island paradise. He also realized that the lost land had many polar features. In Warren's view, the worldwide nature of these descriptions suggested a common physical explanation. An exciting idea of the ice ages provided part of his answer.

Now if, during the prevalence of the Deluge, or later, in consequence of the on-coming of the Ice Age, the survivors of the Flood were translocated from their antediluvian home at the Pole to the great Central Asia "plateau of Pamir," the probable starting-point of historic postdiluvian humanity, the new aspect presented by the heavens in this new latitude would have been precisely as if in the grand world-convulsion the sky itself had become displaced, its polar dome tilted over about one third of the distance from the zenith to the horizon. The astronomical knowledge of those survivors very likely enabled them to understand the true reason of the changed appearance, but their rude descendants, unfavored with the treasures of antediluvian science, and born only to a savage or nomadic life in their new and inhospitable home, might easily have forgotten the explanation. In time such children's children might easily have come to embody the strange story handed down from their fathers in strange myths, in which nothing of the original facts remained beyond an obscure account of some mysterious displacement of the sky, supposed to have occurred in a far-off age in connection with some appalling natural catastrophe or world-disaster.[29]

Warren conjectured that the island paradise myths and their dramatic accounts of a falling sky and worldwide flood were part of the actual history of traumatized populations who had lost their homeland in a geological upheaval. Again and again in the most ancient records, Warren found evidence that the lost land was near the pole.

For example, in 681 CE the Japanese Emperor Temnu ordered the man with greatest memory in the country, Hieda no Are, to recite the most ancient of myths to a scribe. Hieda no Are was the most respected voice of the "guild of narrators" (*katari-be*) and he took his task seriously. O no Yasumaro, the scribe, faithfully transcribed Hieda no Are's words. Their compilation became known as the *Ko-ji-ki* ("Records of Ancient Matters") and appeared in 712. Warren believed that the earliest part of the book contained the notion of an original island homeland near the earth's axis.[30] The *Ko-ji-ki* begins with the "Seven Generations of the Age of the Gods." Each "generation" consisted of a brother and sister. After the seven generations had been created, two more gods, Izanagi and his sister/wife Izanami, were brought into being. They were charged with the task of creating the world out of the porridge-like chaos that was the primordial earth. Warren summarizes the moment when the two celestial deities create the first world. He says the deities,

> standing on the bridge of heaven, pushed down a spear into the green plain of the sea, and stirred it round and round. When they drew it up the drops, which fell from its end, consolidated onto an island. The sun-born pair descended onto the island, and planting a spear in the ground, point downwards, built a palace round it, taking that for the central roof-pillar. The spear became the axis of the earth, which had been caused to revolve by stirring round.[31]

Warren concluded that Onogorojima (Island of the Congealed Drop) was an island somewhere near the pole. The central "roof-pillar" represented, in his view, the earth's axis. A great palace was built on the island, a theme that reappears in the legend of Atlantis. (Later, Izanagi created other islands, including the eight main islands of Japan.)

But why would these people have made their home at the inhospitable pole? Warren answered that at the time the earth was much warmer, its temperature having only recently cooled. Heat was generated from within the planet and combined with surface temperatures to render lands that are now tropical and even temperate far too hot to support life. Only the polar regions were cool enough to invite human habitation.

Warren believed that the polar paradise was destroyed when a critical temperature drop resulted in a worldwide geological upheaval. A huge mass of the earth's interior collapsed inward, pulling sections of the planet's crust with it. The ocean rushed to drown the sunken areas.

The globe then cooled, suffocating the original island paradise in snow and ice.

Because he believed that the entire island had disappeared beneath a polar ocean, Warren dismissed the South Pole as a possible location since the Antarctic continent still existed as land. Instead, he focused his attention on the Arctic Ocean, which to him represented the true "Navel of the Earth."

> Students of antiquity must often have marveled that in nearly every ancient literature they should encounter the strange expression, the Navel of the Earth. Still more unaccountable would it have seemed to them had they noticed how many ancient mythologies *connect the cradle of the human race with this earth-navel.* The advocates of the different sites which have been assigned to Eden have seldom, if ever, recognized the fact that no hypothesis on this subject can be considered acceptable which cannot account for this peculiar association of man's first home with some sort of natural centre of the earth.[32]

Warren believed that the term *Navel of the Earth* referred to the earth's axis. His map of the location of the lost paradise depicts the earth as it appears from the North Pole (see figures 6.1 and 6.2 on page 96).

If Warren hadn't been so fixed on the northern view and had instead looked to the south, he would have seen that Antarctica represents a far more natural Navel of the Earth.

Antarctica sits, like the mythological homeland of the Okanagan, in the "middle of the ocean." Consider these points:

Like the lost island of the Cherokee it lies in the southern hemisphere.

Like the Aztec's Aztlan, Antarctica is "white."

Like Iran's lost paradise, Antarctica is covered "with a thick sheet of ice."

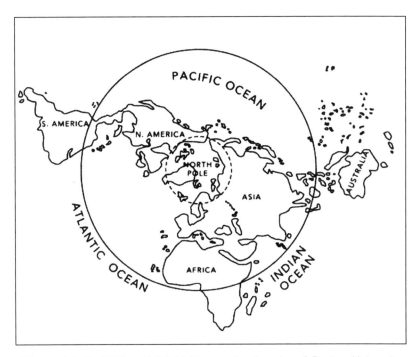

Figure 6.1. Dr. William Fairfield Warren, the founder of Boston University, placed the mythological Navel of the Earth in the Arctic Ocean. Based on Warren, *Paradise Found*, 141.

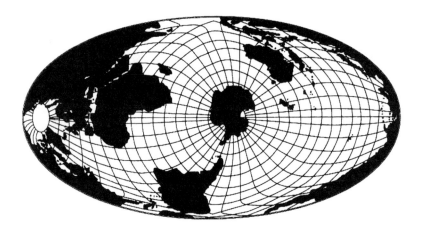

Figure 6.2. A U.S. Navy map of the world depicting Antarctica in the center of the ocean reveals the island continent as the natural Navel of the Earth.

And like the first land of Japanese mythology, Antarctica is close to one of the earth's poles.

Even if Plato had never recorded the legend of Atlantis, the ancient stories told by people scattered around the globe direct us to the island continent of Antarctica. This last-explored continent may well have been the lost island paradise of world mythology.

SEVEN

ATLANTEAN MAPS

In the winter of 332–331 BCE, Alexander the Great, then only twenty-four, led an army of thirty-five thousand through the unrelenting heat of the Sinai Desert. For seven days the procession marched on barren rock. The sound of tramping boots, the clamor of armor, and the snorting of sweat-stained horses were muffled by the vast emptiness and unforgiving heat. Finally, Alexander led his men out of the desert and into the oasis that was Egypt. He had come to conquer this land as he had so many others.

Egypt's ruler, having no troops to oppose him, quickly surrendered. While his men wallowed in wine and soothed their limbs in Egyptian baths, Alexander pondered his future. His old tutor, Aristotle, had impressed on him the wealth of treasures and untold secrets that could be found in the land of the pyramids. His strategic sense told him that Egypt, with desert lying to the west, south, and east, could be an easily defended haven, given adequate equipment and troops. It was settled. He would establish a great city in Egypt to become the western capital of his new empire. It would be called Alexandria.

Alexander eventually left Egypt to pursue and vanquish the Persian armies before marching across even more distant lands. Finally, on the Beas River in present-day India, his exhausted army refused to press onward. They had conquered the known world for their leader. They had had enough. Alexander led them back to Babylon, his eastern capital. There, before his thirty-third birthday, he died, leaving an empire that stretched a distance equal to the breadth of the United States.

Ptolemy, Alexander's childhood friend, returned his body to Egypt. There, Ptolemy established a Greek dynasty that would not end until fourteen kings had ruled and the final queen, Cleopatra, had committed suicide as the Romans seized her domain. Ptolemy wouldn't rest until he had built a great library and museum fit to store all the secrets and treasures of the lands Alexander had conquered. To this end a great effort was made to bring all knowledge together in one place: Alexandria. Preparations for this ambitious task were not made lightly. A hunt through the ancient lands of the Near East was begun, a hunt for long-hidden tablets, mysterious and intriguing maps, the secrets of ancient science, and artifacts to be carried to the museum.

For centuries Alexandria's library was the world's center of learning, sought out by all those who wished to follow the maze of their intellect and curiosity. Drawn like iron to magnets, scholars descended on Alexandria to study the secrets of long-lost civilizations.

One of the earliest librarians, Eratosthenes (ca. 275–195 BCE), must have browsed through some incredible works. The secrets of geography, ancient maps, and accounts of daring travel were all closely guarded within the library's walls. Eratosthenes' great interest in geography took him to the ancient city of Syene on the Nile. While there, he calculated, within a relatively small degree of error, the true circumference of the earth. This feat he accomplished two and one-half centuries before the birth of Christ.

Euclid (ca. 300 BCE), whose name has become synonymous with geometry, studied at the marvelous library. Archimedes (287–212 BCE) the Thomas Edison of the ancient world, spent day after day cloistered inside, unraveling the secrets of the ancient scrolls of Egypt. After his death, any great inventor was dubbed the new Archimedes. But this gifted man was not infallible. He denigrated one of humankind's most significant discoveries.

The fact that the earth revolves around the sun is common knowledge in our age, but in ancient Alexandria this idea was considered ridiculous. Archimedes dismissed with contempt the heliocentric theory of Aristarchos of Samos. Aristarchos (ca. 270 BCE) had come to Alexandria to mine the treasures of the renowned library. He developed the revolutionary idea that the earth was in motion around the sun, an idea that was not accepted for another nineteen hundred years. Perhaps Aristarchos found his inspiration in the pages of the texts of Atlantean sciences that might have lined the shelves of the library.

A series of devastating invasions and fires culminating in the Muslim conquest of 643 BCE during which Caliph Omar decreed that all materials that did not agree with the Koran be burned led to the destruction of this great library. Fortunately many scholars had made copies of important maps, taking them to the safety of the library in Constantinople, the capital of the Byzantine Empire. The surviving ancient maps were of little interest to the Byzantines because they already had lucrative trade routes in place. The science of cartography declined. The maps would lie for centuries gathering dust until an unexpected threat arose from the north.

VIKINGS AND VARANGIANS

The sound of oars slicing through the waters of the misty fjords of northern Europe was heard more and more frequently during the ninth, tenth, and eleventh centuries. The Scandinavians, feeling the tensions of too many people in too little space, launched an invasion that would sweep through Europe. Dragon-prowed ships with red-bearded men at the helm were spied off the shores of England and France and as far south as Italy. These were the Vikings, and their exploits in the southwest would be matched with excursions to Iceland, Greenland, and North America.

The stories of the Vikings' daring voyages into the North Atlantic and their ruthless acts of piracy in western Europe have overshadowed an even more amazing chapter in their history. In the early part of the ninth century, the eastern Vikings, who became known as the Varangians, established a base they called Norovgorod in a city southeast of present-day St. Petersburg. From there they followed the mighty Volga and Dnieper Rivers to the Black Sea and eventually on to Constantinople—jewel of the Byzantine Empire, a city of gold and pageantry, its splendor so renowned that it was known simply as the Big City.

In 860 CE, the Varangians sacked the outer city but failed to penetrate its inner sanctum. After a final attempt at capture failed, an alliance was forged between the Varangians and the Byzantine Empire. By the middle of the tenth century, the Varangians were serving in increasing numbers in Constantinople's Imperial Navy and became the first adventurers to set eyes on the ancient maps that were once housed in Alexandria's library.

It was perhaps inevitable that copies of the maps would have found their way back to the Scandinavian homeland. The western Vikings turned their fellows' bounty to great advantage. Simultaneously as the cartographic treasure chest was opened to them, they made their first discovery of land beyond the Atlantic. Eric the Red (ca. 1000 CE), the discoverer of Greenland, and his son Leif, the first European to reach America, led the long line of explorers who understood the true value of the maps of old Constantinople.

LIBRARIES IN ISLAMIC LANDS

Meanwhile, as the West was suffering the blight of the Dark Ages and enduring the pillages of the Vikings, the Islamic world was thriving in a golden age of learning. Much of the success of this brilliant era can be attributed to the Islamic caliph's vision of an empire stretching from Spain to India.

Abu-l-Abbas Abd-Allah al-Ma'mun was the caliph (ruler) of an empire that stretched west from Baghdad across North Africa into the Iberian Peninsula and east all the way to India. One night the caliph had a dream in which an old man appeared.

It was as though I was in front of him, filled with fear of him. Then I said, "Who are you?" He replied, "I am Aristotle." Then I was delighted with him and said, "Oh sage, may I ask you a question?" He said, "Ask it." Then I asked, "What is good?" He replied, "What is good in the mind." I said again, "Then what next?" He replied, "What is good in the law." I said, "Then what is next?" He replied, "What is good with the public." I said, "Then what more?" He answered, "More? There is no more."[1]

A century after the death of Caliph al-Ma'mun, an Islamic writer told of the effects of the dream. "This dream was one of the most definite reasons for the output of books. Between al-Ma'mun and the Byzantine emperor there was correspondence, for al-Ma'mun had sought aid opposing him. Then he wrote to the Byzantine emperor asking his permission to obtain a selection of old scientific [manuscripts], stored in the Byzantine country."[2]

In 833, on al-Ma'mun's orders, a library known as the House of Wisdom was established. It was located in Baghdad and became for the Arabs what Alexandria had been for the ancient Greeks. The teachings of the Greeks were revived, and scholars not only copied works but also introduced advancements in mathematics and developed the forerunner of chemistry: alchemy.

Many centuries later, in 1559, an Arabic map of the earth was published. Its source is unknown, but it was translated into Turkish by the Muslim cartographer, Hadji Ahmed. The Hadji Ahmed world map outlines the continent of North America in full, including areas that would not be mapped by Europeans until two centuries later.[3] This depiction is remarkable because the technology to measure a continent the size of North America requires an accurate determination of latitude and longitude (see figure 7.1).

Prince Henry of Portugal (1394–1460), one of the great minds of the fifteenth century, is often credited with perfecting the determination of latitude—how far north or south of the equator any given place

a   b

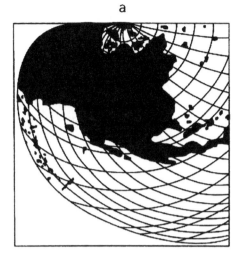

Figure 7.1. Found in 1559, the Hadji Ahmed world map depicted a remarkably accurate North America, long before it was explored by Europeans. It may have been drawn by Atlanteans.

is located. His cartographers knew that the height of the North Star above the horizon gives a close approximation of latitude. If the North Star is at a 50° altitude from the horizon, then the observer is near the 50° latitude. In the Southern Hemisphere, where there is no "South Star" by which to measure, the ship's captain would "shoot the sun" at noon each day to check for latitude. Astronomy provided the answer to determining latitude.

The determination of longitude (how far east or west of the Prime Meridian, at Greenwich, England, which is set at 0°) was a much more complicated affair.

The earth is a sphere divided into 360°. Because it takes twenty-four hours to complete one revolution, one hour's "movement" of the sun equals 15° (360 divided by 24). For example, when it is high noon at Giza, then 15° east of Giza it is 1:00 p.m., and 15° west of Giza it is 11 a.m. This means that to determine when it is noon where we are standing, we must compare that location's time difference to Greenwich time.

Today radio and satellites allow immediate communication with any place on Earth. But in the seventeenth century, if you were sailing the high seas, it wasn't possible to know the time at your home port. This had serious ramifications in 1691 when seven British warships, lost because they couldn't measure their longitude, were shipwrecked off Plymouth. Then in 1694, a British fleet ran aground on Gibraltar for the same reason, and in 1707, two hundred lives and four ships were lost off the Scilly Isles because the British Navy had no way of determining longitude.

In 1714, the British Parliament set up the British Board of Longitude, which offered "a Publick Reward for such a Person or Persons as shall discover the Longitude at Sea." The prize was ten thousand pounds for the invention of a device that could determine a ship's longitude within one degree of an arc. It was upped to twenty thousand pounds if accuracy could be determined within half a degree. Twenty thousand pounds was a huge incentive in 1714, even for such a daunting task. In today's currency it would be equal to nearly two million dollars.

In 1735, John Harrison (1693–1776) designed the first marine chronometer, a highly accurate clock tested on a voyage to Lisbon and found to be accurate. Harrison's fourth, improved marine chronometer underwent its ultimate test on a trip to Jamaica in 1762 and passed easily. But the Board of Longitude, in the tradition of all self-respecting bureaucracies, ensured the perpetuation of its own existence by refusing to grant the money to Harrison. He was given a partial payment of five thousand pounds in 1763, but not until King George III intervened on his behalf did the clever inventor receive the bulk of his reward in 1773. He was eighty years old.

Captain James Cook made good use of the chronometer during his voyages to the South Seas in the 1770s. The device was checked for accuracy at the Greenwich Royal Observatory before his fleet cast off. No matter where they were, the chronometer told exact Greenwich time. All the captain had to do was determine noon, on any given day, and calculate the time difference to that of Greenwich. The difference in time could then be translated into degrees, west or east of Greenwich, to determine longitude. Armed with this new tool, the Europeans could, for the first time, map the shape of continents.

But the fact remains that some maps already depicted the true contours of the continents. As mentioned above, the 1559 Hadji Ahmed map shows the general shape, size, and position of North America, including what had been assumed to be the unexplored northwestern coast. How could such a map exist when the technology required to construct it wasn't available in 1559?

Perhaps the Atlanteans drew the source map for the Hadji Ahmed depiction?

For the people of Atlantis, North America was the least desirable continent. To them it was an unremarkable frozen land, much as Antarctica is regarded today. The discovery of radiocarbon dating after World War II enabled us to understand what North America looked like at 9600 BCE. When we superimpose the 1559 map of the continent over a modern archaeological map of the world of 9600 BCE (see figure 7.2), we see that the ancient document closely depicts what would correspond to an Atlantean view of North America, during the ice age.

If we could show a modern world map to a sailor of the Atlantean fleet, he would be amazed. He would consider Antarctica to be drawn very inaccurately. Its bays, crevices, and archipelago are all hidden on our "modern" map. He would question why the ocean covered so much more land. On the other hand, the sailor would immediately recognize the Hadji Ahmed map of North America as an accurate map of what he would consider a rather dull part of the world.

The existence of the ancient land bridge of Beringia was not confirmed until the middle of the twentieth century. But we find it depicted on the Hadji Ahmed map. It appears that the Arabs had gained possession of an Atlantean map drawn when North America lay frigid beneath polar ice and Antarctica lacked its current coating of ice. It would prove to be not the only map of its kind. Those well-worn maps were passed from hand to hand over generations, sometimes placed reverently in safekeeping by the wise men of the day, sometimes torn and

Figure 7.2. When the Hadji Ahmed map of North America is compared with an estimate of the ice-covered shape of the continent as it was 11,600 years ago, the similarities are pronounced.

crushed by the destructive tide of war. Finally, they surfaced again just as the European age of discovery began.

THE SECRET ROLE OF ANCIENT MAPS
IN THE EUROPEAN AGE OF DISCOVERY

In 812 CE, on January 13, Venice passed from the control of the Empire of Charlemagne to the Byzantine Empire and entered an era of ascendancy that continued for more than a millennium. Venice was ideally situated on the Adriatic Sea. It proved to be the perfect location to profit from the expanding trade flow as Europeans began to develop a taste for the exotic spices and vibrant silks of Asia. Venice would come to dominate that trade for almost four centuries, until the end of the twelfth century, when the Byzantines began to appreciate the advantage of trade with other cities such as Pisa and Genoa. The loss of this rich market provoked the Venetians.

One man in particular, Enrico Dandolo, avenged the loss in a series of operations that led to the first successful attack on the fabulous city of Constantinople.

In 1198, Pope Innocent III was elected. He was obsessed with the idea of a reunion of the Roman Catholic and Greek Orthodox churches. He hoped to accomplish this through the Fourth Crusade, the aim of which was to "liberate" Egypt and Palestine from the Islamic Empire and restore the Holy Land to a united Christianity. To fulfill this ambition he sent letters to all of Europe's kings requesting men and arms. Eventually a contingent of crusaders arrived in Venice, where they came under the command of Dandolo, the doge (chief magistrate) of Venice.

Dandolo was a man consumed by a burning hatred of the Byzantines. His bitterness had been forged into a much more personal vendetta than one over a loss of trade. The doge had nursed his wrath for many years. Thirty years before, he had been captured and "during his stay in Constantinople as a hostage had been treacherously blinded by the Greeks by means of a concave mirror which strongly reflected the rays of the sun."[4]

In *History of the Byzantine Empire: 324–1453,* A. A. Vasiliev summarized the conditions that led to the attack on Constantinople. "Thus, in the preparations for the Fourth Crusade, two men were of first importance: Pope Innocent III, as a representative of the spiritual element in the crusade sincerely wished to take the Holy Land from the hands of the Muhammedans and was absorbed in the idea of union: and the Doge Enrico Dandolo, as a representative of the secular, earthly element, put first material, commercial purposes."[5]

Dandolo had forced the focus of the crusade to the subject of his own wrath until eventually it had nothing to do with the Holy Land. First he unleashed the warriors on the city of Zara, which had recently seceded from the Venetians. Here was a war of Christian versus Christian—a gross pillage.

This "false crusade" then turned toward the ultimate prize: Constantinople. In June of 1203, the crusaders' fleet arrived there. A French soldier described the effect the great city had on Dandolo's troops.

> Now you may imagine that those who had never before seen Constantinople looked upon it very earnestly, for they never thought there could be in all the world so rich a city, when they saw the high walls and magnificent towers that enclosed it round about, the rich palaces and mighty churches, of which there were so many that no one would have believed it who had not seen it with his own eyes— and the height and length of that city which above all others was sovereign. And be it known to you that no man was of such sturdy courage but his flesh trembled: and it was no wonder, for never was so great an enterprise undertaken by anyone since the creation of the world.[6]

Constantinople fell on April 13, 1204. Describing the scene, Vasiliev writes, "After taking the city, for three days, the Latins treated the city with appalling cruelty and pillaged everything which had been collected in Constantinople for many centuries. Neither churches, nor relics, nor monuments of art, nor private possessions were spared or respected . . . many libraries were plundered: manuscripts were destroyed."[7]

Dandolo had his revenge.

Maps, manuscripts, marble statues, and four life-size Alexandrian bronze horses were taken to Venice as the spoils of war. But another treasure, of a different sort, would arrive shortly before the end of the century.

In the late 1290s, Marco Polo, his father, and his uncle returned to Venice after having spent more than two decades living in the heart of the Mongolian Empire of Kublai Khan. Polo had been fifteen when he left home, and he, his father, and uncle were unrecognizable to their families after their long absence. The travelers arranged a great banquet to celebrate their homecoming. The event provided plenty of gossip, as Polo's earliest biographer, John Baptist Ramusio, recorded.

They invited a number of their kindred to an entertainment, which they took care to have prepared with great state and splendor in that house of theirs; and when the hour arrived for sitting down to the table they came forth of their chamber all three clothed in crimson satin, fashioned in long robes reaching down to the ground such as people in those days wore within doors. And when water for the hands had been served, and the guests were set, they took off those robes and put on others of crimson damask, whilst the first were by their orders cut up and divided among the servants. Then after partaking of some of the dishes they went out again and came back in robes of crimson velvet, and when they had again taken their seats, the second suits were divided as before. When dinner was over they did the like with the robes of velvet, after they had put on dresses of the ordinary fashion worn by the rest of the company. These proceedings caused much wonder and amazement among the guests. But when the cloth had been drawn, and all the servants had been ordered to retire from the dining hall, Messer Marco, as the youngest of the three, rose from the table, and, going into another chamber, brought forth the three shabby dresses of coarse stuff which they had worn when they first arrived. Straightaway they took sharp knives and began to rip up some of the seams and welts, and to take out of them jewels of the greatest value in vast quantities, such as rubies, sapphires, carbuncles, diamonds and emeralds, which had all been stitched up in those dresses in so artful a fashion that nobody could have suspected the fact. For when they took leave of the Great Khan they had changed all the wealth that he had bestowed upon them into this mass of rubies, emeralds, and other jewels, being well aware of the impossibility of carrying with them so great an amount in gold over a journey of such extreme length and difficulty. Now this exhibition of such a huge treasure of jewels and precious stones, all tumbled out upon the table, threw the guests into fresh amazement, insomuch that they seemed quite bewildered and dumbfounded. And now they recognized that in spite of all former doubts these were in truth those honored and worthy gentlemen of the Ca'Polo that they claimed to be; and as all paid the greatest honor and reverence.[8]

Shortly after this marvelous occasion the young Polo became involved in one of the many wars that the Italian cities waged between each other. Unfortunately for him, but fortunately for literature and history, Marco Polo found himself a shackled prisoner of war in Genoa. He shared his cell with Rustichello of Pisa, a writer who also had had his freedom sacrificed to war. As they shuffled around the dark jail, Marco reminisced endlessly about his wondrous adventures in the East, where he had been free in body and mind to explore the mysteries of an ancient civilization so strange and incomparable to his own.

The writer in Rustichello was awakened and fascinated. He urged Polo to allow him to record his adventures for posterity. Excitedly, he scribbled page after page and created a book that would fire the imagination of generations who grew thirsty for the treasures of the Orient, spurred on by the glimpses provided by the tales of Marco Polo.

Amid the passion that gripped the Europeans for the silk, spices, gold, and precious stones of the East, a gem of a different sort was inadvertently passed over. Marco Polo had brought back, safely tucked away with his precious jewels, a map of the world that showed a great southern island continent. The map depicts two circles inside a vast ocean. The top circle represents the world of Asia, Europe, and Africa. But it also reveals a southern counterpart.

The notion of another continent located in the far south became, once again, a part of European geographic knowledge. The idea of a great island continent in the Southern Hemisphere had drifted in and out of favor for many centuries. Pythagoras spoke of it in the sixth century BCE, and his tutor, Sonchis, described it in detail to Solon. But during the Dark Ages, knowledge of the island was lost to Western Europe. After the fall of Rome the use of Greek began to decline in the West, and consequently only ancient books written in Latin were consulted.

The only known work in Latin on ancient geography was written by Mela (ca. 43 CE) the famous Roman geographer. He taught that a climatic belt called the Torrid Zone[9] encircled the globe, dividing and separating the northern inhabitable regions from those in the south. He claimed that the Torrid Zone was so hot that the sea boiled. Anyone who attempted to cross from one hemisphere to the other would be swallowed by the scalding waters. These teachings were fully accepted by most Christian priests of the Middle Ages.

However, it seemed to some that the existence of lands in the south, totally inaccessible because of the impassable Torrid Zone, raised serious questions of faith—questions concerning the salvation of the people who Mela claimed lived on the other side of this impassable barrier. If the word of Jesus could not be transmitted to these poor souls, how would they receive salvation? To answer this complex theological problem the priests came up with a simple solution: they burned all maps depicting any southern land.

How many maps of Atlantis were destroyed we can never know. We do know that by the time Marco Polo returned from the Orient with his treasured map, the existence of the great island continent in the south had been forgotten.

The man who first took the terrible risk of exploring this "boiling ocean" was a Portuguese sailor by the name of Gil Eannes. Eannes took the chance, but the inspiration, funding, and will behind the effort originated with Prince Henry of Portugal. The son of King John I and Queen Philippa, Henry had older brothers and so escaped most royal duties. This enabled the prince to pursue his passion for knowledge and discovery. Later generations called him Prince Henry the Navigator, and his name ranks first and foremost in the annals of the modern scientific exploration of the globe.

At Sagres, on the Portuguese coast, Henry created a refuge for scholars. There he voraciously collected all the maps, globes, and accounts of exploration that could be bought. In 1428, his older brother Pedro had been greeted with great respect when he traveled to Venice. He returned with two precious gifts for Henry. The first was a copy of the account of Marco Polo's travels. Henry was delighted with the book, but even more thrilled by the second gift: "a collection of world maps."[10]

It seems probable that some of these maps were once housed in the sacred cartography room of Constantinople and before that the library at Alexandria. These outlines of distant lands sketched across crumbling parchments became Henry's obsession. In his mind the maps were more than lifeless lines drawn by people long dead. He had to know where they led.

The problem wasn't simple. There were plenty of maps on offer that were the work of charlatans more than willing to sell "secrets" to the young prince. To address discrepancies between the various maps, Henry gathered together as many scholars as he could afford, and sometimes more than he could afford.

Finally, Henry concluded that the mystery of the maps' veracity could only be solved by launching a voyage into the void. He equipped vessels and crew for a vast project of exploration. Convinced that the Torrid Zone was passable and that navigation of a southern route to India was possible, Henry instructed his captain, Eannes, to set sail for the south. The crew didn't share Henry's confidence in his secret maps. As the temperature climbed they were convinced that it was only a matter of time before the very seas would be boiling. They returned to Portugal pleading that the voyage was doomed.

Henry decided to speak to the sailors himself. He told them that they would have to sail farther than ever before, but that their fears were unfounded. Tales of boiling waters were fabrications. He appealed to their pride of seamanship and, more pragmatically, their interest in material reward, saying "If there were any authority for them, I could find an excuse for you. But indeed the stories are spread by men of little repute: the type of seamen who know only the coast of Flanders and how to enter well-known ports, and are too ignorant to navigate by compass and chart. Go forth, then, and heed none of their words; but make your journey straightaway. For the grace of God you can gain from this voyage nothing but profit and honour."[11]

The sailors were inspired, and Captain Eannes's voyage to the south dispelled once and for all the notion of an impassable Torrid Zone. A vast door had swung open. The world seemed to shrink.

In 1432, Henry sent Goncalo Velho into the western sea to claim the islands that his maps revealed were there. Velho returned without sighting the Azores and insisted that they didn't exist. The prince ordered the reluctant Velho to retrace his steps, telling him, "There is an island there, go back and find it."[12] Henry's persistence paid off. The Azores were found, and the doorway to the West and the South was open.

In 1453, Constantinople fell to the Turks, and the last scholars fled west. Their arrival in Italy is now considered one of the important incentives for the Italian Renaissance. Others heard with relief that a prince of Portugal would welcome scholars. Intellectual refugees poured into the city of Sagres, and Henry was overwhelmed with plans for potential discoveries. Because of Prince Henry the Navigator's influence, Portugal became the new world center for ancient maps.

In later centuries, several researchers, including Charles Hapgood, claimed that the Portuguese had early knowledge of undiscovered sections of America[13] and Antarctica.[14] It seems that they held accurate maps of undiscovered lands long before Columbus and the rest of the famous explorers set sail. Through a long, treacherous route carved by persecution and barbarism, Atlantean maps had fallen into Henry's hands. He not only saw their value and significance, but was also in a privileged position to act on them.

Sixteen years after Henry's death, a young Italian adventurer was shipwrecked off the coast of Portugal. Having been wounded in a sea battle, Christopher Columbus clung desperately to broken fragments of his ship and swam for ten kilometers until he was washed up on the Portuguese shore. It was 1476, and he was welcomed and nursed back to health by a colony of Italian countrymen from his home city of Genoa. Columbus began a new career in the service of Portugal and settled down in Lisbon to become a mapmaker with his younger brother, Bartholomew. Eventually, Christopher married into one of the most respected families of Portugal. His star began to rise.

Columbus's father-in-law had been a close friend of the now dead Prince Henry, and his mother-in-law was said to have given Columbus some greatly valued maps that her husband had left upon his death.[15] Nowhere on Earth could the young Columbus have been better situated to begin his famous voyage westward. What secret maps he saw and how many of them we don't know (see chapter 1). But despite this great advantage, he never achieved his quest to find a westerly route to India.

The man who did discover the route and who proved the stunning fact that the world was round was a Portuguese seaman who, like Columbus, sailed in the service of Spain after having learned his trade in Lisbon. Ferdinand Magellan was born of a noble Portuguese family in 1480. Magellan became a page to the queen of Portugal and was required, as part of his education, to study all the arts of sailing, including cartography. In 1496, he became a clerical worker in the king of Portugal's marine department. He, even more than Columbus, had access to Prince Henry's wonderful collection of secret Atlantean maps.

Before he left for Spain, Magellan gained entry to the royal chartroom. There he found a globe that showed a strait at the tip of the still *unexplored* edge of South America. When he arrived at the Spanish court Magellan proposed his plan to sail to India via a westerly route. A witness recorded his pitch to the royals: "Magellan had a well-painted globe in which the whole world was depicted, and on it he indicated the route he proposed to take, saving that the straight was left purposely blank so that no one should anticipate him."[16]

Magellan set sail in 1519 with five ships. Crossing the Atlantic he followed the coast of South America to "discover" the straits that now bear his name. He named the Pacific Ocean but did not complete his journey around the globe. He was killed by natives in the Philippines. In 1522, one of his ships made a triumphant return to Spain, the first vessel since the fall of Atlantis to have circumnavigated the globe.

AN EGYPTIAN MAP OF ATLANTIS

In 1976, we came across another Atlantean map. It had been originally discovered by a meticulous researcher, Athanasius Kircher (1601–1680), who claimed that it was an accurate Egyptian map of the lost continent of Atlantis. It may have been stolen by the Romans during the occupation of Egypt and rediscovered by Kircher.

Kircher was born to Anna Gansek and Johannes Kircher, a bailiff of the Abbey of Fulda in Germany. His father was very concerned about the fate of his sixth son, who, it seemed, wouldn't amount to much. Kircher was lazy and showed no special talent, except for getting into trouble. His first application to join the Jesuits was refused on the grounds of "insufficient mental ability." But a series of near fatal accidents brought focus to the boy's life. "One was the near escape from drowning when Athanasius, while swimming in a forbidden pool, was swept down a mill-race and under a mill wheel; another time it was an almost miraculous escape from being trampled to death, when, having worked his way to the front of a great crowd of onlookers, he was pushed out into the path of racing horses; finally there was the severe accident, resulting in a hernia, which came from an abortive attempt to show his skill in ice skating."[17]

Kircher's father impressed on the boy his great fortune in surviving so many near misses, and finally, the man who would come to be known as the "universal genius" settled down to serious study. Eventually, in 1618, he was accepted by the Jesuits. The order demanded physical fitness. Kircher was afraid that his skating injury would jeopardize his position and tried to keep it secret. His limp, however, was noticed by the fathers. He recounted, "The ills from which I was suffering forced me to walk with tottering steps. My superiors immediately noticed this, and I was obliged to tell the whole story. A surgeon was called in. He was horrified at the state of my legs . . . and pronounced me incurable. . . . I was told that since no medical attention could do me any good, I would be sent home from the Novitiate if I did not get better within a month."[18]

For the first time in his life, Kircher prayed for a miracle. Within a few days he could walk with a steady gait. His place within the order was secured.

The Jesuit scientists were among the most educated men in Europe, and Kircher's admission to their ranks ensured him as fine an education as was possible in the seventeenth century. Eventually he would rise "to hold the most honourable place among these scientists of the Society of Jesus."[19] But the road would be a long one. He was showing great promise when the Thirty Years War erupted over Germany. Kircher and his fellow Jesuits were forced to flee from the invading armies in the dead of winter with insufficient clothing and no food. His biographer, Conor Reilly, wrote:

He would never forget the sufferings of that journey. Snow was deep on the roads, and in the devastated countryside the young Jesuits could find little food or shelter. Exhausted and hungry they finally reached the Rhine. The river was frozen over. On the advice of the local people, who took them for deserters from one of the warring armies, they began to cross the ice. It seemed quite solid but Kircher, who was leading the way, suddenly saw open water before him. He turned back, but a gap had opened between him and his companions; he was trapped on an island of ice. The river current caught the floe on which he stood and swung it out into midstream. His companions could do nothing to help: they implored God and his Blessed Mother to save him; they watched as he was swept along, until he was out of sight; then they crossed the river at another point and made their way to a Jesuit College on the west bank of the Rhine.

Hours later, stiff and blue and bruised and bleeding, Kircher struggled up to the door of the college. To the joy of his companions, who had been praying for the repose of his soul, he told how his ice-flow had been jammed among others down stream, permitting him to clamber along toward the further shore. He had had to swim a wide gap before he finally reached dry land.[20]

Kircher's legend was already being forged. He resumed his studies with even greater enthusiasm. Astronomy fascinated him, and through the concentrated use of a telescope, he announced the rather startling idea, at the time, that the sun was made of the same material as the earth. He was the *first* to propose that the sun was an evolving star.

In 1628, Kircher was ordained as a priest. Soon a new interest began to draw his attention—archaeology. One day, while browsing in a Jesuit library, he came upon illustrations of Egyptian obelisks. The hieroglyphic inscriptions fascinated him. Later, he was appointed by successive popes to study and restore the obelisks. Egypt's intimate connection with the Bible made the deciphering of these figures of critical interest to the church, and the popes had chosen a man more than well qualified for the task.

Kircher's other pursuits followed not only the explosive macro-worlds of astronomy and geology but also the silent microworld beneath the lens of a microscope. From these early explorations he introduced the then-revolutionary idea that microbes were the cause of disease. A true Renaissance man, he sought knowledge wherever it led him. After an eruption of Mount Vesuvius, he went so far as to lower himself into the steaming crater to view its violent upheavals firsthand. He also taught physics, mathematics, and Oriental languages at the prestigious College of Rome. In 1643, Kircher resigned his post to devote himself fully to the study of his true love, archaeology.

By 1665, he had produced the first volume of his encyclopedic work, *Mundus Subterraneus*. It was a massive book, brimming with ideas, illustrations, and the results of his intricate research into the mysteries of alchemy.

For a brief time, we owned one of the few copies of this marvelous book.

After selling the contents of our apartment in British Columbia, we'd arrived in London with one trunk and enough money to live out our dream of exploring the city while we studied at the British Museum library. The first catch in our impetuous plan was that the money was only enough to last for three months. The second catch was that in the first flush of excitement, we'd spent a big chunk of that cash on *Mundus Subterraneus*. (Perhaps this was understandable for a couple of writer/librarian characters, but it was more than risky for writer/librarians unemployed in a foreign country!)

We had tracked our prize to a narrow alley near Trafalgar Square that disappeared into some nether land of the city. The location was so far off the beaten track that we were convinced there would be less chance of anyone finding us if anything were to go awry than if we vanished in the transcendent wilds of Canada. As we neared our destination the sounds of London trailed away behind us, and the soot of centuries brushed against our coats. A set of steps built for a dwarf led us into a dank basement. The sound of a cheerful bell belied the mold crawling up the wall as we pushed open a door that begged for a coat of fresh paint.

Inside was a scene worthy of Dickens. Patches of a grubby Persian carpet could be glimpsed between the hundreds of books tilting from floor to ceiling, blocking most of the light from the narrow window—a bounty to delight any bibliophile. Hunched over a cluttered desk in the center of his empire was a man of indeterminate age who obviously didn't have a style or hair salon high on his list of priorities. One look and he probably figured we didn't either. His welcome and firm handshake indicated that if we'd made the effort to get there, not to mention actually find the place, we must be worth helping.

He shuffled into a hobbit-sized cupboard and left us to gaze at his treasures: the writer in us anxious to reach for a book, the librarian in us wondering what mystical cataloguing system he used.

Our host reappeared smoothing the cover of a massive volume. Never was the phrase "you can't judge a book by its cover" more appropriate. Its ugly milky-colored cover stretched across its bulk like a cheap coat two sizes too small. It was curling at the edges like the skin of a Californian too fond of the sun, and despite the bookseller's tender ministrations, there was a tinge of the odor of neglect about it.

Inside lay the magic: page after rustling page of Athanasius Kircher's words, the illustrations delicately detailed, a man's life work beneath our hands.

Juggling it on our laps on the tube trip home wasn't easy. And perhaps it was only our naïveté about the true extent of the treasure we held that kept us laughing as we balanced the *Mundus Subterraneus* between us and congratulated ourselves on our find. It stayed on the table in our bedsit for many months. The map of Atlantis was boldly drawn in Kircher's hand, the symbol of the journey we had made.

But even the pleasures of the *Mundus Subterraneus* had to give way to material necessity if we wanted to stay in London and continue our quest. We ran out of money. And so we carried our treasure to the slick venue of Sotheby's and sat on the uncomfortable chairs and watched as a man with a voice like, well, like an auctioneer, raised his gavel and barked Kircher's book away to an anonymous phone bidder. Within weeks we both had jobs and our three-month sojourn in London turned into five years of fine memories.

HOW NORTH BECAME DOWN

In *Mundus Subterraneus* Kircher claimed that the remains of Atlantis lay beneath the northern part of the Atlantic Ocean. He also revealed the mysterious map of Atlantis that he claimed had been stolen from Egypt by the early Roman invaders (see figure 7.3 on page 120). The inscription

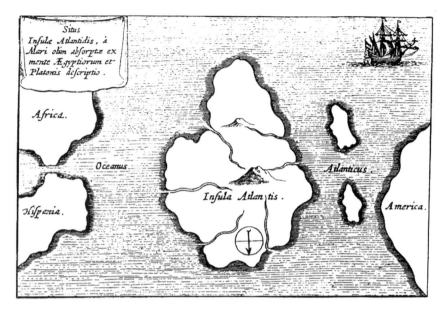

Figure 7.3. In 1665, Athanasius Kircher published this Egyptian map of Atlantis showing north as "down." For generations, researchers have misguidedly turned this map upside down so that America appears on the left and Spain on the right. There is, however, an alternate orientation.

on the map translates as, "Site of the island of Atlantis, now beneath the sea, according to the beliefs of the Egyptians and the description of Plato."

At first glance, the map seems odd to modern eyes because north, as indicated by the downward-pointing compass, is at the bottom of the page. But the ancient Egyptians believed that the most important direction was south, toward the headwaters of the sacred Nile. Therefore south must be "up." Kircher reproduced this belief.

The map appears much more familiar to us if we look at it upside down. What looks like America then appears on the left, with Spain and North Africa on the right—where we are accustomed to seeing them in twentieth-century maps. However, if we lift a modern globe off its hinges and roll it about like a beach ball so that the South Pole faces us, placing South America on our right and South Africa and Madagascar on our left, we can immediately see that the Egyptian map of Atlantis represents an ice-free Antarctica in size, shape, scale, and position (see figure 7.4).

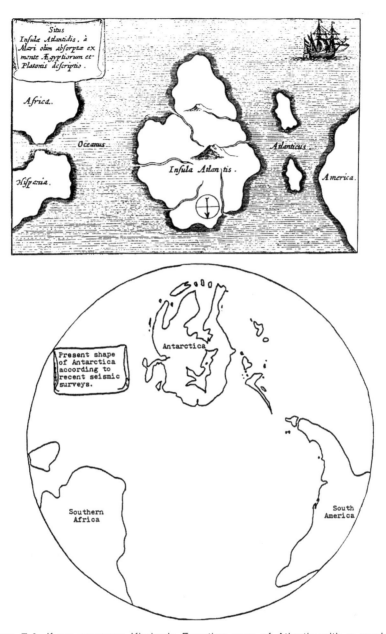

Figure 7.4. If we compare Kircher's Egyptian map of Atlantis with a modern geophysical globe using the South Pole as "up," our perspective changes. With this Southern Hemisphere perspective the segments of the map that Kircher labeled as Hispania (Spain) are actually seen as southern Africa. Africa becomes Madagascar, and America is South America. Atlantis is shown to be Antarctica. Kircher's map was published almost three centuries before we knew the true, ice-free shape of Antarctica, with its offshore islands.

The present shape of Antarctica as depicted is based on the current ocean level, not that of 11,600 years ago. Atlantis did not actually sink beneath the waves. Instead, as the old ice caps melted, the ocean level rose, covering some of the continent's permutations. Further distortions in our modern map, compared with Kircher's, are a result of the weight of today's Antarctic ice sheet. This immense blanket of snow and ice depressed parts of the continent, causing more and more land to fall below the ocean level. Nevertheless, the shadow of Atlantis can still be seen in the modern map of Antarctica.

If the horror of an earth crust displacement were to be visited on today's interdependent world culture, the progress of thousands of years of civilization would be torn away from our planet like a fine cobweb. Those who live near high mountains might escape the global tidal waves, but they would be forced to leave behind, in the lowlands, the slowly constructed fruits of civilization. Only among the merchant marines and navies of the world might some evidence of civilization remain. The rusting hulls of ships and submarines would eventually perish. But the valuable maps they carried would be saved by survivors for hundreds, even thousands, of years, until once again they could be used to guide seamen across the world ocean to rediscover lost lands.

EIGHT

EMBERS
OF HUMANKIND

Numbed with fear, the few shocked and terrified survivors of Atlantis floated lost and confused amongst the debris left in the wake of the earth's nightmare. But the nightmare did not dissipate with the coming of the welcome dawn. There was to be no waking from this dream for many centuries. Instead it was left to those blessed by favorable winds and tides, which carried them to hospitable shores, to bind together and rebuild after the devastation. Only embers of humankind—those who had fled to the mountains—survived.

It is a tribute to the survivor's sheer courage and overwhelming will to live that, adrift, fighting the elements, they somehow began to piece together the tattered remnants of their world. But perhaps the future could offer only hope to their battered hearts. No horror of tomorrow could compete with the devastation they had left behind, buried under the falling snow that was now smothering their island home. But their solitude was not total as they believed, tossed and tormented in their ships, so tiny in the ocean's vastness.

Equally shocked as the Atlanteans were the survivors in the highlands that had escaped the tidal waves. Shivering in their mountain-top shelters were the remaining hunters and gatherers of the earth. Clinging to the comfort of ways that had stood them well for hundreds of thousands of years, little did they suspect that those ancient routines would be overturned in a peaceful revolution brought by strangers from the sea.

The hunters and gatherers were strong, uncoddled people, secure in the proven ways of their ancestors who had carved a living from the bounties of nature wherever they found them. They had fought the ravages of nature before: the droughts, the storms, the famines, and the thousands of dangers of chance. But nothing in their memory had been like this. Nothing had prepared them for the day the earth's crust shifted, carrying them forever away from their familiar existence. And so, shivering in their mountain retreats, they began to eke out a new life in the land, until they were joined by strangers from the sea. They shared nothing with these strangers but a vivid memory of the past that had been swept away by the earth's anger and a mutual fear of the future.

We can only imagine the conflict that raged within Atlantean and non-Atlantean alike at the joy of finding other living souls. Aliens to each other they truly were: but aliens bound together by a mutual need to conquer the circumstances that threatened to destroy them all.

The first task was to secure the future with a stock of food. Maps of the globe would become invaluable in the future, but the survivors of the flood were facing a critical problem—the need to feed themselves. They had to reboot agriculture. The earliest experiments with agriculture began in the *same* century that Atlantis fell. The chances of such a coincidence are astronomical.

Plato, who preserved the legend of Atlantis from ancient Egyptian sources, wrote about those first desperate days after the ocean broke across its boundaries.

ATHENIAN: Do you consider that there is any truth in the ancient tales?

CLINIAS: What tales?

ATHENIAN: That the world of men has often been destroyed by floods, plagues, and many other things, in such a way that only a small portion of the human race survived.

CLINIAS: Everyone would regard such accounts as perfectly credible.

ATHENIAN: Come now, let us picture to ourselves one of the many catastrophes—namely, that which occurred once upon a time through the Deluge.

CLINIAS: And what are we to imagine about it?

ATHENIAN: That the men who then escaped destruction must have been mostly herdsmen of the hills, scanty embers of the human race preserved somewhere on the mountain-tops.

CLINIAS: Evidently . . .

ATHENIAN: Shall we assume that the cities situated in the plains and near the sea were totally destroyed at the time?

CLINIAS: Let us assume it . . .

ATHENIAN: Shall we, then, state that, at the time when the destruction took place, human affairs were in this position: there was fearful and widespread desolation over a vast tract of land; most of the animals were destroyed; and the few herds of oxen and flocks of goats that happened to survive afforded at the first but scanty sustenance to the herdsmen?[1]

Plato's account represents the earliest rational explanation for the appearance of domesticated animals. His theory postulates the emergence of agriculture, beginning with the domestication of animals, as a reappearance of a skill learned long before in Atlantis. As we shall see, the dating of the earliest experiments with agriculture appears to match the century of Atlantis's fall. In the highlands of Turkey two of the worlds' most important crops—wheat and barley—were shaped to humans' design between eleven thousand and twelve thousand years ago,[2] at the time that Plato tells us Atlantis perished.

Plato's vision is also remarkable for the fact that it presents a physical rather than a mythological cause of agriculture. Before his time, all explanations relied upon the intervention of gods and goddesses to account for the beginning of agriculture. In contrast to these mythological origins of agriculture, Plato presents a very different picture. In his view, agriculture *re-emerges* after the destruction of a great and advanced civilization by earthquakes and floods of extraordinary violence. There are no gods or goddesses to suddenly intervene in the affairs of humankind. Instead, Plato sees the emergence of agriculture as a long, slow battle to recover the foundations of a lost civilization. His is a vision of human beings struggling against the vastly transformed physical conditions brought in the wake of the Great Flood.

We've traveled eons in our methods of farming since those first desperate days. In the process we have become dependant on a few key crops and domesticated animals. In North America, the great "breadbasket of the world," only a small fraction of the population toils to harvest the crops. The efforts of these few, with their highly specialized equipment, have transformed the landscape. To create ever more fertile plants, we intervene in the reproductive process of many crops such as wheat, rice, and corn—crops that would soon be swallowed by wild grasses if left to fend for themselves.

Mile after mile of domestic grains, bent to humankind's design, have replaced prairie grasses. From the transformed American prairie to the African savanna and Brazilian jungle, wild vegetation has submitted to the demands of the plow. Squeezed by overpopulation, we continuously strip away the natural garment of the earth and cover it with a cloth of our own weave. Our reliance on agriculture is complete. We can't turn back.

The search to explain the profound mystery of the sudden rise of agriculture on different continents following the climatic changes of 9600 BCE has been one of archaeology's most persistent quests.

THE MODERN SEARCH FOR AGRICULTURAL ORIGINS

In 1886, Alphonse de Candolle took a botanical approach to the problem of the origins of agriculture. He wrote, "One of the most direct means of discovering the geographic origin of a cultivated species is to seek in what country it grows spontaneously, and without the help of man."[3]

A dedicated, and ultimately doomed, Soviet botanist, Nikolai Ivanovich Vavilov (1887–1943), saw the possibilities in de Candolle's approach. For two decades, Vavilov patiently gathered a collection of over fifty thousand wild plants. He chose plants that are genetically linked to the domesticated variety we rely on today. Vavilov discovered "eight *independent* centers of origin of the most important cultivated plants." They were located on the earth's highest mountain ranges. He wrote, "It is clear that the zone of initial development of the most important cultivated plants lies in the strip between 20° and 45° north latitude, near the high mountain ranges, the Himalayas, the Hindu Kish, those of the Near East, the Balkans, and the Appennines. In the Old World this strip follows the latitudes while in the New World it runs longitudinally. In both cases conforming to the general direction of the great mountain ranges."[4] Although he was unaware of it, Vavilov's meticulously measured results support Plato's claim that mountain elevations were crucial to the reemergence of agriculture (see figure 8.1).

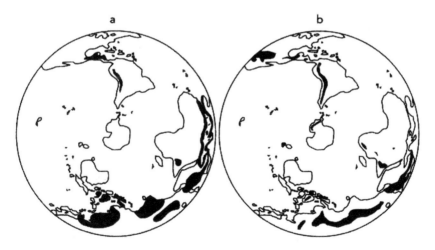

Figure 8.1. When we place Antarctica at the center of a world map, we can see (a) the sites where agriculture originated according to the Russian botanist Nikolai Vavilov. Most domesticated plants were originally domesticated in (b) sites at 1,500 meters (4,920 feet) above sea level.

In the cruellest of ironies Nikolai Vavilov was targeted by Josef Stalin as a scapegoat for the horrendous famine that the dictator's wild policies had inflicted on the Russian people and died of starvation in a prison cell in January 1943.

We aren't the first world culture to become ensnared in a dependency on sophisticated agricultural techniques. The Atlanteans also were accomplished farmers. They constructed elaborate canals to irrigate immense areas for cultivation. But when the end came, only a few possessed the skill to select the wild plants in the new lands that would sustain them. Those few would be enough.

In the tropics, three areas (in South America, Thailand, and Ethiopia) offered climatic stability and security (see figure 8.2). All were critical sites in the history of tropical agriculture. In addition, all three:

- Lay midway between the former and current path of the equator
- Received the same amount of annual sunlight both before and after the earth crust displacement
- Were located over 1,500 meters above sea level.

Let's consider two of these sites. Tropical agriculture suddenly bloomed in South America and Southeast Asia around the same time on exactly opposite sides of the globe. This puzzling phenomenon remains a deep archaeological mystery, but earth crust displacement provides the central missing piece of the puzzle. Rand offered this answer in an article published in the *Anthropological Journal of Canada* (see appendix). His interest lay in the significance of the uncanny locations of agriculture's earliest sites. This paper was the first to note that potatoes and rice were domesticated in tropical sites that are *antipodal.**

Of course, the chances of being published in an academic journal if even the whisper of the word *Atlantis* rippled its pages was impossible. Rand made the decision to present only the scientific facts of the

---

*The term *antipodal* means "on opposite sides of the earth." The North Pole is antipodal to the South Pole. Each place on the earth's surface has an antipode.

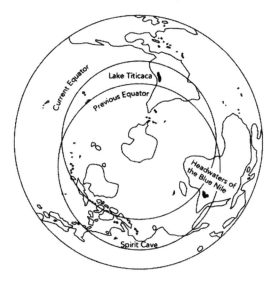

Figure 8.2. Seen from Antarctica, the path of the equator shifted with the last earth crust displacement. Lake Titicaca in the central Andes, Spirit Cave in the highlands of Thailand, and the highlands of Ethiopia were all midway between the current and former path of the equator. These favorable sites were climatically stable and supplied the survivors with raw crops that became potatoes, rice, and millet. The earliest agricultural sites date to 9600 BCE, the same time that Plato says Atlantis perished.

research and thereby eliminate the inevitable prejudice against the new ideas. This strategy worked. The article was accepted for publication as the lead article despite the fact that Rand wasn't an anthropologist. The abstract read, *"A climatic model, based on archaeological evidence is applied to the question of agricultural origins and the sequence of independent civilizations, on a global scale."*[5]

LATIN AMERICA

In Latin America, as we have seen elsewhere around the world, agriculture was established in about 9600 BCE. For instance, in the highlands of ancient Mexico, maize, one of the world's most important cereals, was suddenly and abruptly domesticated at about that time.[6]

Let's look at the appearance of agriculture in other places in Latin America. What made them likely sites for this flowering?

Incan mythology weaves a tale about the arrival of godlike men from the *south* who introduced a crop-growing civilization immediately after the Great Flood.[7] As we have seen, it's probable that these people came from Atlantis, but lets' examine in more detail how they brought the idea of raising crops rather than hunting for food and the impact of this change.

In 2007, in an area of South America that lies between the current and former locations of the equator, archaeologists unearthed early agricultural remains that included squash, cotton, peanuts, and other "founder crops" such as beans, manioc, chili peppers, and potatoes.[8] Charred remnants of the plants were discovered in houses that date to 11,650 years ago—very close to the date (9600 BCE) that Plato says Atlantis was destroyed and agriculture was rebooted.

One unique plant was also found—quinoa. Designated a "super crop" by the United Nations, quinoa is a remarkably nutritious plant containing a high-protein content. The Inca called it *chisaya mama,* or mother of all grains. Its bitter-tasting shell discourages the attentions of rodents and insects. Someday botanists might be able to reproduce this strategy for protecting crops and free us from our ubiquitous use of chemicals. Each year the Incan emperor used a golden hoe to sow the seeds from this most precious of plants. Archaeologists believe that quinoa was originally domesticated around Lake Titicaca *before* 9,200 years ago.

South America was the closest continent to Atlantis. Survivors reached its shores first. Edible crops appeared there shortly after 9600 BCE.

Farming was coaxed to life again near Lake Titicaca, where the amount of annual sunshine remained the same as before the earth crust displacement. Why didn't the climate change? Prior to the catastrophe Lake Titicaca lay about 1,000 miles (1,600 km) north of the equator. After the crust's movement, it was dragged 1,000 miles (1,600 km) south of the equator. As a result—even though South America was dramatically impacted by the shifting crust—Lake Titicaca maintained its relative distance from the equator. This meant that plants and animals from this zone—like potatoes, llamas, and guinea pigs—continued to thrive.

OTHER CLIMATICALLY FAVORABLE SITES

Africa suffered fewer latitude changes than the other continents. In the Ethiopia highlands, around the headwaters of the Blue Nile, the amount of annual sunshine was unaltered after the last earth crust displacement. Because it was roughly the same distance from the equator after the catastrophe as before, it became an oasis of survival. The highlands of Ethiopia may yet yield surprises for archaeologists. Here millet was first domesticated. These highlands would have been an excellent site for the survivors of Atlantis to settle because here, as in Lake Titicaca, the climate was not dramatically changed as a result of the earth crust displacement. Atlanteans may have survived here and eventually followed the Blue Nile down to Egypt to participate in the development of Egyptian civilization.

Rice is one of our most precious crops, providing food daily for almost half the population of the planet. Some of the earliest remains of domesticated rice were found at Spirit Cave[9] in the highlands of Thailand, on the opposite side of the earth—the antipode—from Lake Titicaca. Besides Thailand, early centers of rice cultivation have been found in the Himalayas, eastern India, and southern China.[10] Strangely, it is as if people in all these regions of Asia simultaneously recognized the value of this crop.

After the catastrophe, Egypt shared a common fate with Crete, Sumer, India, and China. This great crescent of land, extending from Egypt to Japan, adjoined an area to the north that remained temperate both before and after the displacement (see figure 8.3 on page 132). "The abrupt and dramatic changes in climate during the Holocene caused human migrations in many areas."[11] Can it be mere coincidence—blind chance—that the first five great civilizations all shared a common climatic fate?

The veil obscuring this mystery slips away if we allow that survivors

Figure 8.3. A vast crescent of land extending from Egypt to Japan was tropical before the earth crust displacement and temperate afterward. This favored crescent was the birthplace of the world's first known civilizations.

of Atlantis, carrying the knowledge of agriculture and their ancient skills with them, arrived from their destroyed homeland and reinvented agriculture in these viable zones.

BANANAS AND SUGAR

At Kuk in the central highlands of New Guinea something remarkable happened around the time of the fall of Atlantis. So momentous are these discoveries that the area has been designated a World Heritage Site.[12]

New Guinea is the third largest island in the world after Antarctica and Greenland. A mysterious land, Europeans did not penetrate its central highlands until the 1930s and only then using air power. However, New Guinea has been occupied for at least forty thousand years.[13] During the first thirty thousand years the people lived by hunting and gathering. But abruptly, around ten thousand years ago, they suddenly moved into the highlands, taking with them plants that had always been cultivated at sea level. They cleared the land and systematically drained a swamp that eventually would become the birthplace of several important domesticated crops, most notably bananas and sugar cane.

Why would people who had been living as hunters and gatherers for thousands of years suddenly climb high up to the central plateau of New Guinea, drain a swamp, and plant bananas, a crop that can take twenty years to become viable? Why would people who had been perfectly adapted to the land for thirty thousand years suddenly abandon their long-established and successful means of subsistence and opt for agriculture? And why did they find it necessary to leave the coastal regions at all?

These questions haunted the Australian archaeologist Jack Golson, who has spent a lifetime trying to solve this New Guinea riddle.[14] Golson and his partner on the quest, Phillip Hughes, became convinced of the radical idea that Kuk was deliberately created as a cradle for agriculture. At an early stage they made the remarkable discovery of a "paleochannel," a sophisticated landscaping device for draining a swamp to create tillable land.*

Once again, the occurrence of an earth crust displacement makes sense of the sudden appearance of these advanced tools. Kuk lies at an altitude of 1,560 meters, making the temperature there several degrees cooler than in the hot lowlands, where its transplanted wild plants originated. When New Guinea moved some 20° closer to the equator as a result of the earth's crust shifting around 9600 BCE, the sudden rise in annual temperatures forced the New Guineans to adapt. Their obvious solution was to move to the highlands. For every 150 meters they climbed the temperature dropped by one degree.† At 1,500 meters they could reestablish their settlements and enjoy the temperatures that had previously prevailed at sea level.

---

*One of their students, Tim Denham, was not convinced that the paleochannel was in fact man-made. He undertook tests that called into question the artificial attributes of the channel. Nevertheless, whether it was by design or just good luck, the people of the highlands of New Guinea made very constructive use of land that was once a swamp. And they certainly did become very effective water manipulators as time went on.
†Temperature drops as one goes up in altitude varying from 1 degree Celsius in "dry" areas to half a degree in "damp" areas for each 150 meters. In the case of Kuk, the temperature is around 6–10 degrees Celsius cooler than temperatures at sea level.

Is the mystery of Kuk reflecting a distant mirror of a long-lost civilization? Plato tells us that the people of Atlantis were masters at manipulating the flow of water to sustain agriculture. After 9600 BCE, when Atlantis perished, early agricultural experiments sprung up around the globe, followed eventually by vast water engineering projects designed to enhance crop production. In Central and South America, Egypt, Sumer, India, and China all of the early civilizations relied on massive water engineering projects. Is this mere coincidence?

NINE

THE RING OF DEATH

Seen from space, our planet is a tiny turquoise jewel in a midnight black setting. But one landmass stands out from most of the others—the shining snow-covered continent of Antarctica. The continent of Antarctica is immense, covering a greater area than the mainland United States. But it is a mysterious and hostile place where few humans dare to venture. Cold, nightless summers fade into freezing, sunless winters. And always there is the wind, the constant howling wind of a land forgotten. Most of the earth's precious fresh water is locked within its ice cap. The very existence of this vast ice cap points to a climatic conundrum. At the same time it provides a clue to the great convulsions that have seized the earth in the past.

Geographers distinguish between "Lesser Antarctica" and "Greater Antarctica" (see figure 9.1 on page 136). Lesser Antarctica, the tail of land that points toward South America, is characterized by its mountains, relatively thin ice sheet, and heavy snowfall. The body of the continent, Greater Antarctica, groans beneath a massive weight of ice. The ice is over two miles thick, even though the area receives very little annual snowfall. It is, in fact, a polar desert (see figure 9.2 on page 136). This puzzling disparity between annual snowfall rates and the great depth of its ice sheet reveals that Antarctica's climate must have been radically different in the past, that there must have been a time when snowfall was commonplace.

Each spot on the earth's surface has an "antipodal" point, that is,

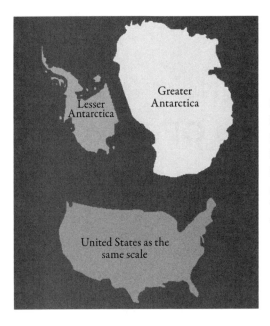

Figure 9.1. The island continent of Antarctica is comparable in size to the lower forty-eight states of the United States. Geographers separate the continent into "Lesser Antarctica" and "Greater Antarctica."

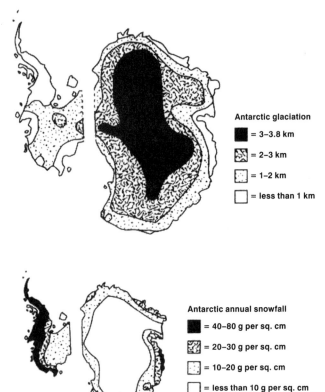

Antarctic glaciation

■ = 3–3.8 km
▨ = 2–3 km
▦ = 1–2 km
□ = less than 1 km

Antarctic annual snowfall

■ = 40–80 g per sq. cm
▨ = 20–30 g per sq. cm
▦ = 10–20 g per sq. cm
□ = less than 10 g per sq. cm

Figure 9.2. Today's climate conditions cannot account for the shape of the ice sheets on Antarctica. Lesser Antarctica has the least ice but the most annual snowfall, while Greater Antarctica holds the most ice yet experiences the least snowfall. Antarctic glaciation data from Strahler, *Introduction to Physical Geography*, 355. Antarctic annual snowfall data from Rubin, "Antarctic Meteorology," 161.

a point exactly on the opposite side of the planet. If a line is drawn through one point on the earth, through the exact center of the earth, that line will emerge at its antipodal point. The North Pole is antipodal to the South Pole. England and New Zealand are antipodal. North America and the southern part of the Indian Ocean lie on the opposite sides of the earth. Greenland, covered with the largest ice sheet in the northern hemisphere, is very close to being antipodal to the great ice cap on Greater Antarctica. The area of thickest ice on Greenland overlaps the area of thickest ice on Antarctica. In every case, the points that are antipodal share the same amount of annual sunshine and thus similar temperatures.

Like its cousin in the south, Greenland's current snowfall does not match its ice cap. The current climate cannot possibly account for the ice sheets on Greenland and Antarctica, and yet there has not been any explanation for this "odd" placement of the ice sheets. The problem is ignored. The present largest ice sheets are antipodal yet lopsided relative to the earth's axis. This suggests a displacement of the earth's crust—to be expected when lands shift in and out of the polar regions.

Earth crust displacement does, in fact, provide an answer to the problem. As the earth's crust shifts, it moves through the climatic zones. Some lands that had enjoyed mild climates before the shift were dragged into the polar zones. As a result, they received more snow. Other lands were released from the polar zones as they were shifted into warmer climates, causing their ice sheets to melt. Greenland and Greater Antarctica were locked into the polar zones before *and* after the displacement. Since these lands experienced polar conditions longer than any other parts of the world, they accumulated the greatest ice sheets. The overlapping old and new Arctic and Antarctica circles (it is actually the crust that moves, not the polar zones) leave the old ice sheets intact.

Until 9600 BC, Lesser Antarctica was outside the polar zone. This area has hardly been explored for two reasons. First, three nations (Argentina, Chile, and the United Kingdom) all lay claim to it. No system of law has been established and territorial disputes overlap. Second, most scientists focus on studying Greater Antarctica's vast ice sheet. Because of limited data about the area of the continent that is most important to the mystery of Atlantis, we must gauge Lesser Antarctica's past climate using the antipodal argument.

Greenland, smothered by the largest ice sheet in the Northern Hemisphere, lies in an antipodal position to the great ice cap on Greater Antarctica. Its area of thickest ice corresponds to the thick ice on Antarctica (see figure 9.3). It is also a polar desert that receives minimal snowfall. Unexpectedly, neither ice sheet is centered at a pole.

Climatologists insist that the colossal size of these antipodal, lop-

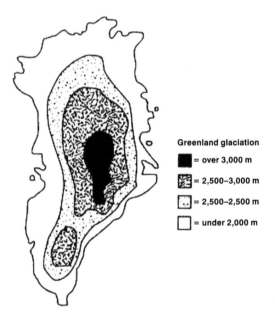

Greenland glaciation

■ = over 3,000 m

▨ = 2,500–3,000 m

▦ = 2,500–2,500 m

☐ = under 2,000 m

Figure 9.3. Greenland's massive ice cap cannot be explained by the annual snowfall patterns. Greenland glaciation data from Strahler, *Introduction to Physical Geography*, 354. Greenland annual snowfall data from Rumney, *Climatology and the World's Climate*, 116.

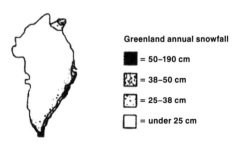

Greenland annual snowfall

■ = 50–190 cm

▨ = 38–50 cm

▦ = 25–38 cm

☐ = under 25 cm

sided ice caps couldn't possibly be realized under current snowfall conditions. They must have been formed by some other phenomenon. This glaring anomaly has *never* been explained by geologists.*

Charles Hapgood's theory of a sliding crust and/or mantle is the tool that can unlock the mystery of aberrant glaciation patterns. As the earth's crust shifts, it moves through the climatic zones. Land that had previously enjoyed a mild climate is dragged into polar zones, exposing it to more snow. Other areas are released from frigid zones and shift into warmer climes, causing ice sheets to melt.

Central Greenland and Greater Antarctica are the only regions on Earth that remained within polar zones both before and after the last displacement. As a result there has never been an opportunity for their ice to melt. Antipodal, lopsided ice sheets are exactly what we would expect if the earth's crust is dramatically shifted over a relatively short period of time with no opportunity for the ice-locked land to thaw.†

ANTARCTICA'S ANTIPODES

Only a few thousand people live on Antarctica at any given time. They are primarily preoccupied with astronomical and climatic studies that rely on ice-core dating, a discipline fraught with difficulties.[1]

In contrast, we know a great deal more about the Arctic, where Russian, European, American, and Canadian scientists have studied the climate extensively. The wide range of scientific data gathered from the north has been used to provide models of the climate that ruled the polar south in the past. (Most American scientists approach the problem from the opposite direction. They attempt to explain climatic conditions in places like Siberia and Beringia by using ice core dating from Antarctica.)

---

*The only competing theory is that of a radical shift of the Earth's axis (see chapter 13).
†This anomaly has remained unaddressed by geologists for nearly two centuries. The problem is simply ignored because there is no acceptable geological theory to address it. Without a competing theory, the logic of science dictates that any theory that can address the problem must be taken seriously, yet Hapgood's work goes largely unrecognized.

After the Cold War ended, more Russian scientists joined the international research community. They brought with them the startling finding that American ice-core dating conclusions about Siberia did not match their own evidence. European scientists are also challenging current assumptions about the past climate of the far north.

In 1993, at a site 250 kilometers north of the Arctic Circle, Norwegian zoologists Rolv Lie and Stein-Erik Lauritzen discovered polar bear bones dating to the last ice age. The find was surprising because geologists assume that arctic Norway was under a vast ice cap between eighty thousand and ten thousand years ago. No life could survive such a barren environment. The bones were not supposed to be there! Carbon-14 and uranium dating confirmed that the remains must be at least forty-two thousand years old. Further excavations revealed the remains of wolves, field mice, ants, and tree pollen. "The wolf needs large prey like reindeer," said Lie. "Reindeer in turn, must be able to graze on bare ground. The summers must have been relatively warm and the winters not excessively cold . . . the area wasn't under an icecap as we believed."[2]

The existence of these animals and the plants that they needed to live challenges common notions about the last ice age. How could an area that was supposedly frozen in the polar zone exhibit characteristics only found in much warmer climates? These difficulties disappear if we surrender the presupposition of a stable earth's crust and recognize that it is subject to abrupt movement. Then it is possible to see that reindeer, wolves, and ants once thrived in an area that today cannot sustain them.

If we peer through a glass globe and align the North Pole with the South Pole, we can see those parts of Antarctica that are antipodes to lands in the north (see figure 9.4). This juxtaposition reveals the possibility that Lesser Antarctica once enjoyed a temperate climate capable of supporting Atlantis, similar to the past climate shown by the Norwegian evidence.

The Norwegian discovery was not the only evidence that would challenge our ideas about the Arctic climate before 9600 BCE. Off

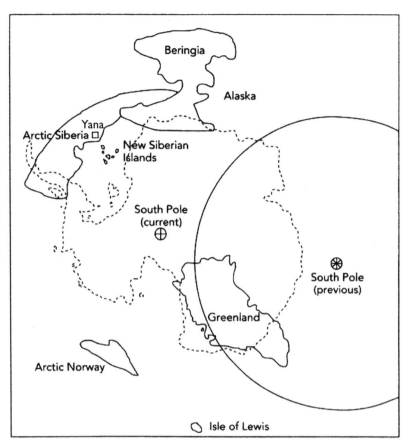

Figure 9.4. A glass globe allows us to see those areas of Antarctica that are antipodal to areas of Alaska, Beringia, northern Siberia, arctic Norway, and Scotland's Isle of Lewis. Since established scientific evidence of temperate zone conditions has been found in the northern areas, it stands to reason that large parts of Antarctica must have enjoyed temperate conditions prior to 9600 BCE as well.

the northwestern coast of Scotland lies the remote Isle of Lewis. In 1984, two scientists made the unexpected discovery that it was unglaciated between thirty-seven and twenty-three thousand years ago. They wrote, "Models of the last ice sheet showing Scottish ice extending to the continental shelf edge depict the north of Lewis as being covered by 1,000–1,500 metres of ice, but our evidence demonstrates that part of this area was actually ice-free."[3]

When we shift our gaze to arctic America, the evidence continues to build toward a new understanding of the world before 9600 BCE. In 1982, Dr. R. Dale Guthrie, at the Institute of Arctic Biology, was struck by the variety of animals that thrived in Alaska before 9600 BCE. He wrote, "When learning of this exotic mixture of hyenas, mammoths, sabre-toothed cats, camels, horses, rhinos, asses, deer with gigantic antlers, lions, ferrets, saiga, and other Pleistocene species, one cannot help wondering about the world in which they lived. This great diversity of species, so different from that encountered today, raises the most obvious question: is it not likely that the rest of the environment was also different?"[4]

In 2004, nine Russian scientists reported a remarkable discovery at Yana in northern Siberia. Located at nearly 71° North, the site lies well within the Arctic Circle. Thirty-three thousand years ago humans cohabited in Yana with a host of animals that could not possibly survive in the harsh climate that dominates now. These include "mammoths, rhinoceros, Pleistocene bison, horse, reindeer, musk-ox, wolf, polar fox, Pleistocene lion, brown bear, and wolverine."[5] The authors of the report, most of whom are with the Russian Academy of Science, noted that "only the reindeer and wolf still inhabit this area."

When we compare Yana's current latitude (71° N) to where it would have been *before* the last earth crust displacement, we find that during the time period when the current North Pole was at Hudson Bay, the latitude for Yana would have been 43° N—well outside the polar zone. Notable cities at 43° N today include Vladivostok; Marseilles; Madison, Wisconsin; and Concord, New Hampshire. The animals that lived in Yana thirty-three thousand years ago could survive in the climatic conditions of any of these modern cities.

The significance of the Yana site was not lost on two physicists. Professor Emeritus W. Woelfli of the Institute for Particle Physics in Zürich and Professor W. Baltensperger of the Brazilian Center for Physics Research in Rio de Janeiro both cite the Yana evidence in support of the idea of a radical shift of the earth's axis around 11,500 years ago. They repeatedly make the point that Arctic East Siberia must have had a lower latitude in the Pleistocene[6] and mention Hapgood's work.

These scientists understood that Siberia must have been located at a radically warmer latitude before 9600 BCE. Our fixation with the belief that the earth's crust has always been stable in relation to its axis blinds us to the legacy left in ancient Alaska and the traces of the past to be found in Siberia's flora and fauna. The evidence collected from Yana proclaims that *temperate,* not polar, conditions must have prevailed in Siberia.

OSSIP'S DISCOVERY

In the summer of 1799, while searching for ivory in the isolated wilderness of Siberia, a Tungus chief named Ossip Shumakhov encountered, complete with preserved hair and flesh, the ice-encapsulated carcass of a mammoth. The chief was terrified. Legend foretold that any whose gaze fell on one of these creatures would soon die. As predicted, within a few days Shumakhov grew ill. However, to his own and everyone else's surprise, he made a complete recovery.

With renewed courage, Shumakhov set out to revisit the frozen mammoth, this time taking along several curious Russian scientists. Excited to discover that Shumakhov's fantastic account was true, they shipped the remains of the incredible creature to St. Petersburg, where it can still be seen today.

On the heels of this sensational discovery, the New Siberian Islands, in the Arctic Ocean, gave up the desolate graves of thousands of large animals. The find created confusion among scientists. How could these huge creatures, requiring vast amounts of vegetation to fuel their daily existence, thrive in such large herds on barren dunes of ice? And what incredible force had destroyed them?

One of the first and most distinguished scholars to accept the challenge of these questions was Georges Cuvier (1769–1832) a French naturalist. Cuvier had already created a sensation by unearthing and reassembling a prehistoric elephant from the ground beneath Paris. This was only one of the amazing discoveries that the inquisitive Cuvier would reveal to a startled Europe. By his midthirties he had become the dominant scientific thinker of his era, clearing new paths in virtually all of the natural sciences.

Cuvier's flamboyant character, combined with his colorful discoveries, made him a favorite object of gossip in the fashionable salons. It was said that late one night Cuvier's students decided to play a practical joke on him. One of them, dressed in a red cape to represent the devil, artificial horns secured to his head and hooves tied to his feet, burst into the sleeping professor's chambers shouting that he had come to devour the learned scientist! Cuvier awoke, calmly examined the spectacle before him and pronounced, "You have horns and hooves; you can only eat plants."

Cuvier labored long hours over the mystery of the ancient bones from Siberia and the inevitable questions they raised. He became more and more convinced that the world had experienced a catastrophe of unspeakable dimensions and that man "might have inhabited certain circumscribed regions, whence he repeopled the earth after these terrible events; perhaps even the places he inhabited were entirely swallowed up and his bones buried in the depths of the present seas, except for a small number of individuals who carried on the race."[7]

The unexpected discovery of frozen giants in the wastelands of Siberia excited Cuvier's genius and proved to him that the earth had suffered sudden, destructive convulsions and upheavals.

> These repeated eruptions and retreats of the sea have neither been slow nor gradual; most of the catastrophes that have occasioned them have been sudden; and this is easily proved, especially with regard to the last of them, the traces of which are most conspicuous. In the northern regions it has left the carcasses of some large quadrupeds, which the ice had arrested, and which are preserved even to the present day with their skin, their hair, and their flesh. If they

had not been frozen as soon as killed they must quickly have been decomposed by putrefaction. But this eternal frost could not have taken possession of the regions that these animals inhabited except by the same cause, which destroyed them; this cause, therefore, must have been as sudden as its effect. The breaking to pieces and overturning of the strata, which happened in former catastrophes, shew [*sic*] plainly enough that they were sudden and violent like the last; and the heaps of debris and rounded pebbles which are found in various places among the solid strata, demonstrate the vast force of the motions excited in the mass of waters by these overturnings. Life, therefore, has been often disturbed on this earth by terrible events—calamities which, at their commencement, have perhaps moved and overturned to a great depth the entire outer crust of the globe, but which, since these first commotions, have uniformly acted at a less depth and less generally.[8]

At the time Cuvier put forward his theory, geologists were involved in an intense debate with the church over the role of catastrophes in the earth's history. Although he was greatly respected, Cuvier's theory of an earth crust displacement was unacceptable to the scientific establishment. It was associated with the idea of a supernatural force (God) that could overturn the laws of nature at will. It was also unacceptable to the religious fanatics, who, although they liked Cuvier's earthquakes and floods, didn't accept his timing, which placed these events far earlier than the Bible proclaimed. And so Cuvier's theory that mass extinctions were caused by displacements of the earth's crust was suffocated in the heated debate between religious extremists and defensive scientists.

However, one man who based his studies on Cuvier's theory developed what is still an accepted concept: the idea of the ice ages. Naturalist and geologist Louis Agassiz (1807–1873) was born in Motier, Switzerland. From an early age Agassiz was blessed with the ambition and determination to make his unique mark on the history of science.

Only twenty-two when his first work, *Brazilian Fish,* was published, he dedicated the book to Cuvier, "whom I revere as a father, and whose works have been till now my only guide." Cuvier responded to the young scientist with a complimentary letter suggesting additional lines of investigation.

With this encouragement, Agassiz continued to study the evolution of fish while maintaining the medical career urged on him by his parents. In October 1831, in what was to be a sadly ironic turn of events, he seized the opportunity to travel to Paris to study a grim cholera epidemic. He wasted no time in presenting himself to Cuvier. The great man was impressed with Agassiz's work and took a liking to the enthusiastic young Swiss, perhaps seeing reflections of his younger self in the bold-featured youth nervously spreading his research before him.

Cuvier turned over to Agassiz one of his elaborately equipped laboratories and all his personal notes on the subject of their mutual interest. The topic of fish fossils also held a fascination for Cuvier, and realizing that Agassiz had independently arrived at similar conclusions, he was unceasingly generous in his aid, providing advice and encouragement whenever needed, even the occasional meal at his home, where many contemporary original thinkers mingled over wine and cigars.

In May of 1832, tragedy struck. Cuvier was taken by the very cholera Agassiz had originally come to Paris to study. The impact of this painful event on Agassiz was profound. "With Cuvier's death, whatever sense of intellectual independence Agassiz had known disappeared. The fact that the great naturalist had turned over important fossils to him for description and publication made Agassiz think of himself as Cuvier's disciple. He determined to mode his intellectual efforts after the pattern set for him by Cuvier."[9]

Agassiz adopted Cuvier's conclusion that the earth's history had been periodically marked by great catastrophes that had destroyed existing plants and animals and wiped clean the slate for the creation of new creatures by God. These ideas, known as *catastrophism* and *special creation,* were concepts Agassiz would hold for the rest of his life and were fundamental to his physical view of the world. The first, catastro-phism, was a conclusion based on the fossil record, an interpretation of the known facts. But the second idea, special creation, drifted from the precision of scientific data into the murky arena of theology.

Agassiz's adoption of Cuvier's notion of special creation violates one of the basic principles of modern science: the concept of the invariance of physical laws. Scientists today assume that the physical laws govern-ing our planet (for example, gravity) apply throughout the universe and are constant throughout time and space. Catastrophists assume that supernatural forces (God) can, and do, intervene in the affairs of our planet. Physical laws, in their view, are subject to the whims of super-natural forces. They also assume that the Bible is the ultimate authority as to the age of the earth. Many, even today, believe that the world was created in seven days and that it is only thousands of years old. The idea of special creation goes one step further: life is specially created *after* catastrophes.

Catastrophism (as it was understood by Agassiz and Cuvier) was an accepted geological assumption based on the teachings of the Bible. It has now been rejected by the vast majority of scientists. The tradi-tion that eventually overtook and replaced catastrophism was created by a Scottish amateur geologist, James Hutton (1726–1797). He realized that over great periods of time, even small changes caused by the daily impact of forces such as wind and water would eventually transform the face of the earth.

However, Hutton's motives in proposing a new approach to the earth sciences were not the strictly scientific ones that we are now led to believe. He lived in a time before the notion of progress, so funda-mental to our own era, was widely accepted. The Bible was still the ulti-mate authority on questions of the earth's history. The biblical account of the Great Flood was believed to be the key to understanding geol-ogy. Common thinking was that time brought only decay, not prog-ress. It was generally assumed that the history of the planet could be divided into three phases. "Firstly, there had been a period of generation extending from the Creation up to the Fall of Man; secondly, there was the prolonged and present period of degeneration initiated by the Fall; and thirdly, there was the eagerly awaited period of regeneration that would be ushered in by Christ's Second Coming."[10]

Hutton challenged this view by arguing in the first volume of the *Transactions of the Royal Society of Edinburgh* that the earth's history was very long and would extend indefinitely into the future. He wrote, "We find no vestige of a beginning—no prospect of an end."[11] He saw the earth as a vast machine created by the Almighty for the *purpose* of maintaining life (as opposed to the Catastrophists, who believed that the Almighty could destroy life).

His famous book *Theory of the Earth with Proofs and Illustrations* (1795) was an attempt to show that the earth was the handiwork of God. In that book, Hutton wrote,

> If we believe that there is almighty power, and supreme wisdom employed for sustaining that beautiful system of plants and animals which is so interesting to us, we must certainly conclude, that the earth, on which this system of living things depends, has been constructed on principles that are adequate to the end proposed, and procure it a perfection which it is our business to explore.[12]

Hutton rejected the biblical idea of a deluge or Great Flood *because* he believed that this was contrary to God's design. If the purpose of the earth was to sustain life, God would not violate his plan by allowing deluges to wreak havoc with his creation. "But, surely, general deluges form no part of the theory of the earth; for, the purpose of this earth is evidently to maintain vegetable and animal life, and not to destroy them."[13]

What was radical in Hutton's theory was his assumption that the earth's design was a more accurate reflection of the Almighty's intention than was the Bible. And even more unusual was his belief that all geological phenomena could be understood as the products of a perfectly designed machine that was operating today as it has always operated. For Hutton, "the present was the key to the past." Given a vast amount of time, even small changes could produce significant results. Here we have Hutton writing as most geologists would like to remember him.

Not only are no powers to be employed that are not natural to the globe, no action to be admitted of except those of which we know the principle, and no extraordinary events to be alleged in order to explain a common appearance, the powers of nature are not to be employed in order to destroy the very object of those powers; we are not to make nature act in violation to that order which we actually observe, and in subversion of created things. In whatever manner, therefore, we are to employ the great agents, fire and water, for producing those things which appear, it ought to be in such a way as is consistent with the propagation of plant and life of animals upon the surface of the earth. Chaos and confusion are not to be introduced into the order of nature, because certain things appear to our partial views as being in some disorder. Nor are we to proceed in feigning cause, when those seem insufficient which occur in our experience.[14]

Hutton wished to replace the chaos of the Great Flood with a world order more worthy of God. His idea of gradual change operating over vast amounts of time would come to be known as uniformitarianism.

Charles Lyell (1797–1875), in *Principles of Geology* (1830 and 1832), took Hutton's idea of uniformitarianism, refined it, expanded it, and demonstrated it in language and with illustrations that were accessible to the nonscientist. He dealt a fatal blow to the notion that physical laws could be subject to the whims of supernatural forces. In opposition to catastrophism, he wrote, "In our attempt to unravel these difficult questions, we shall adopt a different course, restricting ourselves to the known or possible operations of existing causes: feeling assured that we have not yet exhausted the resources which the study of the present course of nature may provide, and therefore that we are not authorized, in the infancy of our science, to recur to extraordinary agents."[15]

In his time, and for more than a century, Lyell's prohibition against the consideration of geological forces that cannot be observed in the present served the fledgling science of geology well. But Lyell was blind to the fact that these rigid boundaries need not exclude the investigation of extraordinary upheavals that can be explained without reference to a supernatural force, that is, dramatic geological upheavals (still subject to the physical laws of the earth) that result in accelerated rates of change.

These "spurts" of change occur as a result of physical events operating within the confines of natural laws.[16] Today, Cuvier's theory should be recognized as being far ahead of his time, but geologists grouped his ideas with those of the catastrophists, and his notion of a great geological upheaval was forgotten. His student, Agassiz, took up the banner with his theory of the ice ages.

Four years after Cuvier's death, Agassiz was exploring Switzerland's sheer crevices and towering mountains with two friends who were students of Alpine glaciers. The germ of an idea was planted as the two persuaded Agassiz that the dominating boulders they were climbing over had been pushed, heaved, and hauled to their positions by glaciers. Agassiz saw the possibilities at once, and in 1837 he announced his theory of the ice ages to an unsuspecting Europe. "Siberian winter," he declared, "established itself for a time over a world previously covered with rich vegetation and peopled with large mammalia, similar to those now inhabiting the warm regions of India and Africa. Death enveloped all nature in a shroud, and the cold, having reached its highest degree, gave to this mass of ice at the maximum tension, the greatest possible hardness!"[17]

Although the term *ice ages* has become part of our modern vocabulary, it was an unusual and startling concept when Agassiz first proposed it. Hand in hand with our concept of the ice ages comes the meaning of the term *glacial*. Today it is generally accepted as indicating a ponderous, slow movement, an inch-by-inch advancement (and thus losing its original sense of catastrophe). But Agassiz, in first proposing that the earth had suffered traumatic periods of extreme cold, insisted that the ice ages had descended on the earth suddenly and catastrophically, plunging it into its darkest winter. He wrote, "A sudden intense winter, that was to last for ages, fell upon our globe; it spread over the very countries where these tropical animals had their homes, and so suddenly did it come upon them that they were embalmed beneath masses of snow and ice, without time even for the decay which follows death."[18]

To Agassiz this theory of catastrophic ice ages cleared the overgrown trail leading to the heart of the mystery of extinctions. The onslaught of a sudden deadly ice age would have entombed massive creatures where they stood, mute witnesses to a season of disaster.

When Agassiz first presented the idea of ice ages to the scientific community in 1837, he was met with great skepticism. However, he proved that the movement of glaciers could account for the placement of massive boulders. The skeptics were forced to accept that the earth had indeed once been gripped by deadly winters. The trigger for these paralyzing winters remained a puzzle. Agassiz had recognized this obstacle from the beginning.

> We have as yet no clew [sic] to the source of this great and sudden change of climate. Various suggestions have been made—among others, that formerly the inclination of the earth's axis was greater, or that a submersion of the continents under water might have produced a decided increase of cold; but none of these explanations are satisfactory, and science has yet to find any cause which accounts for all the phenomena connected with it.[19]

This grand cycle of destruction may have been the cause of periodic bouts of mass extinctions. There have been many of these disasters, each one of which has had a profound impact upon the course of evolution. The late Pleistocene extinctions, which occurred shortly after 9600 BCE, have been studied in detail by scientists attempting to solve the mystery of these deadly events.

One line of inquiry puts the blame on humankind. Charles Darwin's codiscoverer of the theory of natural selection, Alfred Russel Wallace (1823–1913) advanced the idea that the extinctions at the end of the last ice age were caused not only by climatic changes but also by humans. In 1911, he wrote, "The extinction of so many large Mammalia is actually due to man's agency, *acting in co-operation with those general causes* which at the culmination of each geological era has led to the extinction of the larger, the most specialized, or the most strangely modified forms."[20]

Like Darwin, Wallace was strongly committed to the Hutton/Lyell model of strict, gradual change in the earth's history. But even Lyell couldn't ignore the problems in resting all the terrible responsibility for extinctions on humans. "It is probable that causes more general and powerful than the agency of Man, alterations in climate, variations in the range of many species of animals, vertebrate and invertebrate, and of plants, geographical changes in the height, depth, and extent of land and sea, or all of these combined, have given rise, in a vast series of years, to the annihilation . . . of many large mammals."[21]

Despite Lyell's warnings, the idea of humankind as the cause of extinctions has a great following among anthropologists and paleontologists. The modern spokesman for the "overkill hypothesis" is Dr. Paul S. Martin of the University of Arizona. He believes that human migration to the New World caused the mass extinctions. North America did experience massive extinctions at this time. The great bears, saber-toothed tigers, mammoths, and mastodons all became extinct shortly after 9600 BCE. (Many archaeologists believe that people first arrived in the New World shortly after 9600 BCE, an idea we will examine in detail in chapter 10.) Martin conjectures that the animals that humans encountered had not developed the necessary skills to escape the newcomers' hunting techniques and were consequently slaughtered to extinction.[22] In contrast, the animals of the Old World, especially in

Europe and Africa, had evolved evasion strategies to deal with hunters, thereby avoiding the fate of their counterparts in the New World.

It is perhaps a natural view to adopt in the twenty-first century, given our shameful record in annihilating so many species, but the overkill hypothesis can only explain one set of mass extinctions. It can't explain those that occurred earlier than the Pleistocene. Nor can the overkill hypothesis explain the deaths of vast numbers of large animals that once thrived in temperate northern Siberia, land that is now barren tundra. To support these animals Siberia's climate must have been much warmer than it is today. Russian scientists are convinced that humankind played little or no role in their extinction and that only a dramatic climate change can account for so many deaths.[23]

The physical facts are not in dispute. Various continents have experienced different rates of extinction at different times. Nearly twelve thousand years ago, North America, South America, Australia, and the Arctic regions suffered massive extinctions, while at the same time there were relatively few in Europe and Africa.[24] These varying rates of disappearance would seem, at first glance, to support the overkill hypothesis. "The lack of synchroneity between the extinctions on different continents and their variable intensity, for example, heavier in America than Africa, appears to eliminate as a cause any sudden extraterrestrial or cosmic catastrophe."[25]

But an earth crust displacement would cause extinctions to occur on different continents at different rates as a result of varying changes in the world's latitudes. Some continents experience great climatic change, while others are largely unaffected. Changing climates produce extinctions as creatures succumb to different temperatures and alien seasons.

Hapgood's data permits us to see the Pleistocene extinctions in a clear light. Using his determination of the location of the earth's crust before 9600 BCE, we can observe the latitude changes that occurred after the displacement. An imaginary circle drawn around the globe through the locations of the current and previous positions of the North and South poles reveals the area that experienced the largest latitude change, thereby suffering the greatest trauma. We call it the *line of greatest displacement* (LGD) or *ring of death*. This line runs through North America, west of South America, bisects Antarctica, travels through Southeast Asia, goes on to Siberia, and then back to North America (see figure 9.5). The ring of death corresponds directly with those regions of the globe that suffered the most extinctions.

The *line of least displacement* (LLD) intersects with those climatic regions that remained relatively stable both during and after the catastrophe. It runs through Greenland, Europe, and Africa before cutting between Australia and New Zealand, passing Hawaii, and then returning to Greenland. This LLD corresponds directly with those regions that experienced the least extinctions (see figure 9.5).

Unlike the overkill hypothesis, the theory of earth crust displacement provides a model for the study of mass extinctions in general. The same principle can be applied to earlier geological periods and is not dependent on our guesses as to the ability of animals to avoid human hunters. An earth crust displacement randomly determines which species will survive and which will perish. The remnants of species that

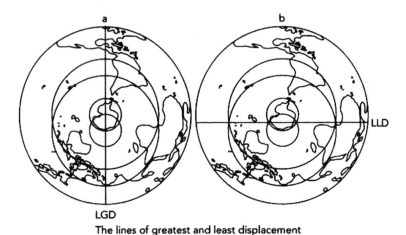

LGD

The lines of greatest and least displacement

Figure 9.5. Each earth crust displacement results in dramatic climatic changes. Some regions experience far more dramatic latitude change than others. The last displacement left a path of extinction across the line of greatest shift. Along the line of least displacement extinctions were few. North America lost large mammals such as mammoths and saber-toothed tigers, while Africa's elephants and lions survived.

survive the destruction of an earth crust displacement represent smaller gene pools, increasing the probability of the development of new species because mutations can take a better "hold" within small communities. Ocean creatures stand a much greater chance because they can swim to climates to which they are already adapted. Land animals, however, have their mobility hampered by mountains, deserts, lakes, and oceans. With escape cut off they must adapt or extinction is inevitable. This explains why evolution appears to occur faster on land than within the oceans.

The most recent earth crust displacement left its evidence in a ring of death around the globe. All the continents along the line of greatest displacement experienced mass extinctions, while the continents closest to the line of least displacement experienced relatively few. The mass graves of so many giant creatures bear last witness to the great upheavals that periodically shatter our planet.

TEN

BROKEN PARADIGM

On July 4, 1996, geologist Dr. Tim Heaton was excavating in an abandoned bear cave at the northern tip of Prince of Wales Island in the Alaska panhandle. The site known as On Your Knees Cave had been discovered in 1993 by a logging survey team. Just a kilometer from Sumner Strait and 125 meters above sea level, the cave's small entrance concealed two tunnels, one of which held a small spring. It was the final day of the excavation, and Heaton was filling his last bag of sediment when he came across the lower jaw and pelvis of an ancient human.

The bones were that of a man about twenty years old who had died in that beautiful, isolated spot some ten thousand years before. The discovery of the oldest skeleton in Alaska and Canada generated much discussion within the archaeology "club" and the media. The assumption was that the existence of this ancient mariner provided positive proof in support of the Pacific Coast theory of the peopling of America. One of the stone tools found with the body was geologically unlike anything else from Prince of Wales Island, suggesting that this young man had not been a local.

A mystery emerged. Where did he come from?

In 2008, DNA evidence extracted from the remains revealed that he was genetically unique and in all probability had died a very long way from home. Less than 2 percent of First Nations peoples hold the unique DNA signature of these bones. Known as Haplogroup D4h3a, this group "is mostly found in South America with the exception of eight samples from Mexico and two found in California."[1]

Our ancient mariner may have traveled from as far a way as Tierra del Fuego. It is there that we find the Yaghan people, one of the few groups who have this unique genetic makeup.[2] Terra del Fuego is the closest large landmass to Antarctica. A large island* about the size of Massachusetts and New Jersey combined, it lies south of the South American landmass.

The Yaghan people have a rich and varied culture that may stretch back to 11,600 years ago, to the very century of the destruction of Atlantis. They commonly cremate the bodies of their dead so no ancient remains from Tierra del Fuego have yet been found. But physical evidence for human occupation of this land, so close to Lesser Antarctica, dates to 11,880 (plus or minus 250 years) at a site called Tres Arroyos.[3]

Today there is only one person, Cristina Calderón, still fluent in the Yaghan language, which is remarkably rich in vocabulary and has been classified as an "isolate," meaning that it appears to be unrelated to any other known language in the world. It contains more than thirty-two thousand *concepts,* and its unique grammar allows for the creation of several hundred thousand words.[4] When one considers that only 850 words are necessary to speak basic English,[5] the volume of Yaghan words is nothing short of amazing.

The Yaghan's rich mythology records "three world cataclysms: a glaciation, a world conflagration and a flood."[6] This association of a flood with glaciation is rare. In our research of world mythology we have only discovered one other instance: the ancient Vedic story of Airyana Vaêjo (see chapter 6), which was said to have been covered with a thick blanket of ice at the time of the Flood, when a "dire winter" destroyed the island paradise.

The Yaghan society was based in the closest place on Earth to the former site of Atlantis. However, is there a possible connection between the Yaghan people and the Atlanteans other than location? To find out, let's examine both culture's gender roles. One of the modern features of ancient Atlantis was the role that women played in the community. In

---

*48,100 square kilometers, or 18,572 square miles

The First Sex, Elizabeth Gould Davis notes that Plato related that the Atlanteans enjoyed equal rights. "In *Critias* he had spoken of the former primacy of the goddess and of the equality of men and women in ancient times. In the *Republic* he envisions a similar criterion for leadership where women will have all the advantages of education and all the opportunities for advancement available to men. 'Public offices are to be held by women as well as men,' as was the way of the ancients."[7]

As for the Yaghan, their women held powerful roles as shamans and dictated the final say over important matters because they were thought to rule the sea[8] Only women learned to swim. Men were forbidden to marry within the tribe and were expected to embark on sea quests to find wives. The young mariner found at On Your Knees Cave may have been on one of these long canoe searches for a wife when he died on Prince of Wales Island.

In 1931, after years of study, anthropologist E. M. Loeb concluded that there were rituals, ceremonies, and rites of passage that the Yaghan of Tierra del Fuego shared with some of the tribes of California.[9] Loeb could not have known, in 1931, that his theory of a connection between the two groups would be confirmed using genetic evidence. In California many of the First Nations people, including the Chumash tribe, practiced a Kukusu Cult ritual of dance and masks and appeals to the spirit world. In 2008, it was reported that the Chumash possess the same distinct Haplogroup D4h3a genetic marker as the Yaghan.[10]

Bears were important animals in the Kukusu Cult. Bear caves were considered ideal sites in which to follow spirit quests. Given what we know of the Yaghan's mastery of the sea, their long quests for mates, and their adventurous nature, it is not impossible that the young man with the D4h3a genetic marker found on Prince of Wales Island may have traveled from Tierra del Fuego. If so, then this discovery, along with a host of other excavations, has the potential to break open the prevailing paradigm of the peopling of America.

This entrenched paradigm dictates that North America was colonized *before* South America. On the contrary, human migration may well have moved in the opposite direction. Increasingly, evidence from South America points to this radical conclusion.

THE PEOPLING OF AMERICA

Our perceptions of how people originally came to America have been forged by European- and North American–centered prejudices and a long view of history that became more and more narrow until very recently.

The story begins in 1552, when Cortes's secretary and biographer, Francisco Lopez de Gomara, wrote *Historia general da las Indies,* in which he informed the world that the Aztec's original island homeland of Aztlan was one and the same as Atlantis. It was, he argued, a white island in the ocean and must have been the very same lost island continent that was the subject of Plato's writings. In 1572, the historian Pedro Sarmiento came to the same conclusion based on his understanding of South American mythology. Thanks to their writings, for nearly forty years (1552–1589) Atlantis was widely believed to be the original homeland of the native people of America.[11]

Joseph de Acosta, a Jesuit missionary who had lived in Peru, wrote *Historia natural moral de las Indies,* (1589) in which he pondered the question of the origins of the people and animals of America. His religion told him that Noah's ark was the only ship to have survived the Flood, but evidence pointed to the conclusion that some people and animals had escaped the Flood and reached America. Acosta's faith in the Bible was so complete that he determined that some descendants from Noah's ark must have reached America by way of a land bridge, either in the far south or north. His idea would come to bear fruit in the twentieth century, as we will shortly see.

In 1607, another writer, Gregorio Garcia, took a different approach. He assumed that shipbuilding was an ancient art that had survived Eden's destruction by the Great Flood. He wrote, "The art of navigation has been invented by Noah and was therefore as old as man."[12] If ancient man could indeed travel by sea, then perhaps the Aztec and

Incan civilizations were offshoots of other civilizations. Egypt became the "motherland" of choice because the Egyptians had boats, built pyramids, and worshipped the sun, as did the people of Mexico and Peru. Moreover, Egypt's founding god, Osiris, was said to have traveled far, taking civilization to the rest of the world.

The idea of Mexico and Peru owing their civilizations to the influence of the Old World appealed to Europeans. Perhaps it served to rationalize their brutal plundering of the New World: destroying them was not such a sin. What was given could be taken.

THE LAND BRIDGE

After a century of speculation about the "diffusion" of culture from the Old World to the New World, an event occurred that permanently changed the common notion of how the original people had arrived in America. In 1728, Vitus Bering, a Danish navigator serving the Russian czar, Peter the Great, reached the northeast limit of the Asian continent. His discovery of the Bering Strait between Siberia and Alaska would eventually revolutionize the debate about the origins of Native Americans. Now, one could easily imagine the people of Siberia crossing this narrow stretch of water and populating the New World. The Atlantic Ocean avenue to America was effectively ruled out.

After World War II, anthropologists and archaeologists confirmed the discovery of a former land bridge between Siberia and Alaska called Beringia. This land, now lost to the ocean, seemed to vindicate Acosta's original idea that people came to America by land. After World War II the idea of the land bridge route became the official explanation for the peopling of America and as with all things "official," it soon became sacrosanct. Any suggestion that people came from anywhere other than Siberia was ignored.

Initially, the land bridge theory did dovetail with the physical evidence unearthed that characterized the first Americans as big game hunters. These supposed "first" Americans used a "clovis" blade (named after an excavation site near Clovis, New Mexico). A paradigm, known as the clovis first theory,[13] soon gripped the archaeological establishment. It assumed that at approximately 9500 BCE the earliest native people of America arrived as big-game hunters from Asia. They traveled across the Beringia land bridge through an ice-free corridor that passed between the massive ice sheets that otherwise blocked their way (see figure 10.1).

Let's consider these ice sheets and the possible ice-free corridor. At the same time that arctic Siberia was full of life and largely free

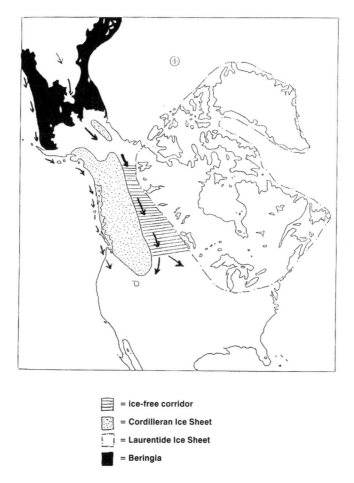

☰ = ice-free corridor

▨ = Cordilleran Ice Sheet

⌐¬ = Laurentide Ice Sheet

■ = Beringia

Figure 10.1. The long accepted theory of the peopling of America states that 11,600 years ago an ice-free corridor opened between the western and eastern ice sheets of North America allowing people from Siberia to make their way between the ice sheets to reach the central plains. A more recent theory suggests that people in boats may have followed the Pacific coast to arrive in America.

of ice, two vast ice sheets bore down on North America. At its height the Laurentide Ice Sheet, centered on Hudson Bay, was larger than Antarctica's current ice cap. It covered most of Canada as well as the states that border the Great Lakes. In the west, the Cordilleran Ice Sheet lay along the Rocky Mountains, covering southern Alaska, almost all of British Columbia, and a good share of Alberta, Washington State, Idaho, and Montana. The lower ocean level created the Beringia land bridge, which connected an ice-free Alaska with an ice-free Siberia.

At that time, an ice-free corridor between the ice sheets was believed by archaeologists to be the sole avenue of entrance to America by people coming from Siberia. While we do not subscribe to this theory, we note that the existence of the ice-free corridor has never been explained. Why should this region be ice-free? Archaeologists and geologists have no idea. Hapgood supplies a simple answer: The crust was in a different position when the corridor was formed. The sun would rise from the direction of the Gulf of Mexico and set toward the Yukon. This arc of sunshine cut a path through the ice and melted the snow that fell there. The appearance of the ice-free corridor is no longer so "odd" (see figures 10.2–10.5).

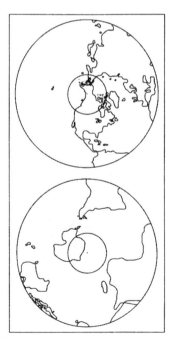

Figure 10.2. Before 91,600 BCE, the Arctic Circle was centered on the northwest corner of North America. In the Southern Hemisphere, that part of Greater Antarctica that lies toward Africa was under ice. Much of Lesser Antarctica was ice free. The Cordilleran Ice Sheet of northwest North America was created at this time.

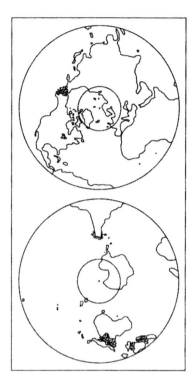

Figure 10.3. After the first displacement, in the years from 91,600 BCE to 50,600, the Arctic Circle contained much of Europe and all of Greenland. Passage from Asia to America was open. Northwestern Siberia, Beringia, and Alaska enjoyed a mild climate. In the Southern Hemisphere, the part of Greater Antarctica leaning toward New Zealand was under ice.

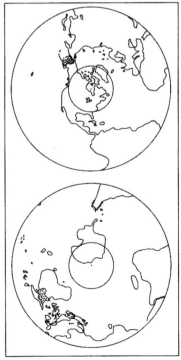

Figure 10.4. After the second displacement, between 50,600 and 9600 BCE, North America felt the grip of the Arctic Circle. Most of Greenland remained in the polar zone. The massive Laurentide Ice Sheet on North America was created at this time. Lesser Antarctica, the site of Atlantis, along with Siberia, Beringia, and Alaska, was ice-free except at high altitudes. During this time migration from Asia to the New World was open.

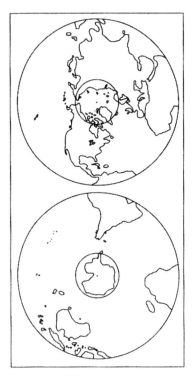

Figure 10.5. After the third earth crust displacement in 9600 BCE, North America was freed from the icy grip of the polar zone, which left the Great Lakes in its wake. Greenland was for the third straight time trapped inside the Arctic Circle (except for the southern tip), accounting for 90 percent of the ice in the Northern Hemisphere. Siberia, for the first time, was brought into the polar zone. All of Antarctica was encapsulated by the Antarctic Circle, causing a "dire winter" on the island continent, as recorded in the Vedic story of the lost island paradise of Airyana Vaêjo.

So after consideration of these earth crust displacements, was there an alternate ice-free corridor into America, rather than a corridor down the center of Canada? Consider this: In the March 1994 issue of *Popular Science,* Ray Nelson reported on an important archaeological find in New Mexico. Dr. Richard S. MacNeish, along with his team from the Andover Foundation for Archaeological Research, excavated a site at Pendejo Cave, in southwestern New Mexico. They found eleven human hairs in a cave about one hundred meters above the desert. Radiocarbon testing dated them at fifty-five thousand years ago.[14]

MacNeish's find is important because it confirms that migration to North America from Siberia was possible between 91,600 BCE and 50,600 BCE (see figure 10.3) and again after the next earth crust displacement at 50,600 BCE (see figure 10.4). This displacement dragged eastern North America into the polar zone but left islands off the Pacific coast free of ice. The Arctic Circle then lay over Hudson Bay. Greenland remained in the polar zone. Theoretically, from 91,600 BCE to 9600 BCE, people travelling in boats could have moved from Siberia to America along the Pacific Coast where they could navigate between the ice-free islands (see figure 10.6).

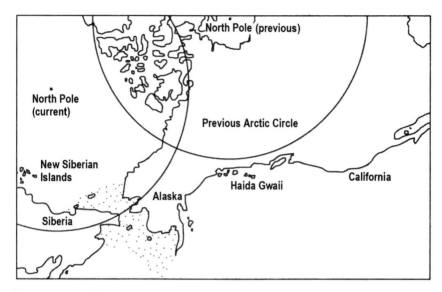

Figure 10.6. Directions change with each earth crust displacement. Before the last catastrophe, the Pacific side of North America was actually the south, while the Arctic Circle was centered on Hudson Bay. Seen from this perspective, the migration of people from Siberia, across Beringia, and along the Pacific coast would be a movement from west to east. Seen from Haida Gwaii, the sun would appear to rise from the direction of California and set in the direction of Alaska.

This Pacific waterway to America was open and inviting and has, since the publication of the first edition of this book in 1995, become the prevailing theory of how people arrived in America. But these archaeological theories have a serious blind spot. None of them take any account of what the people themselves say.

If we listen with respect to the tales that the people of the First Nations of America tell then we find no stories of ice walls or traveling through ice. Instead, we discover an entirely different scenario from that favored by archaeologists. It is a scenario of violent upheaval from a homeland that was destroyed (see chapter 5). There are stories of arrival in ships and others that tell of ancient ancestors who were already in

America and were forced to climb mountains to save themselves from the rising ocean.

In the past decade the clovis first theory of the peopling of America has fallen apart as each of its assumptions was challenged by physical evidence. This evidence has come primarily from South America, which has more "pre-Clovis" sites than North America.[15] The contradictions between the physical evidence in South America and the theories from North America have only recently come to light because a whole new generation of Latin American archaeologists has entered the field.

It was Plato who first commented on the conditions that permit the exploration of the past. "The enquiry into antiquity are first introduced into cities when they begin to have leisure, and when they see that the necessaries of life have already been provided, but not before."[16]

The prosperity of North America gave its theorists an advantage in archaeology for it allowed universities in the United States and Canada to turn out waves of archaeologists whose focus was North America. The far fewer numbers of Latin American archaeologists were at a disadvantage. Theories were developed primarily in the United States and were applied to Central and South America even before excavations had been carried out. Argentine archaeologist Vivian Scheinshon complained in 2003, "South American hunter-gatherer archaeology has been strongly influence by North American archaeology. Automatic application of North American models in South America and a tendency to overemphasize similitude on both continents were the consequences."[17]

The most notable site, only accepted after some nasty squabbling by the defenders of the clovis first theory, is in Chile and has been clearly dated to at least 14,500 years ago.[18] The Monte Verde site broke through the wall established by Clovis and opened up the possibility that people had been in America long before 9500 BCE.

The clovis first theory has been falsified, and we who have long believed that the First Nations of America origins date to much farther back than 9600 BCE have been vindicated. But the prevailing paradigm that assumes that all the first people of America came from Asia has yet to be challenged.

Physical evidence increasingly points to South America as the first entry point to America. Could these people have come from Antarctica? The idea is as unacceptable today as pre-Clovis entry-point sites were just a few years ago. But if we listen to the mythology of the people of Lake Titicaca, we learn that their ancestors came from the south at the time of a Great Flood (see chapter 6). If we take seriously the mythology of the Okanagan people, who say their ancestors came from a vast island in the middle of the ocean (see chapter 3), then we might just begin to look at the ancient age of South America in a new light.

ELEVEN

FINDING ATLANTIS

There has been a cycle in the quest for knowledge. We began in humility, appealing to the gods to protect us from the unknown. Later, we imagined a world perfectly ordered by God's divine will. But it was faith in reason that transformed us from believers in supernatural intervention into followers of the creed of progress. And now we have come full circle, once again humbled by the immensity of the universe. We no longer cast spells to protect us against the unknown. We cast spacecraft into the void.

The story of our search for order and pattern has been lost in the mute, unwritten past. For before science, there was magic. Magic was a tool of the hunter when he drew stark images of animals over fire-lit walls. Through magic the shaman hoped to secure the future, but a future that never dared to challenge the elder's myths. It was taboo to doubt the gods. This inhibition was the fatal flaw in the design woven by these early magicians. All was explained, but little was truly understood. The power of magic was destined to flounder, for without the freedom to cast doubt on an idea, there can be no genuine inquiry. And without inquiry, magic could not evolve into science.

The hunger to command and the need to pilot our own fate have been among humankind's most persistent traits. Science has shone a great light along the shadowy road, but it has been a bumpy ride. Unlike shamans or the priests, scientists must by the very nature of their calling be willing to tamper with taboos. From this struggle there emerged a new way of seeing the world and a new way of learning and knowing.

For millennia, our worldview was clouded by the mist of magic and myth. But then, quite suddenly, six centuries before the birth of Christ, came a clearing. On the eastern shore of the Mediterranean Sea, the Ionian Greeks burst forth with a fresh and energetic way of seeing the world. They heralded the death of magic and the birth of science.

The first "immortal" to be struck down by the new sword of science was the Olympian god of the sea, Poseidon. As master of the ocean he commanded the respect, awe, and honor of all seafaring Greeks. Poseidon was a violent god who carried within his arsenal the dreaded weapon of the earthquake. Since the land of the Greeks had often fallen victim to earthquakes, Poseidon was not only worshipped but also feared. It is not surprising then, given this fear, that the Greeks were disturbed when one of the seven wise men, Thales (ca. 636–546 BCE), dared to suggest that the fearful rumbling of the earth was not controlled by the powerful Poseidon.

Thales may have acquired his materialistic explanation of the cause of earthquakes while visiting Egypt. We are told, "He went to Egypt and spent some time with the priests there."[1] Thales set no bounds on his curiosity and delved into the enigmas of the soul as well as solutions to the mysteries of the universe. These lines attributed to him touch the depth of his intellect: "Of all things that are, the most ancient is God, for he is uncreated. The most beautiful is the universe, for it is God's workmanship. The greatest is space, for it holds all things. The swiftest is mind, for it speeds everywhere. The strongest, necessity for it masters all. The wisest, time, for it brings everything to light."[2]

But above all Thales dared to doubt. He argued that the island-earth was like a great ship at sea that, as it rocked on the waters, experienced earthquakes. Thales had proclaimed the unthinkable. He had usurped the role of a god by providing a physical explanation for a natural phenomenon. Thales thus became the world's first acknowledged scientist.*

---

*A case can be made for giving this title to Sonchis, whose materialistic explanation for the destruction of Atlantis invoked physical events rather than supernatural forces as the cause of the Great Flood (see chapter 4).

He began the long, relentless battle that, even in our time, is waged between faith and reason, myth and science.

It is accepted opinion today that mythology and science are like oil and water: they don't mix. But like Thales we should always be willing to cast doubt on accepted opinion. If we use science as our torch, a pathway can be made through the darkness of mythology: myth and science need not always collide.

Thales found order within the universe: he showed that gods and goddesses were no longer needed to unravel the powers of nature. Human beings could do it alone. However, it would take centuries before this radical notion was to find its proper place in history. Until then another explanation for the mystery of the actions of the gods was needed.

In the fourth century BCE, a Sicilian by the name of Euhemerus wrote *Sacred History,* in which he argued that the exploits of the gods and goddesses of ancient times were simply exaggerated tales of the real deeds of former kings and queens. Thus was born the first school of mythology. The idea was simple but provocative. Myths were signposts to the past. They might be used to recapture the lost lines of history. They were disguised truths that might lead us to hidden treasures, lost cities, perhaps even lost continents. But this "lost history" school of mythology never became widely accepted. The people of Rome preferred to believe in the reality of their gods and goddesses. Later, Christians would seek paradise in the afterlife, not on earth.

The first great mythologist of the modern age was the son of an Italian bookseller. Giambattista Vico (1668–1744) was a self-educated scholar who saw myths as valuable keys to understanding human culture and the workings of the mind. Vico believed that societies move through various stages of development and that each stage produced a corresponding level of mythology. He wrote, "The fables originating among the first savage and crude men were very severe, as befitted the founding nations emerging from a state of fierce bestial freedom."[3]

In this anthropological approach myths are vital keys to under-standing culture. Each culture is seen as a unique and self-contained unit. Vico recognized the limitations of his interpretation and aug-mented it by comparing myths from around the world. "Uniform ideas originating among entire peoples unknown to each other must have a common ground of truth."[4]

Also, Vico offered the prospect of finding common ground in the nature of the human mind. "There must in the nature of human things be a mental language common to all nations, which uniformly grasps the substance of things."[5]

This psychological school of mythology found forceful proponents in the English anthropologist Sir Edward Burnett Tylor (1832–1917) and the psychiatrists Sigmund Freud (1856–1939) and Carl Jung (1875–1961). More recently the French anthropologist Claude Levi-Strauss (born 1908) and the American mythologist Joseph Campbell (1904–1987) have enriched this approach to myths.

For Tylor the fascination lay within the commonality of myths from around the world. "The treatment of similar myths from differ-ent regions, by arranging them in large compared groups, makes it pos-sible to trace in mythology the operation of the imaginative processes recurring with the evident regularity of mental law; and thus stories of which a single instance would have been a mere isolated curiosity, take their place among well-marked and consistent structures of the human mind."[6]

Freud believed that the mind filters memories to suit its present state and distrusted myths as an inaccurate representation of real events.

One is thus forced by various considerations to suspect that in the so-called earliest childhood memories we possess not the genuine memory-tree but a later revision of it, a revision which may have been subjected to the influences of a variety of later psychical forces. Thus the "childhood memories" of individuals come in general to acquire the significance of "screen memories" and in doing so offer a remarkable analogy with the childhood memories that a nation preserves in its store of legends and myths.[7]

Jung took the idea of myths as doorways to the mind even further than Freud. Like Vico, Jung was fascinated by the appearance of similar myths around the globe. "Although traditional transmission by migration certainly plays a part there are, as we have said, very many cases that cannot be accounted for in this way and drive us to assume the existence of a collective psychic substratum. I have called this the *collective unconscious.*"[8]

Like Freud and Jung, Levi-Strauss seeks clues in myths to the workings of the mind. "The purpose of myth is to provide a logical model capable of overcoming a contradiction."[9]

Campbell summarized the contribution of this school of mythology. "The bold and truly epoch-making writings of the psychoanalysts are indispensable to the student of mythology; for, whatever may be thought of the detailed and sometimes contradictory interpretations of specific cases and problems, Freud, Jung, and their followers have demonstrated irrefutably that the logic, the heroes, and the deeds of myth survive into modern times. In the absence of an effective general mythology, each of us has his private, unrecognized, rudimentary, yet secretly potent pantheon of dream."[10]

For Campbell the myths provide pathways to ethical wisdom and offer beacons of spiritual guidance. In his view, to look at them as potential lost history is missing the spiritual dimension altogether.

From Vico to Campbell, mythologists have sought the key to the puzzle of the nature of imagination and thought. In this book we have examined many myths that speak of the lost island paradise and have explored the significance of what we call the "sun-deluge motif". These are stories which blame the great flood on a dramatic change in the sun's path. But we do not offer the myths as concrete evidence. However, we do believe that these ancient renditions represent something more than just evidence of the similarity of humanity's mental makeup. We propose that certain myths do indeed represent lost history, but this conjecture is based on the capacity of the earth crust displacement theory to provide order to recognized, long-standing problems in science.

The noted sociologist of science Thomas S. Kuhn lists five key characteristics of a good scientific theory. "Accuracy, consistency, scope, simplicity and fruitfulness—are all standard criteria for evaluating the adequacy of a theory."[11]

The simplicity of the theory of earth crust displacement drew Albert Einstein to Hapgood's idea. Hapgood replaces the presupposition of a relatively stable crust with the notion that the crust shifts. Using this simple assumption, the theory is capable of accurately and consistently addressing a wide scope of established problems. It provides a framework with which to comprehend the mysterious myths of the lost island paradise and the worldwide appearance of the sun-deluge motif. And it offers an explanation of why some ancient maps are so strangely accurate—maps that appear to have originated from an unknown civilization.

The theory also points to Lesser Antarctica as the site of Atlantis. But what have others believed about the lost continent?

ATLANTIS THEORIES

After Plato's death his student Aristotle (384 BCE–322 BCE) became the foremost philosopher in Athens. Aristotle was said to be highly skeptical about Homer's famous legend of Troy, declaring, "He who brought it into existence can also cause it to disappear."[12]

These words were applied by Aristotle's followers to discredit Plato's account of Atlantis, giving rise to the idea that Atlantis was entirely the product of Plato's lively imagination.* A more sophisticated branch of this "imaginary" school was founded by the second-century Greek

---

*Aristotle wrote nothing about Atlantis.

philosopher Numenius. He argued that Plato wrote the story as an allegory. This approach still has supporters today.

But as we have shown, the compelling idea of Atlantis is found woven again and again into the myths of peoples with whom Plato could not possibly have had any contact. The Haida and Okanagan myths of a lost land and the Cherokee story of a floating island in the Southern Hemisphere are not ideas that Plato could have borrowed. Nor is it possible, if Plato's story were simply an allegory, that he could give an accurate geographic account of the world as seen from Antarctica.

Crantor (ca. 300 BCE) was one of the first to write extensively about Plato's dialogue *Timaeus,* which contained the legend of Atlantis. He was convinced of the truth of the account and went so far as to send envoys to Egypt to verify the story. When the messengers returned, they confirmed that the legend had been found "written on pillars which are still preserved."[13]

Crantor believed that Atlantis was a real place that had existed in the North Atlantic Ocean. As time went by, this became the most popular location for the lost continent—an idea, as we have seen, based on a misunderstanding of the term *Atlantic Ocean.* The age of discovery opened up land to the west and the intriguing possibility that the vanished continent would surely be found in Central America, North America, or Brazil. Or as new territory was explored, South Africa, Ceylon, Greenland, and so on.

Eventually, however, the North Atlantic Ocean reemerged as the favorite site. Athanasius Kircher, the Jesuit who discovered the Egyptian map of Atlantis, was also convinced that it lay beneath the North Atlantic Ocean. His influence was great because he was widely believed to be the most learned man in the world. After his death in 1680, the dialogue was reduced to a debate between those who thought, like Kircher, that Atlantis had sunk beneath the ocean and was lost forever and those who held out hope that some yet undiscovered land would prove to be the lost paradise (see figure 11.1).

All this changed in 1882 with Ignatius Donnelly's book *Atlantis:*

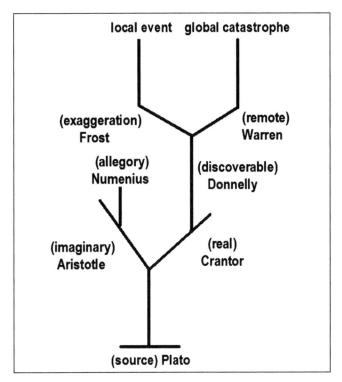

local event   global catastrophe

(exaggeration)   (remote)
Frost   Warren

(allegory)   (discoverable)
Numenius   Donnelly

(imaginary)   (real)
Aristotle   Crantor

(source) Plato

Figure 11.1. The legend of Atlantis was first recorded by Plato, and it was his student, Aristotle, who may have been the first skeptic by suggesting that Atlantis was imaginary. Numenius was the first to suggest Atlantis was meant as an allegory. Crantor was the first to insist that Atlantis was real, while the American writer Ignatius Donnelly proposed that it was not only real but also still discoverable. The founder of Boston University, William Fairfield Warren, created the school of thought we support by suggesting that Atlantis had been lost in a global geological event and could still be found in a remote area of the globe. The modern approach was formulated by K. T. Frost, who suggested that the account was an exaggeration of a local event. Drawing by Rand Flem-Ath and Rose Flem-Ath.

The Antediluvian World. Donnelly (1831–1901) is one of the most colorful figures in the story of the search for Atlantis. Born in Philadelphia, he studied law before moving to Minnesota, where he was elected lieutenant governor at the age of twenty-eight. He was then elected to the U.S. Congress and spent most of his time absorbed by the rich resources of the Library of Congress. Like Kircher, Donnelly believed that Atlantis lay beneath the North Atlantic Ocean, and he was excited by the idea that a marvelous new invention, the submarine, would transform the search into a reality.

Donnelly's popular book boldly asserted that the description of Atlantis offered by Plato was not, as had long been supposed, a fable, but was based on actual history. He believed that Atlantis "became, in the course of ages, a populous and mighty nation, from whose overflowings the shores of the Gulf of Mexico, the Mississippi River, the Amazon, the Pacific coast of South America, the Mediterranean, the west coast of Europe and Africa, the Baltic, the Black Sea, and the Caspian were populated by civilized nations."[14]

The idea of Atlantean colonies was a popular one in a newly independent America. However, even if it were true, the remains of such colonies would have perished long ago. We have recovered barely enough artifacts from the oldest known civilization, Sumer, to piece together its history. Most have disintegrated into the dust of time. Any Atlantean colonies would be at least twice as old as Sumer and highly unlikely to survive nearly twelve thousand years of weathering.

Donnelly also surmised "that the oldest colony formed by the Atlanteans was probably in Egypt, whose civilization was a reproduction of that of the Atlantic island."[15] The newly discovered ancient age of the Great Sphinx as documented by John Anthony West gives support to this claim.[16]

Donnelly's book sent America spinning into an Atlantean fever. In 1883, New Orleans devoted its Mardi Gras to the Atlantis theme.[17] Donnelly was elected to the American Association for the Advancement of Science. By 1890, the book had gone to press for twenty-three editions. It is still in print today.

Three years after the publication of Donnelly's work, the founder and president of Boston University, William Fairfield Warren (1833–1929) published *Paradise Found: The Cradle of the Human Race at the North Pole*. This book used comparative mythology and the latest theories of geology to tackle the question of the lost paradise, of which Atlantis is but one story. His geological idea did not survive, and consequently his whole investigation has been ignored, despite the fact that it was much more comprehensive than Donnelly's. Because he believed that "paradise" was once at the North Pole, Warren didn't restrict his investigation to lands on either side of the North Atlantic Ocean. He examined myths from around the globe, finding a great deal of mythology that associated the lost paradise with the pole. He launched the research tradition that treated the lost land as a real place located in a remote region of the world that had been destroyed by a global catastrophe.

Unlike this "remote" school of thought, which derives its momentum from a geological theory of catastrophe colored by comparative mythology, the most recent investigations of Atlantis take an entirely different line. The "regional" school of thought finds its strength in archaeological evidence of a vanquished civilization and geological support for a local catastrophe that destroyed it.

Although unaware of it, Charles Lyell, the great uniformitarian geologist, was the first scientist to lay down the arguments that would eventually form one of the backbones of the regional approach to the problem of Atlantis. In his *Principles of Geology* Lyell was concerned with the worldwide stories of a Great Flood. His uniformitarian beliefs led him to belittle them. "The true source of the system must be sought for in the exaggerated traditions of those partial, but often dreadful catastrophes, which are sometimes occasioned by various combinations of natural causes."[18] This idea of exaggeration would come to play a central role in the "modern" thought about Atlantis.

The concept of a small, localized Atlantis was launched after Sir Arthur Evans (1851–1941) excavated the remains of the Minoan civilization on Crete. Nine years later, on February 19, 1909, an article appeared in the London *Times* under the title "The Lost Continent." It was written by K. T. Frost, a young man who was on the staff of Queen's University in Belfast. He argued that Evans's discovery meant that Crete might have been Atlantis. Frost was killed in action in World War I. His idea was taken up again on the threshold of World War II.

In 1939, Professor Spyridon Marinatos, director of the Greek Archaeological Service, presented the theory that a volcanic explosion had occurred on the island of Thera, just north of Crete. In the 1950s and 1960s, Professor Angles Galanopoulos dated the debris from the Thera eruption to 1500 BCE, a time corresponding with the fall of the Minoan civilization. Was Thera Atlantis?

The classical account of the theory of Thera/Crete as Atlantis was written in 1969 by I. V. Luce, a classics and philosophy lecturer at Trinity College in Dublin. In *The End of Atlantis: New Light on an Old Legend*,[19] Luce treats Plato's account as an exaggeration of the actual fall of Crete, which, in turn, was triggered by the volcanic explosion on Thera.

Luce's theory fails on several counts. Plato's Egyptian priest described Atlantis as being larger than Libya (North Africa) and Asia (the Middle East) combined. It is an island continent. Such an immense landmass could never be found within the confines of the Mediterranean Sea. Moreover, Plato's account directs our attention to Atlantis as located *beyond* the Pillars of Heracles (Strait of Gibraltar) and in the "real ocean," of which the Mediterranean Sea is but a small harbor. The Crete theory ignores the sun-deluge motif and distorts the timing of events by a factor of ten.

The idea of misrepresenting the age of Atlantis by a factor of ten makes sense to modern eyes because we use Arabic numbers, in which, for instance, the numerals 10 and 100 seem visually similar. However, the ancient Egyptians at the time of Plato (and of Solon and Pythagoras) did not use an Arabic system. The difference between the written forms of 1,000 and 10,000 in Egyptian hieroglyphics is extreme, and they could not possibly be mistaken.

Finally, Luce's theory ignores the description of Atlantis's great mountains and high altitude. While it may be true that a volcanic explosion on Thera destroyed Crete, there is no justification in tying it to the legend of Atlantis.

In 1979, Harald A. T. Reiche, a professor of classics and philosophy at Massachusetts Institute of Technology, published "The Language of Archaic Astronomy: A Clue to the Atlantis Myth?" in which he argues that the layout of the city of Atlantis mirrors "features of the southern circumpolar sky." In other words, the various rings of the city of Atlantis equate to the layout of the stars in the *Southern* Hemisphere. Reiche sees in Plato's account "an embellished version of what in original intention was a map of the sky."[20]

Reiche died in 1994 at age seventy-two, but in 2006 an expanded version of his article, previously unpublished, was released by the Epigraphic Society.[21] In the expanded paper, he emphasized the immense water management system that the Atlanteans constructed. Their canals extended from the mountains and covered an area measuring 2,000 by 3,000 stades (1 stade = 606.75 feet). That's an area equal to the size of the state of Nebraska. The layout of the city of Atlantis, according to Reiche, mirrored "the southern sky from the south pole to about the latitude of 50° and is to be equated with the central island of the Atlantis myth."[22]

In 1996, after the first edition of this book had been in print for a year, we received a letter directing our attention to *The First Sex,* written in 1971 by a librarian in Florida, Elizabeth Gould Davis (1910–1974). Davis was inspired by the British writer Harold John Massingham (1888–1952), who had argued that civilization "was consciously planted by 'ancient mariners.'"[23] In her book, which was the first to suggest Atlantis was in Antarctica, Davis wrote:

> Writing in the early years of this century, Massingham was daring enough in his attribution of world travel to a people of the third millennium BCE, but now we know that the "ancient mariners" belonged to an even more remote period in history than Massingham assumed. For, incredible as it may seem, these ancient mariners drew an accurate map of a continent, Antarctica, that disappeared under three miles of solid ice at least 6,000 years ago.
>
> Modern scientific instruments have affirmed that the continent

of Antarctica became glacierized no later than 4000 BC and that it has lain under an impenetrable mountain of ice ever since. This fact, plus the probability that Antarctica lay in temperate latitudes prior to 4000 BCE combined with the further fact that tremendous coal deposits have been detected indicating forest growth, leads to the incredible thought that Antarctica must have been mapped by an *Antarctican—prior* to its glacierization [*sic*] 6,000 years ago. Was this Antarctic cartographer an Atlantean? And was the vast continent of Antarctica once the vast continent of Atlantis?[24]

To support her idea of Antarctica as Atlantis, Davis cites Hapgood's *Maps of the Ancient Sea Kings* and in particular the maps of Antarctica that Hapgood studied. There exists a prevalent misconception that Hapgood believed Antarctica had been Atlantis. The fact is that he thought Atlantis lay in the mid-Atlantic and the remnants of the lost land would be discovered under the islands of St. Peter and St. Paul.

Again and again people return to Plato's famous account to squeeze yet another clue from it. Why have these attempts always failed?

As we have seen, the original meanings of the Greek terms *Atlantic Ocean* and *Pillars of Heracles* have been consistently misunderstood. These mistakes restricted the search to either the North Atlantic Ocean or the Mediterranean Sea. But Atlantis was in the real ocean, the world ocean of oceanographers. And it wasn't until the earth's violent history was known that we could look beyond the Northern Hemisphere for the lost land.

The theory of earth crust displacement provides a mechanism for the destruction of Atlantis, and Plato's account points to Antarctica as the former site of the lost land. But Atlantis was also a city as well as a continent. Where on Antarctica might the remains of this ever fascinating city be found?

TWELVE

CITY OF ATLANTIS

We now ask the gentle reader's indulgence in a writers' flight of fancy as we introduce you to a sailor of the Atlantean fleet. Courtesy of Plato's description[1] as entrusted to Solon by the Egyptian priest Sonchis, we will follow a young man's journey into the deepest recesses of the most compelling city of them all—Atlantis.

The Sailor

The chill of the ocean wind stiffened his bones. His lips were cracked and sore from long months of exposure to bitter sea salt. But there was a gleam in his pale eyes as the sailor squinted across the ship's deck. There she was, only a few hours' travel away, shining against the horizon, a vision he had only dimly seen in his dreams for all the months he'd toiled and done his duty at sea. Atlantis. The shining city. Capital of an empire. Home.

The mountains of the continent rose in defiance of the waves, reassuring him with their eternal lines that dominated the sky, the sea, and the land itself. The austere welcome of the rigorous peaks was softened by their beauty, reaching so high they seemed to invite a duel with the sun.

The last hours seemed interminable, but as the fleet drifted toward port the clamor from the harbor and the surrounding merchants' quarter was carried to the crew by the wind. The ceaseless din, the calls and demands of anxious traders, the cries of animals, and the clanging of wares were a sweet tune to the sailors of the colossal Atlantean fleet. From their pivotal location in the belly of the ocean, the Atlanteans had access to every corner of the world. But to the weary sailor, no land, however exotic or fascinating, could compare with Atlantis.

The buildings clustered atop the forbidding outer wall were infused with the brilliance of the approaching sunset as the ship's crew began their familiar preparations to enter the first of the great canals that would guide them through a ten-kilometer route to the city center. Pungent odors from bustling stalls gradually replaced the bracing sea air. The increasing din of the marketplace signaled a return to civilization as the monotony of the sea gave way to the frantic activity of the merchants' section stretched along the great wall.

The clamor and excitement were to be expected at the port of a capital as renowned as Atlantis. Here the distribution of the goods to sustain a vast empire kept this vital section of the city a scene of constant activity. Providing the lifeblood of the empire, the prospering merchants' quarter enveloped three-fourths of the outer city. Trade and barter hummed constantly as foreign fleets crowded the massive docks dominating the port.

These docks were an integral part of a fortress equal to any ever conceived. Built in defense of the Atlanteans' precious material and spiritual treasures, they were carved from the white, black, and red rock of the land itself. A masterpiece of ingenuity, their pattern was continued in the substance of the towers and gates guarding the entrance. The business conducted in this extensive, noisy section of the city was responsible in no small part for the prosperity and leisure enjoyed by all Atlanteans.

Noise from the market receded as the fleet entered the confines of the canal. Incoming ships were dwarfed by the cliffs that towered on either side of the canal, an intimidating welcome indeed to any foreigner. The ship and her anxious crew were now on their way to their final destination, the inner sanctum of the great capital itself. But in order to reach their haven, ships must travel a slow route through a farther complex series of canals [see figure 12.1].

The young sailor's impatience to reach the city's legendary center was tempered by the comfort of being once again within the embrace of his home. His ancestors had constructed a capital befitting their

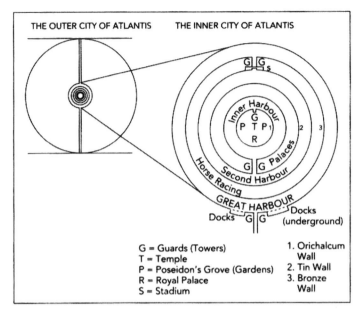

THE OUTER CITY OF ATLANTIS   THE INNER CITY OF ATLANTIS

Inner Harbour

Horse Racing

Second Harbour

Palaces

GREAT HARBOUR

Docks   G   G   Docks (underground)

G = Guards (Towers)
T = Temple
P = Poseidon's Grove (Gardens)
R = Royal Palace
S = Stadium

1. Orichalcum Wall
2. Tin Wall
3. Bronze Wall

Figure 12.1. The city of Atlantis consisted of rings of land that were, in turn, ringed by water. The inner city housed royalty and included gardens, racing tracks, palaces, and a temple. The outer city was populated by merchants and traders.

reputation. The city of Atlantis was an incredible example of city planning on a scale that the twentieth century has yet to match. They were experts at manipulating the most abundant and obvious of power sources— water—to serve their most important needs. All the city's commercial and transportation needs were met by an intricate system of canals that reached beyond the city into the great plain and farther up to the source of the bountiful waters, the mountains. Ironically, the forces of water were to write their epitaph.

THE MARVELOUS CITY

But that epitaph was still in the unknown future at the time that this unnamed sailor came home. And the city he returned to had no rival in the ancient world. Neither Rome nor Alexandria nor Constantinople, the capital of the Byzantine Empire, could outshine Atlantis for sheer

size and beauty. In diameter alone, the city covered twenty-three kilometers. A massive carved wall crowned with dwellings traced a seventy-
two-kilometer girth around the city. Most of London's famous sites
would fit comfortably within the dimensions of the inner section of the
city of Atlantis (see figure 12.2). And unlike the haphazard core of the
United Kingdom's capital, Atlantis was a masterpiece of planning.

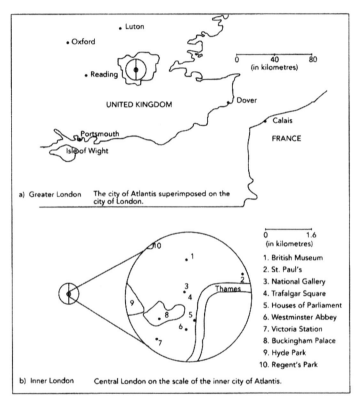

Figure 12.2. The capital city of Atlantis was as large as modern-
day greater London.

The towers and gates of outer Atlantis would have seemed fairly
easy obstacles compared with what lay before any invader intent on
unveiling the mysteries of the inner city. Whether enemy or friend, no
one could fail to be impressed as he or she sailed across the stretch of
water half a kilometer wide that separated the inner city from the mer-

chants' quarter. This expanse led to a shining wall of brass that concealed the only entrance to the inner city.

Once granted admittance, the full spectrum of the great civilization could be glimpsed. The first ring of land contained a racing stadium, gymnastic areas, and gardens blooming with exotic flowers, plants, and trees from around the world. Beyond this leisure area the pattern of water and land was repeated. The next belt of land was elevated and surrounded by a wall of tin. It protected the palaces, gardens, and fountains of the lesser noblemen of Atlantis.

And then, as if the Atlanteans had deliberately tempted any unwary traveler with the promise of ever more wonderful sights, the last belt of water, girdled by still higher land, came into view. This area was also surrounded by a wall, this time covered in orichalcum, a metal unique to Atlantis that was said to sparkle like fire. It was from this central island, the pinnacle of the pyramid city of shining walls, that the Atlantean Empire was ruled.

On the central island the Grove of Poseidon surrounded the temple. Hot and cold water flowed through the gardens, providing cooling pools in the summer and warm baths in the winter. The temple and palace were protected by a gold-encrusted wall, and the temple itself was coated with silver. Its interior was graced by statues, including a gigantic depiction of the god of the sea, standing on a chariot, its reins connected to six winged steeds. One hundred sea nymphs astride dolphins accompanied the sea god across the ocean.

At the altar of the temple of the sea god were enshrined the laws governing the ten princes of the ten provinces of Atlantis. They were engraved on a pillar of orichalcum, and the king and princes gathered "alternatively every fifth and sixth year (thereby showing equal respect to both odd and even numbers), consulted on matters of mutual interest and inquired into and gave judgement on any wrong committed by any of them."[2]

These intense deliberations were followed by elaborate rituals meant to reinforce the rulers' mutual commitment to the laws of Atlantis. "When darkness fell and the sacrificial fire had died down they all put on the most splendid dark blue ceremonial robes and sat on the ground by the embers of the sacrificial fire, in the dark, all glimmer of fire in the sanctuary being extinguished. And thus they gave and submitted to judgement on any complaints of wrong made against them; and afterwards, when it was light, wrote the terms of the judgement on gold plates which they dedicated together with their robes as records."[3]

The Atlanteans lived in peace and prosperity, enjoying and exploiting their empire, and "their wealth was greater than that possessed by any previous dynasty of kings or likely to be accumulated by any later."[4]

In his dialogue *Critias,* Plato repeats the words of the Egyptian priest who spoke to Solon about the lost city of Atlantis. The priest offered five physical clues to the location of the city:

1. On a large plain
2. Near the ocean
3. Midway along the continent's greatest length
4. Toward the islands
5. Surrounded by mountains.

Using these five clues and the climatic facts deduced from the theory of earth crust displacement, we can narrow the search for the city. The maps in figure 12.3 depict the area of Antarctica that lay outside the Antarctic Circle when Atlantis thrived. More than half of the island continent was under ice at that time. The city would not be found here. Thus the search can be restricted to Lesser Antarctica.

Plato tells us that the city was near the ocean, along the continent's greatest length, and opposite the islands of Atlantis. It was completely surrounded by mountains and sat on a large plain on a small hill. The Antarctic mountain range runs along the coast on the same side as the small islands. Therefore, in figure 12.3, the plain on which the great city probably stood is shown in black.*

---

*It is within this area that, using the "Atlantis Blueprint," we located the possible circular remains of the city under the ice.[5]

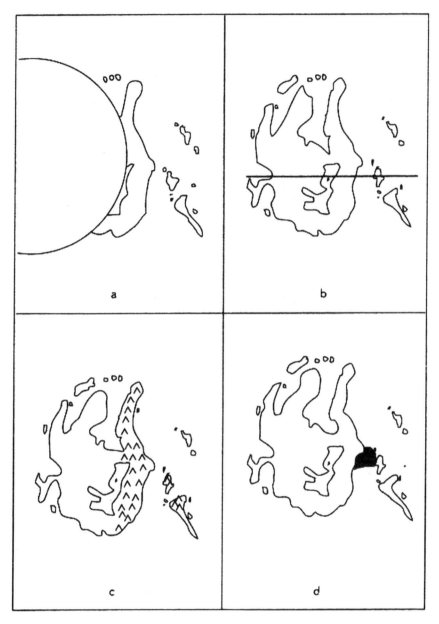

Figure 12.3. The plain on which the capital city of Atlantis stood will be found in a relatively small area of Antarctica once we view the continent without its ice. Charles Hapgood's theory of earth crust displacement points to Lesser Antarctica because there was ice on Greater Antarctica during the reign of Atlantis (a). The Egyptian priest tells us that the city of Atlantis was at the midpoint of the main island toward other islands (b). The city was surrounded by mountains (c). The black area is the probable location of the city of Atlantis (d).[6]

Such were the physical attributes of Atlantis according to the learned Egyptian priest. But its culture and civilization remain an intriguing mystery. Though a few tantalizing details are revealed by Plato, it remains the task of modern archaeology to excavate life from the cold grave of the lost city. It is to the icy, dark waters of Antarctica that we look to find answers about the very roots of civilization itself, answers that may yet be preserved in the frozen depths of the forgotten island continent of Antarctica.

THIRTEEN

WHY THE SKY FELL

What was the force that propelled the earth's crust to displace? How often has it happened? How long did it take to happen? Will it happen again, and if so when? Did the axis change? Why did the sky fall? These are the questions that haunted both Charles Hapgood and Albert Einstein* from November 1952, when they began their correspondence, until April 1955, when Einstein died.

Earth crust displacement is not the first geological theory formulated without addressing the mechanism that initiated it. As noted in chapter 9, when Louis Agassiz introduced the notion of ice ages, he was met with extreme skepticism. Agassiz's ice ages were catastrophic events that struck the planet out of the blue. Like his mentor, Georges Cuvier, Agassiz formulated his theory in an attempt to explain the sudden demise of animals in Siberia.[2] But Agassiz had no explanation for what caused the ice ages.

The geological establishment, lead by Charles Lyell, saw the importance of Agassiz's theory. It offered an explanation for several longstanding problems such as the existence of large boulders in seemingly odd locations. But Lyell would have nothing to do with the notion of a cataclysm and so toned down Agassiz's theory. As the result of Lyell's

*For Hapgood the quest began in 1949 and only ended with his death in 1982. Einstein grappled with the problem from November 1952 until his death in April 1955. The Hapgood-Einstein correspondence is discussed in chapter 1 of *The Atlantis Blueprint*.[1]

influence in geology the term *ice age* and the related term *glacial* have became synonymous with "ponderously slow change." Agassiz's theory has been successfully tamed to fit the fixation that all geological change is gradual.

Even without a mechanism to explain it, the ice age theory took its place as one of the underlying assumptions of modern geology. The quest for a mechanism to explain the cause or causes for ice ages has been going on for more than a century and a half—without success. Eventually nongeologists got into the quest for a mechanism that could explain the ice ages.

ICE AGES—THE SEARCH FOR A CAUSE

In 1842, the first astronomical clue was discovered by a mathematician working as a tutor in Paris. Joseph Alphonse Adhemar (1797–1862) knew that the earth passes through four cardinal points (the spring equinox, the summer solstice, the fall equinox, and the winter solstice) during its orbit around the sun. One season changes to another as the earth crosses these points.

The cardinal points gradually shift over a grand, twenty-two-thousand-year cycle due to the gravitational pull of the sun, moon, and planets on the earth. Adhemar knew that the earth is closest to the sun on January 3 and farthest away on July 4. At the present point in the orbit's grand cycle, those in the Northern Hemisphere are nearest to the warmth of the sun, resulting in relatively mild winters. But eventually, in thousands of years, the earth will be drawn closer to the sun around the time of the summer solstice, precipitating sweltering summers and frigid winters. Adhemar believed that this gradual shifting of the cardinal points, which scientists today call the *precession of the equinoxes,* instigated the ice ages by depriving the earth of the sun's genial influence at critical times.

In 1843, another French scientist, Urbain Leverrier (1811–1877), detected a second astronomical feature related to the ice ages. He realized that the distance from the sun at which the earth traveled was affected by the actual *shape* of the earth's orbit. Over a one-hundred-thousand-year cycle, the orbit's shape is gradually altered, again by the gravitational influences of the sun, moon, and other planets. It ranges from a near-perfect circle, as it is today, to a more oval orbit in which our world is carried farther from the sun, allowing the ice ages to gain a grip on the vulnerable earth.

Despite these breakthroughs in astronomy, there was still no agreement about the cause or timing of the ice ages. An unlikely source provided the third and final clue. Scotsman James Croll (1821–1890) was forced to drop out of school at the age of thirteen to help his mother raise their family. But although his formal classes had ended, he undertook an ambitious self-education program during which he mastered the fundamentals of the physical sciences. In 1859, after holding numerous jobs, from millwright to insurance salesman, he finally arrived at the position from which he made his monumental contribution to science: Croll became the janitor in the Andersonian College and Museum in Glasgow. He wrote, "My salary was small, it is true, little more than sufficient to enable me to subsist; but this was compensated by advantages for me of another kind."[3]

The janitor had access to the college's science library. It was all he needed. The untutored Croll decided to turn his talents to the puzzle that still eluded the scientific establishment: What had actually caused the ice ages? With the publication of his book *Climate and Time* in 1872, Croll introduced the third astronomical key to the mystery: change in the earth's axis.

The angle of the earth's tilt determines the amount of sunshine received by various parts of the planet. Changes in the tilt result in temperature changes on the earth's surface. Today the axis is angled at 23.5°. But the tilt gradually changes, varying from a minimum of 21.8° to a maximum of 24.4°.

Milutin Milankovitch (1857–1927), a Serbian engineer who in 1911 was working as a professor of mathematics at the University of Belgrade, used these astronomical factors to calculate the amount of solar radiation that would reach the earth at any particular time in its history. He believed that ice ages resulted when winter ice did not melt the following summer because the earth was not receiving enough warmth from the sun. Over successive seasons the ice sheets would thicken, slowly smothering the land beneath.

In 1976, Croll and Milankovitch's ideas were validated by James Hay, John Imbrie, and Nicholas Shackleton, who published a paper showing that the geological evidence of the ice ages matched the astronomical cycles (see chapter 10). They showed that normally the earth is gripped by an ice age. But we now enjoy an interglacial period—that is, a very mild climate compared with what the planet normally endures.

Our present interglacial period, which began almost twelve thousand years ago, is destined to be only a short-lived melting period. During the last 350,000 years there have been four interglacial periods occurring roughly 335,000, 220,000, 127,000, and 11,600 years ago. Three astronomical cycles must coincide to bring about an interglacial period: the planet's tilt must reach approximately 24.4°, the orbit's shape must be elongated by at least 1 percent, and the earth must be closest to the sun in the month of June.

The Croll/Milankovitch astronomical theory of the ice ages is today gathering widespread support as an explanation for the *timing* of large-scale glacials. But it addresses only part of the question. Of equal importance is the *geography* of glaciations. It is here that the long-neglected theory of earth crust displacement plays its role in unraveling the mystery.[4] According to Hapgood's theory, the areas of the globe that experience the coolest climates are those that are thrust into the polar zones.

In his foreword to Hapgood's book Einstein explains the mechanism that might dislocate the crust. "In a polar region there is continual disposition of ice which is not symmetrically distributed about the pole. The earth's rotation acts on these unsymmetrical deposited masses, and produces centrifugal momentum that is transmitted to this rigid crust of the earth. The constantly increasing centrifugal momentum produced this way will, when it reaches a certain point, produce a movement of the earth's crust over the rest of the earth's body, and this will displace the polar regions toward the equator."[5] And such a movement will, simultaneously, shift some temperate areas into the polar zones, freezing them until they are freed by another earth crust displacement.

Einstein, although convinced that displacements had occurred, doubted that the weight of the ice caps alone would produce sufficient force to dislodge the crust. Hapgood gave up searching for the cause of the displacements and concentrated on demonstrating how his theory could explain unsolved problems in geology and evolution.

The Croll/Milankovitch theory of ice ages suggests the combined extraterrestrial gravitational pull of the planets, sun, and moon and the terrestrial influence of the weight of the ice caps as a cause of the crustal displacements. We suggest that if the shape of the earth's orbit deviates from a perfect circle by more than 1 percent, the gravitational influence of the sun increases because the earth's path narrows at certain points. The sun exercises more pull on the planet and its massive ice sheets. The ponderous weight alternately pushes and pulls against the crust, and this immense pressure, combined with the greater incline in the earth's tilt and the sun's increased gravitational pull, forces the crust to shift.

After each displacement the ice sheets melt, raising the ocean level. This melting is compounded if the displacement coincides with the beginning of an interglacial period when worldwide temperatures climb. Such was the case 11,600 years ago following the last earth crust displacement. Eventually, as snowfall again accumulates within the repositioned Arctic and Antarctic circles, the ocean returns to a lower level and the cycle begins all over again.

The last earth crust displacement occurred 11,600 years ago when all three astronomical cycles meshed, ushering in the present interglacial epoch. The dominant cycle relating to these events is that of the earth's tilt (now thought to move from the minimum of 21.8° to the maximum of 24.4° every 41,000 years).[6] We believe other earth crust displacements occurred during the last glacial epochs at 11,600, 52,600, and 93,600 years ago.

Such a theory, coupled with Hapgood's geomagnetic evidence for the location of the poles, accounts for the unique geography of glaciations. Those areas, trapped within the polar zones both before and after the displacements, accumulate unusually large amounts of glaciations.

Hapgood's theory is simple, coherent, and fruitful. These are all features that Thomas Kuhn recognizes as being characteristics of what he termed a paradigm shift. The problem of the ice ages is transformed once we use Hapgood's theory. The explanation is simple. Those parts of the earth's crust that shift into the polar zones experience ice ages. Today there is an ice age in Siberia, Greenland, and Antarctica.*

CONTINENTAL DRIFT AND PLATE TECTONICS

In 1915 Alfred Wegener (1880–1930) introduced a radical new idea to geologists.[7] Noticing how Africa and South America seemed to be two pieces of an ancient puzzle, he suggested that the continents had drifted apart over millions of years. The idea was greeted with scorn by geologists, who called it "geo-poetry."

For almost half a century the idea lay dormant until discoveries in the 1950s transformed the theory into what is known as plate tectonics. The new science of paleomagnetism began to support Wegener's idea that there had once been a single continent that had drifted apart. In 1953, geomagnetic dating proved that India has once been in the southern hemisphere—a fact that Wegener had predicted. Today ice ages and plate tectonics are fundamental components of modern geology.

---

*Theories that assume an overall lowering of the globe's temperature are presented with the problem of how the earth's atmosphere generates enough evaporation to create snow. The earth crust displacement theory provides a mechanism for this problem. In Hapgood's theory there are always tropical zones hot enough to cause evaporation and thus generate the snowfall inside the Arctic and Antarctic Circles.

SOLAR TYPHOONS

In 2001, with the publication of *The Atlantis Blueprint* in the United States, Rand began correspondence with Jared Freedman, who suggested a mechanism for earth crust displacements. Freedman is a computer professional and inventor who worked with electromagnets. He is aware that the earth itself is a gigantic magnet possessing a metal core. When any magnet passes through an electromagnetic field, heat is generated. In an article titled "Solar Typhoons and Earth Crust Displacements," he wrote, "If the Earth's magnetic field received such a tremendous distortion of its magnetic field, over a prolonged period of time, it would generate immense amounts of heat within the Earth's core as the Earth spun through the force that was causing the magnetic field disruption. The only force that can collapse the Earth's magnetic field is the Sun's magnetic field."[8]

In the article, Freedman noted that the sun has climatic variations of its own, but because of the immense size of the broiling star, they happen over longer periods of time. Solar storms can theoretically last for "days, weeks, or even more." If the earth passes through electromagnetic waves coming from the sun, then force would be applied steadily to one of the poles. That energy would be carried into the Earth's core where it could liquefy the solid nickel. Flows of metal to the earth's surface could transform the asthenosphere from a sluggish tar into a liquid. He wrote, "Perhaps it is not the disruptions of the Earth's core that cause fluctuations in the Earth's magnetic field, but rather disruptions of the Earth's magnetic field cause fluctuations in the Earth's core."[9]

There are several advantages to Freedman's theory. Einstein had doubted that the weight of the earth's ice sheets would be sufficient to dislodge the crust. He also doubted that an abrupt shift of the entire axis was the explanation because any force that could accomplish that would probably shatter the planet into thousands of pieces. What he sought was a steady force applied for a sustained period to the earth's crust.

Freedman's theory addresses all these problems and also provides a mechanism for stopping the displacements. Once the earth leaves the path of the electromagnetic storm, it cools, turning the liquid-like asthenosphere once again into a tarry substance, which prevents the crust from shifting any farther.*

2012

In his article, Freedman also mentioned the cataclysms predicted for the year 2012.

> A blast of energy was emitted that was strong enough to collapse the Earth's magnetic field on April 11th and 12th of 2001. Luckily, these missed us. As you know, the sun goes though 11-year cycles, and these cycles correspond to the Mayan calendar. Every 11 years, as the sun flips its magnetic field, it winds up the big magnetic field within the Sun. Some say that every 11 years, the repercussions of the Sun field flip are stronger, with this year being the biggest display of solar activity ever in recorded history. From what I understand, the Mayan calendar says this age will end in the year 2012, which is a Sun magnetic field flip solar cycle year.[10]

There have been more than one thousand such "flips" since the last earth crust displacement, making the odds that 2012 will see an earth crust displacement at least one thousand to one against.

While Freedman's concept of a solar typhoon provides a compelling mechanism for earth crust displacements, we are not supporters of the idea that the Mayan calendar predicts such a catastrophe. We note that Hapgood believed that earth crust displacements take five or six thousand years to happen. He *never* connected his idea with the Mayan

---

*Freedman's theory also makes sense of the stories told around the globe that attribute the Flood to a change in the sun (please see chapter 3).

calendar. This, however, has not stopped opportunists from claiming so in the latest orgy of scare mongering and exploitation aimed at selling books, DVDs, or television programs.

Because we believe that displacements correlate to times when the earth's tilt is at its maximum of 24.4° (as in 9600 BCE), we do not expect another earth crust displacement for at least another 29,500 years. Neither Hapgood nor Einstein ever suggested that there would be an earth crust displacement in 2012.

CRUST OR AXIS SHIFT?

As noted in chapter 9, Professor Emeritus W. Woelfli of the Institute for Particle Physics in Zürich and Professor W. Baltensperger of the Brazilian Center for Physics Research in Rio de Janeiro suggested in a series of articles from 2006 to 2008 that the earth experienced a radical change in its axis 11,500 years ago.

This was based on compelling evidence demonstrating temperate conditions in Siberia during the last ice age. They concluded that Siberia's latitude must have been "lower before the end of the Pleistocene"[11] in order to explain the existence of mammoths and humans who lived at 71° N during an ice age.

The physicists propose that an unknown planet was destroyed 11,500 years ago when it plunged into the sun after passing by Earth. As this gigantic planet passed by Earth, it caused our world to twist and turn in response to gravitational forces, dramatically altering the location of Earth's axis. They propose that before this catastrophic axis change the North Pole was located at central Greenland. The new position of the axis (in today's Arctic Ocean) resulted in North America being moved farther from the pole and Siberia being dragged into the Arctic Circle.[12]

These two scientists—though not geologists—are attempting to use an axis shift theory to explain a real problem. They are to be applauded, but their theory falls short. A central Greenland pole cannot explain the vast Cordilleran Ice Sheet that was located on the west coast of North America.* The pole would be too far away (see figure 13.1).

Some physicists might reply that the overall world temperature was lower. But that explanation faces the daunting problem of how to get enough evaporation in the tropics to create the amount of moisture needed in the atmosphere in order to create snow.

The theory of earth crust displacement, however, can explain all these anomalies. Looking at the map of North America in Figure 10.2, we see that before 91,600 BCE the Arctic Circle was centered in the Yukon. All of Alaska, British Columbia, and parts of Washington and Idaho were under ice. The Cordilleran Ice Sheet was the remnant of that polar zone. Figure 10.3 shows Greenland and Europe within the polar zone from 91,600 to 50,600 BCE. And in Figure 10.4, we see Greenland and most of North America within the polar zone from 50,600 to 9600 BCE. The configuration of ice age North America's vast ice sheets (see figure 10.1) was the natural consequence of the previous positions of the polar zone.†

Future research may take the theory of earth crust displacement in unexpected directions, just as happened to Agassiz's theory of catastrophic ice ages or Wegener's theory of continental drift. The theory is young and waits a new generation unencumbered by the current fixations of geology.

What we are dealing with is not just another lost civilization, it is a lost *advanced* culture, one possessing scientific knowledge that we have yet to comprehend. Who knows what problems might be solved by the discovery of the lost sciences of Atlantis? And one can only wonder about the lost art, sculpture, and architecture lying beneath the

---

*The authors do not give a specific location on central Greenland for the pole. For the map in Figure 13.1, we used the location on Greenland where the ice sheet is thickest (72° N, 38°W).

†As a result of the various positions of the earth's crust (see figures 10.2, 10.3, and 10.4) and the former positions of the Antarctic polar zone, Antarctica's ice cap is thickest in the area that gets the least amount of snow and thinnest in the area that gets the most amount of snow—conditions that defy expectations (see figure 9.2).

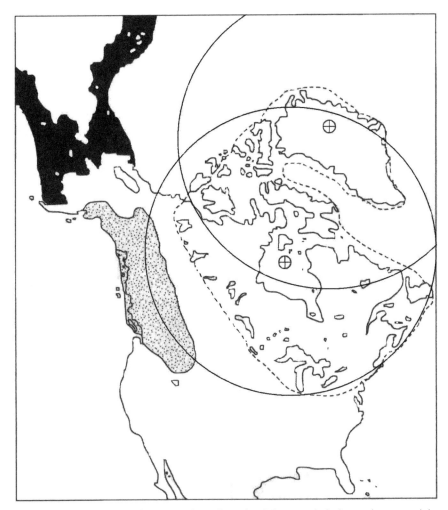

Figure 13.1. An axis shift centered on Greenland (upper circled cross) can explain the ice sheets on Greenland and eastern Canada (within dotted lines), which also would have covered parts of Europe, but it cannot explain the existence of the Cordilleran Ice Sheet in Alaska, British Columbia, Washington, and Idaho (dot-shaded area). Earth crust displacement theory proposes that the Arctic Circle was centered on the Hudson Bay (lower circled cross). This would account for not only the formation of the ice sheets on Greenland and eastern Canada but also the Cordilleran Ice Sheet. Drawing by Rand Flem-Ath and Rose Flem-Ath.

ice. Whoever takes up the search should remember that the remains of Atlantis might cradle an unimaginable heritage.

But already the promise of treasure of another sort—minerals, fishing grounds, unique laboratory conditions—have led to polite grumbling around the negotiating table as claim and counterclaim to slices of the last continent are argued.

We surely must proceed with caution if we decide to disturb this pristine place. Behind the deceptively rigid white mask lies a continent that is home to many forms of life bound in a delicate chain vulnerable to the brutal mechanics of technology.

It is ironic that beneath Antarctica—center of one of our most dramatic environmental alarms, the depletion of the ozone layer—may lie the smothered evidence of the most overwhelming environmental disaster.

Beneath the splendor of the Southern Lights, human garbage already scums the gleaming snow and the giant skeleton remains of machinery rusts against the horizon. Plastic containers float in the black sea and dynamite blasts rip through the eternal silence. This place offers great promise and a great opportunity—maybe a last chance for human beings to touch with some dignity, some sensitivity, the creatures that still live there. Perhaps this unique exploration, unlike so many of the others we have seen in these pages, can be tempered with mercy. We might start by declaring Antarctica an international park, the responsibility of us all. We could use only the most sophisticated, least intrusive, instruments to peer beneath the ice. If evidence of civilization is found, a surgical probe could be made. We would hold our breath as we waited to glimpse the ancient city locked in ice.

- The quest would be reborn.
- Our past and future would meet.
- Science and myth might merge.

POSTSCRIPT TO THE NEW EDITION

We're very proud that the first edition of *When the Sky Fell* is one of the few books to be found in the libraries of all seven continents—including an Australian base in Antarctica! Even more rewarding has been the opportunity to introduce the idea of Atlantis in Antarctica to the popular imagination, triggering the talents of artists, musicians, and other writers.

The mail regularly brings paintings, sketches, and poems from talented amateurs and tempered professionals, all keen readers whose muse was awoken by *When the Sky Fell*.

Clive Cussler gave us *Atlantis Found* (and a kind e-mail), in which James-Bond-like superhero Dirk Pitt travels to Antarctica and fights neo-Nazi villains over the remains of Atlantis. Later, Cussler teamed with Paul Kemprecos to write *Pole Shift,* a novel that envisioned terrorists who are hell-bent on artificially displacing the earth's crust. Stel Pavlou created the exciting *Decipher,* in which Richard Scott travels the world cracking ancient hieroglyphics, including those found in the city of Atlantis two miles beneath the ice of Antarctica.

Thomas Greanias wrote *Raising Atlantis,* in which an astro-archaeologist teams with a Vatican linguist on a quest to find Atlantis in Antarctica. In 2007, a book by Jeremy Robinson, *Antarktos Rising,* imagined a present-day Earth crust displacement that frees Antarctica from the polar zone, revealing the formerly iced continent and awakening the hibernating civilization that lies beneath.

On television, the long-running science fiction series *Stargate SG-1* (1997–2007) and its spinoff, *Stargate Atlantis* (2004–2009), both assumed a close connection between Atlantis and Antarctica. This connection yielded an unexpected invitation to Hollywood, complete with a personal tour of the old MGM studio, which was a fun surprise not often imagined while one is hunched over a manuscript for long hours checking for typos!

On the big screen, *AVP: Alien vs Predator* (2004) and *AVPR: Alien vs Predator—Requiem* (2007) were both predicated on the idea that Antarctica was once the site of an advanced civilization. And Rand's expertise on Charles Hapgood was tapped for the recent film *2012*.

As for music, the Canadian rockers Atlantis Blueprint are enjoying success. And in Australia, the group When the Sky Fell continues to gather fans.

Tom Miller's evocative painting of scientists retrieving artifacts from beneath Antarctica's ice was inspired by *When the Sky Fell* and was featured on the cover of the bestselling issue of *Atlantis Rising* magazine.

Over the years many people have written to share their thoughts and ask questions. Thank you. At times this has been a raucous debate. Fortunately, most people "get it" that in the end it is how we treat each other that counts. Scoring intellectual points never needs to exclude common courtesy and goodwill.

We continue to welcome your input and look forward to our evolving adventure together at www.flem-ath.com.

AFTERWORD

By John Anthony West

An afterword presupposes that readers have already read the book under discussion—apart from that minority of browsers who like to nibble fore and aft before biting into the bait.

If you have indeed read this book through, you may have come to the same conclusion I have: the evidence assembled by the Flem-Aths is compelling.

Anyone reading or researching deeply into the distant past soon comes up against glaring anomalies in the currently accepted scenario of pre-history. Deluge myths are universal around the world, and the mythologies of widely separated peoples tell, over and over again, variations of the same story of global cataclysm. Plato's infamous Atlantis legend, in all its precise detail, sits there, thumbing its nose at all those modern attempts to write it off as still another instance of the inflamed and disordered ancient imagination.

Beginning with Cuvier back in the eighteenth century, a succession of daring intellectual explorers have been braving the disapproval—sometimes the opprobrium and derision—of their academic colleagues, trying to account scientifically for these anomalies and to write the true scenario of the shattering events responsible for all those myths and legends.

The situation is like a gigantic jigsaw puzzle with most of the pieces originally missing. Early attempts to assemble the puzzle ended up with more holes than pictures and were relatively easy to ignore or dismiss. But as modern science develops, new pieces to the puzzle keep turning up. Successive attempts to put the whole picture together grow increasingly cogent.

The Flem-Aths are perhaps the most persuasive and daring of the contemporary "Atlantologists." Underpinned by the absolutely irrefutable fact of mass mammal extinctions around 10,000 BCE and the precise, detailed, and no less irrefutable testimony of the Piri Reis's and other maps of the pre-catastrophe world, the picture becomes increasingly coherent. A spectrum of relevant disciplines—geology, paleoclimatolgy, cartography, astronomy, comparative religion—all contribute to the puzzle, and Hapgood's earth crust displacement theory seems to provide the *modus operandi* that accounts for the whole, huge, worldwide scenario in a single stroke.

Will the Flem-Aths' contemporary portrait finally take root and prevail? It is a big question. All of our human distant past hangs in the balance, along with the true story of the evolution of human civilization on earth.

A GLOBAL
CLIMATIC MODEL

for the Origins of Agriculture and
the Sequence of Pristine Civilizations

This is the original text submitted in the spring of 1981 to *The Anthropological Journal of Canada* and accepted for publication. It contains *more* information than the edited and published text (see Flem-Ath, "Global Modal") and appears here in full for the *first* time.

ABSTRACT

A climatic model orders archaeological evidence on the origins of agriculture and the sequence of independent civilizations on a global scale.

Why did agriculture become the preferred means of subsistence following the termination of the Pleistocene? Why did the civilizations of the New World take so much longer to evolve despite the fact that their early agricultural experiments are contemporary with those of the Old World? This paper will attempt to shed light on these problems with the aid of the little-known climatic model of Hapgood[1] in conjunction with the stress model of Harris.[2]

Cohen[3] has argued, quite rightly, that it is no longer adequate to explain the "where" and the "when" of agricultural origins but to address ourselves to the more important question of "why?" Why did mankind, in both the Old and New Worlds, almost simultaneously shift from their highly successful and traditional subsistence of hunting and gathering to agriculture? Why were certain areas of the world more suitable to this adaptation than others? Any theory, which attempts a global approach to this problem, must confront the question of "why" in such a manner as to illuminate the data concerning the "where" and "when" of the origins of agriculture.

Global theories, which have addressed this problem, have fallen into three categories: the diffusion models; the population/ecological models; and what I term the "traditional" climatic models. Why have these models failed to account for major significant archaeological evidence?

The fact that ". . . all agricultural origins fall about 10,000 ± 2000 years ago,"[4] well before the first civilizations, coupled with the evidence demonstrating more than one center of early agricultural experimentation[5] has seriously undermined the concept of diffusion as an important model for the origins of agriculture. Until a theory is developed which can overcome these two problems the theory of diffusion will remain untenable as a global model.*

Cohen attempted to apply a population/ecological model on a global scale. Following Boserup[6] who first put forward the idea of population density as a causal feature of technological change, thus reversing the traditional Malthusian model, Cohen argued that population growth worldwide reached a saturation level, which in turn created a stress condition, forcing the adoption of agriculture as a new strategy of food supply. This thesis suffers from three very serious drawbacks: first, it flies in the face of anthropological data, which, as shown, indi-

---

*The reader will appreciate that Rand could not mention the word *Atlantis* in a paper for a scientific journal and still expect to be published. Traditional diffusion theories assume civilization spread from Egypt, Sumer, or India, and sometimes China. Diffusion from Atlantis took place thousands of years before these civilizations emerged.

cate that hunter-gatherers *normally* maintain equilibrium with their environments;[7] second, given that the population of density of the Old World was significantly greater than the New World, Cohen's theory fails to explain why the ecological thresholds were reached *at the same time;* and finally it does not address itself to the evidence of Vavilov,[8] which shows a direct correlation between high altitudes and the centers of agriculture. In short, although Cohen has addressed the problem of "why," his model does not shed light on the "when" and "where" aspects of the problem.

The diffusion and population/ecological global models have difficulties in explaining archaeological data and so we now turn to the "traditional" climatic models. These theories, such as Childe[9] and Binford[10] have suffered as Cohen correctly pointed out,[11] from two problems: they are regional in scope and thus cannot account for the data on a broader perspective; and they are repetitive processes, which fail to explain why the particular changes of the post-Pleistocene period resulted in agriculture, when similar events in the past had not done so. Any new climatic theory must address these two problems.

Before we proceed to the primary thesis of this paper it may be helpful to describe the type of theory that is required. We need a theory that can explain "why" the process of agriculture began in the New and Old Worlds at approximately the same time yet led to much different rates of cultural evolution. The model must not only address this "when" evidence and especially the long-neglected correlation between altitude and centers, but the theory, if it is a climatic one, must address itself to the traditional limitations of repetitive and regional effects outlined by Cohen. Finally the theory should address the data on a global scale.

A climatic model based on the geological theory of Hapgood in conjunction with the stress model of Harris can meet all the requirements stated above. The sad state of affairs is that Hapgood's geological work has simply been ignored despite the fact that the original volume was prefaced by the late Albert Einstein. Einstein's preface is an excellent summary of the basic theory and since the book is now out-of-print, I have taken the liberty of quoting him:

> I frequently receive communications from people who wish to consult me concerning their unpublished ideas. It goes without saying that these ideas are very seldom possessed of scientific validity. The very first communication, however, that I received from Mr. Hapgood electrified me. His idea is original, of great simplicity, and—if it continues to prove itself—of great importance to everything that is related to the earth's surface.
>
> A great many empirical data indicate that at each point of the earth's surface that has been carefully studied, many climatic changes have taken place, apparently quite suddenly. This, according to Hapgood, is explicable if the virtually rigid outer crust of the earth undergoes, from time to time, extensive displacement over the viscous, plastic, possibly fluid inner layers. Such displacements may take place as the consequences of comparatively slight forces exerted on the crust, derived from the earth's momentum of rotation, which in turn will tend to alter the axis of rotation of the earth's crust.[12]

It should be noted that the process of earth crust displacement (ECD) refers only to a movement of the earth's crust and *not* to the mantle, core, or pole of rotation. Put simply, ECD is a process, which results in various parts of the earth's crust being shifted, at different times, over the earth's axis (the North and South Poles).

Working on the assumption that the earth's magnetic fields are usually located in close proximity to the pole of rotation, Hapgood collected geo-magnetic rock samples from different parts of the globe indicating those areas of the crust, which were at the poles from the last three ECDs. Hapgood found evidence that the most recent ECD occurred between 17,000–12,000 BCE, at which time the crust displaced resulting in the North Pole's relocation to its current place in the "Arctic" Ocean after having been located previously in the Hudson Bay region of northern Canada. More recent climatic data from different sources have been brought together[13] indicating at dramatic climatic change at 12,000 BCE, which coincides with Pleistocene extinctions, rising ocean levels, the close of the ice age, and the origins of agriculture.

A displacement of the earth's crust causes dramatic climatic changes, but it should be noted that these variations are not all equal in their impact. There were areas of the globe following the ECD of 12,000 BCE that were tropical before *and* after the event. Taken in conjunction with the data of Vavilov[14] I have labeled these areas as "Micro-Centers" because the further one travels from the midpoint between the current and previous equators, the less likely that one will be able to survive the harsh ecological changes (see figure A.1).

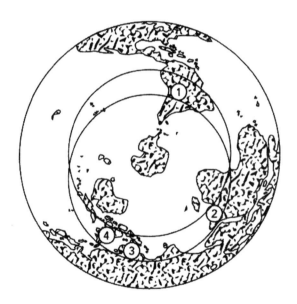

ECD-zones	before 12,000 B.P.	after 12,000 B.P.	Description of Lands
Micro-Centers	tropical	tropical	1. Central Andes 2. Ethiopian Highlands 3. Thailand Highlands 4. NE Borneo Highlands

Figure A.1. Tropical agricultural origins.

Vavilov found a direct correlation between agricultural origins and land over 1,500 meters above ocean level. This long-neglected data is explicable in terms of ECD because the displacement of the crust results in immense tidal waves. Survivors of the event have a strong motive for staying in high mountains. The Micro-Centers listed in figure A.1 are over 1,500 meters above ocean level.

Important archaeological discoveries in three of the four Micro-Centers date agricultural developments to approximately 12,000 BCE. MacNeish[15] reviews the archaeological evidence in Peru dating to this time range, while Pickersgill and Heiser[16] delineated the number of important crops, which were domesticated in the Lake Titicaca region of Bolivia/Peru. The same sort of data comes from the antipode of Lake Titicaca in the highlands of Thailand. Early agricultural experiments at Spirit Cave, Thailand, are reviewed by Solheim[17] and Gorman.[18] Similar evidence near the Ethiopian highlands is found in Wendorf.[19] The model suggested here indicates that more excavations might be profitably undertaken in the highlands of northeastern Borneo.

ECD creates a situation where mobility is limited and important plants and animals for man become extinct.[20] This is exactly the condition that Harris argues leads to the process of agriculture. According to his model, an immobile population creates population pressures, which intensify wild-food procurement with eventual improved seasonal scheduling. A resource specialization coupled with improved technological innovations and a cultural selection of specific plants or animals may develop into a genuine food-producing system. If mobility is restored this last phase may not take place and a reversion to hunting-gathering can take place.

Harris's model can also be applied to the areas in high altitudes, which were temperate *both* before *and* after the ECD of 12,000 BCE. Figure A.2 shows the conditions that prevailed in the northern hemisphere following the last ECD (see figure A.2).

The absence of important early agricultural experiments in the "Non-Center" shown and described in Figure A.2 is entirely in line

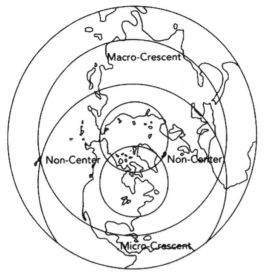

ECD-zones	before 12,000 B.P.	after 12,000 B.P.	Description of Lands
Macro-Crescent	tropical	temperate	Old World lands N of Tropic of Cancer and N of former Tropic of Cancer
Micro-Crescent	temperate	tropical	North America S or Tropic of Cancer and N of former Tropic of Cancer
Non-Center	temperate	temperate	North America N of Tropic of Cancer, Europe (not Crete and S. Greece), NW Africa, and Asia N of Tropic of Cancer

Figure A.2. Temperate agricultural origins.

with climatic conditions proposed by Hapgood and the stress model of Harris. Since this area was temperate *both* before *and* after the ECD of 12,000 BCE, it did not take long for mobility to be reestablished. Cohen reviews the literature showing the preference for the hunting and gathering way of life over the more labor-intensive means of agriculture.

The area labelled "Macro-Crescent" was the most favorable area for agricultural experiments following the ECD of 12,000 BCE. Since this area was formerly tropical and *newly* become temperate, the possibility of expansion into this zone from the Old World Non-Center was especially favorable. People who had gone almost all the way to food-producing during the population pressures in the high mountains around the Black Sea could move from a region, which was temperate *both* before and after the ECD, into a *newly* temperate zone. Such expansion would favor the use of agriculture since the indigenous plants and animals had been depleted.

The situation in the "Micro-Crescent" of the New World was entirely different. Here expansion to the south was into a zone that was formerly temperate but that had become tropical. Expansion into this zone was slow because of the radically different climatic conditions compared to the North American Non-Center. This fact accounts for the time-lag of New World civilizations (see figure A.3).

ECD-zones	before 12,000 B.P.	after 12,000 B.P.	Civilizations	Dates
Macro-Crescent	tropical	temperate	Sumeria	3500 B.C.E.
			Egypt	3200 B.C.E.
			Indus	2600 B.C.E.
			Minoan	2100 B.C.E.
			China	1800 B.C.E.
Micro-Crescent	temperate	tropical	Olmec	1200 B.C.E.
Micro-Center	tropical	tropical	Chavin	900 B.C.E.
Non-Center	temperate	temperate	none	none

Figure A.3. Sequence of pristine civilizations.

Figure A.3 demonstrates the utility of ECD as a model for accounting for the sequence of early independent civilizations. It will be noted that the first five civilizations appeared within the Macro-Crescent and that later societies fall into place according to the climatic conditions delineated. The first four civilizations were dependent upon plants and animals that were first domesticated near or in mountains and in the vicinity of the Black Sea. China is here seen as an off-shoot of the Thailand highland Micro-Center, which brought high altitude plants from a tropical zone into a low altitude temperate zone.

This paper has restricted itself to addressing the questions of the origins of agriculture and the sequence of pristine civilizations as seen through the climatic model of Charles H. Hapgood and population stress model of David R. Harris. Why previous ECDs have not led to agriculture can be accounted for by two factors: the fact that only two ECDs (12,000 BCE and 55,000 BCE) have occurred within the lifespan of Homo sapiens; and because lower overall population levels in the past allowed for a reversion to hunting and gathering.

It is my conviction that the theory of earth crust displacement constitutes a scientific revolution as defined by Kuhn.[21] It is a theory that has a wide application to various persistent problems in different scientific fields, and in the field of archaeology it orders data on a global scale and suggests new lines of investigation. Hapgood applied the theory to the problems of the ice ages, mountain building, extinctions, and the process of evolution. Recent developments in solar physics[22] are suggestive[23] of a mechanism for the displacements. This paper has applied the theory of ECD to the two persistent problems of: the "why," "where," and "when" of the origins of agriculture; and the sequence of pristine civilizations. In future papers I hope to expand the model to other problems in archaeology.

NOTES

INTRODUCTION

1. Evans, "Electronic Publications."

CHAPTER 1.
MEMORANDUM FOR THE PRESIDENT

1. Hapgood, memorandum to President Eisenhower.
2. Inan, *Life and Works of the Turkish Admiral: Piri Reis.*
3. *Illustrated London News,* "Columbus Controversy," February 23, 1932.
4. Yusuf, "Turkish Interest in America," 307.
5. Arlington Mallery with moderator Matthew Warren and M. I. Walters in a 1956 radio show sponsored by Georgetown University. In White, *Poleshift,* 36–49.
6. Hapgood, *Maps of the Ancient Sea Kings,* 2.
7. Ohlymeyer, letter to Charles Hapgood.
8. Burroughs, letter to Charles Hapgood, in Hapgood, *Maps of the Ancient Sea Kings,* 243.
9. Hapgood, letter to Rose and Rand Flem-Ath.
10. Sobel, *Longitude.*
11. Hapgood, letter to Arch C. Gerlach.
12. Burroughs, letter to Charles Hapgood, in Hapgood, *Maps of the Ancient Sea Kings,* 244.
13. Flem-Ath, "Piri Reis Map."

14. Statement of James H. Campbell, 1893, cited in Hapgood's Memorandum to President Eisenhower.
15. Hapgood, *Maps of the Ancient Sea Kings,* Preface.
16. Concas, "Report," vol. 2, 1500.

CHAPTER 2. THE EARTH'S SHIFTING CRUST

1. Einstein, letter to Charles H. Hapgood, in Hapgood, *Path of the Pole,* 328.
2. The Einstein–Hapgood correspondence is covered in detail in Flem-Ath and Wilson, *Atlantis Blueprint.*
3. Einstein, "Report on Hapgood."
4. Einstein, letter to Charles H. Hapgood, in Hapgood, *Path of the Pole,* 341, no. 5.
5. Einstein, in Hapgood, *Earth's Shifting Crust,* Foreword.
6. Hapgood, *Earth's Shifting Crust,* Foreword.
7. Ibid.
8. Horgan, "Profile," 40.
9. Kuhn, *Structure of Scientific Revolutions,* 5.

CHAPTER 3. THE WAYWARD SUN

1. Powell, "Mythological Philosophy."
2. Boas, *Kutenai Tales,* 281.
3. Ibid., 287.
4. Turney-High, *Ethnology of the Kutenai,* 96.
5. Baker, *Forgotten Kueteni,* 7.
6. British Columbia Department of Education, *Kootney.*
7. Turney-High, *Ethnology of the Kutenai,* 11–12.
8. Boas, *Kutenai Tales,* 281.
9. Ibid., 231.
10. Bancroft, *Native Races,* vol. III, 153–54.
11. Lowie, *Anthropological Papers,* 293.
12. Farmer, *Beginnings,* vol. XX, part III, 127.
13. *Dictionary of Indian Tribes of the Americas,* vol. 3, 455–60.
14. Freund, *Myths of Creation,* 11.
15. Dockstader, "Pima," in *Dictionary of Indian Tribes of the Americas.*

16. Over, *Sun Songs*, 30–31.

17. Ibid., 28.

18. Alexander, "North America," in Gray, Moore, and MacCulloch, *Mythology of All Races,* vol. X, 222.

19. Clark, *Indian Tales,* 42–43.

20. Ibid., 14–15.

21. Ibid., 31–32.

22. Dixon, "Achomawial Atsugewi Tales," 169.

23. Dixon, "Ahasta Myths," 36.

24. Mooney, *Myths of the Cherokee,* 252–54.

25. Olcott, *Sun Lore of All Ages,* 60.

26. Bancroft, *Native Races,* vol. III, 154.

27. Freund, *Myths of Creation*, 10.

28. *New Larouse Encyclopedia of Mythology,* 445.

29. Zarte, *Discovery and Conquest of Peru,* 49.

30. Alexander, "Latin America," in Gray, Moore, and MacCulloch, *Mythology of All Races,* vol. XI, 202.

31. de Leon, *Incas of Pedro de Cieza de Leon,* 27.

32. Banelier, *Islands of Titicaca and Koati,* 257.

33. Bingham, "Story of Machu Picchu," 183.

34. Ibid., 181.

35. Ibid., 185.

36. Ibid., 183.

37. Bingham, *Lost City of the Incas,* 35.

38. Canby, "Anasazi." See also: Sofaer, *Sun Dagger.*

39. MacCulloch and Machal, *"Celtic, Slavic,"* in Gray, Moore and MacCulloch, *Mythology of All Races,* vol. III, 12.

40. Over, *Sun Songs,* 165.

41. Homberg, "Finno-Ugric, Siberian," in Gray, Moore, and MacCulloch, *Mythology of All Races,* vol. IV, 312.

42. Muller, "Egyptian," in Gray, Moore, and MacCulloch, *Mythology of All Races,* vol. XII, 82.

43. Ibid., 39.

44. Plumley, "Cosmology of Ancient Egypt," 25–26.

45. Kirk and Raven, *Presocratic Philosophers,* 13.

CHAPTER 4. ATLANTIS IN ANTARCTICA

1. Plato, *Timaeus of Plato*, 65.

2. Plutarch, *Lives of the Noble Grecians and Romans*, 54–55.

3. Ibid., 38.

4. Ibid., 69.

5. Laertius, *Lives of Eminent Philosophers*, vol. II, 343.

6. Lewis, *Continent for Science*, 3.

7. Ovid, *Metamorphoses*, 341.

8. Plato, *Timaeus of Plato*, 69–70; Plato, *Critias, Cletophon, Menexenus, Epistles*, 31–33; Plato, *Timaeus and Critias*, 34–35.

9. Plato, *Timaeus of Plato*, 70; Plato, *Critias, Cletophon, Menexenus, Epistles*, 33; Plato, *Timaeus and Critias*, 35.

10. Aristotle, "On the Universe," 208.

11. Anikouchine and Sternberg, *World Ocean*, 2.

12. Plato, *Timaeus of Plato*.

13. Pindar, in Warmington, *Greek Geography*, 77.

14. Plato, *Timaeus of Plato*, no. 8, 141.

15. Whitaker, *Almanack*, 1176.

16. *Encyclopedia Americana: International Edition*, vol. 7, 688.

17. Plato, *Timaeus of Plato*, 79; Plato, *Critias, Cletophon, Menexenus, Epistles*, 41; Plato, *Timaeus and Critias*, 37.

18. Plato, *Timaeus and Critias*.

CHAPTER 5. THE LOST ISLAND PARADISE

1. Fedje and Josenhans, "Drowned Forest and Archaeology," 101.

2. Flem-Ath and Flem-Ath, "A Knife that Shut Up," 9–16.

3. Alexander, "North America," in Moore, Gray, and MacCulloch, *Mythology of All Races*, vol. X, 249–50.

4. Barbeau, *Haida Myths*, 187.

5. Greenberg, Turner, and Zegura, "Settlement of the Americas," 479.

6. Ruhlen, "Voices from the Past," 10.

7. Moore, "Pre-Neolithic Farmer's Village," 62–70.

8. *New Larouse Encyclopaedia of Mythology*, 55.

9. Ibid., 62.

10. Moore, Gray, and MacCulloch, *Mythology of All Races,* vol. VI, 208.

11. *New Larouse Encyclopaedia of Mythology*, 62.

12. Bibby, *Looking for Dilmun,* ch. 2.

13. Brinchurst, "Poem of the Elders," 75.

14. Ernst-Martin, Feldkeller, and Russell, "Ankylosing Spondylitis," 1–5.

15. Stykes, *Seven Daughters of Eve.*

CHAPTER 6.
AZTLAN AND THE POLAR PARADISE

1. Posnansky, *Tihuanacu,* vol. 1, 11.

2. Ibid., 89–90.

3. West, *Serpent in the Sky.*

4. Roberts, "Riddle of the Sphinx," 27.

5. Bauval and Gilbert, *Orion Mystery.*

6. Scham, "World's First Temple."

7. See the Collins interview, "Göbekli Tepe," and Schoch's article, "Searching for the Dawn."

8. La Berre, "Aymara Indians," 9.

9. de Leon, in Heyerdahl, *American Indians in the Pacific,* 231.

10. Mylrea, "Computer Helps Preserve Language," 8.

11. Barnes, "Ancient Purity and Polyglot Programs," 13; see also Atamiri Multilingual MT–System, www.atamiri.cc/en (accessed August 19, 2011).

12. Posnansky, *Tihuanacu* vol. 1, 2.

13. Burland, *Montezuma,* ch. 6 and 10; and Collins, *Cortes and Montezuma,* ch. 5.

14. Burland, *Montezuma*, 183.

15. Ibid., 165.

16. Ibid., 169–70.

17. Collins, *Cortes and Montezuma,* 56–60.

18. del Castillo, *Discovery and Conquest of Mexico,* 32.

19. Bancroft, *Native Races,* vol. III, 469.

20. Brundage, *Fifth Sun,* 6.

21. Sorenson, "Significance of an Apparent Relationship," 239.

22. Donnelly, *Atlantis,* 326.

23. Palmer, *Dictionary of Mythical Places.*

24. Alexander, "North America," in Moore, Gray, and MacCulloch, *Mythology of All Races,* vol. X, 113–14.

25. Prescott, *History of the Conquest of Mexico,* 693.

26. Shirer, *Gandhi,* 85.

27. Tilak, *Arctic Home in the Vedas,* 419.

28. Ibid., 72.

29. Warren, *Paradise Found,* 193–96.

30. Ibid., 141.

31. Ibid., 140–41.

32. Ibid., 225.

CHAPTER 7. ATLANTEAN MAPS

1. Al-Nadim, *Fihrist of al-Nadim,* 583.

2. Ibid., 584.

3. Hapgood, *Maps of the Ancient Sea Kings,* 41–42, 101.

4. Vasiliev, *History of the Byzantine Empire,* 452.

5. Ibid., 453.

6. Ibid., 459.

7. Ibid., 461.

8. Yule, *Book of Ser Marco Polo,* 5.

9. Kish, *Source Book in Geography,* 128.

10. Sanceau, *Henry the Navigator,* 117.

11. Cameron, *Lodestone and Evening Star,* 107.

12. Sanceau, *Henry the Navigator,* 111.

13. Hapgood, *Maps of the Ancient Sea Kings,* ch. 1–3.

14. Ibid., ch. 4.

15. Morison, *Admiral of the Ocean Sea,* 39.

16. Bourne, *Spain in America,* 119.

17. Connor, "Father Athanasius Kircher," 459.

18. Ibid., 460.

19. Ibid., 458.

20. Ibid., 460–61.

CHAPTER 8. EMBERS OF HUMANKIND

1. Plato, *Laws,* vol. 1, book III, 167–73.
2. Zedar, "Domestication and Early Agriculture," 11597–604.
3. de Candolle, *Origin of Cultivated Plants,* 8.
4. Vavilov, "Origin, Variation, Immunity, and Breeding of Cultivated Plants," 20.
5. Flem-Ath, "Global Model," 2–7.
6. Matsuoka et al., "Single Domestication for Maize," 6080–84.
7. de Leon, *Incas of Pedro de Cieza de Leon,* 27.
8. Dillehay et al., "Preceramic Adoption," 1890–93.
9. Gorman, "A Priori Models and Thai Prehistory," 321–56.
10. Londo et al., "Phylogeography of Asian Wild Rice."
11. Gupta, "Origin of Agriculture," 58.
12. Muke, Denham, and Genorupa, "Nominating and Managing a World Heritage Site," 324–38.
13. Denham, "Envisaging Early Agriculture," 162.
14. Denham, "Food for Thought," issue 4.

CHAPTER 9. THE RING OF DEATH

1. Please see Flem-Ath and Wilson, *Atlantis Blueprint,* app. 6, 345–51.
2. Associated Press, "Bear-Bones."
3. Sutherland and Walker, "Late Devonsian Ice-Free Area," 701–3.
4. Guthrie, "Mammals of the Mammoth Steppe," 309.
5. Pitulko et al., "Yana RHS Site," 55.
6. Woelfli and Baltensperger, "Arctic East Siberia."
7. Cuvier, in Silverberg, *Mammoths, Mastodons and Man,* 101.
8. Cuvier, "Revolutions and Catastrophes," 11.
9. Lurie, *Louis Agassiz,* 63–64.
10. Davies, *Earth in Decay,* 6.
11. Hutton, *Transactions of the Royal Society of Edinburgh,* 273.
12. Hutton, *Theory of the Earth,* vol. I, 275.
13. Ibid., 273.
14. Ibid., vol. II, 547.
15. Lyell, *Principles of Geology,* vol. III, 2–3.

16. Gould, "Is Uniformitarianism Necessary?" 223–28.

17. Agassiz, in Moore, *The Earth We Live On,* 140.

18. Agassiz, in Lurie, *Louis Agassiz,* 98.

19. Agassiz, *Geological Sketches,* vol. I, 210.

20. Wallace, *World of Life,* 264.

21. Lyell, as quoted by Hester, "The Agency of Man in Animal Extinctions," 189.

22. Martin, "Prehistoric Overkill," 396.

23. Vereschain and Baryshnikov, "Quaternary Mammal Extinctions," 483–515.

24. Stuart, "Who (or What) Killed the Giant Armadillo?" 29–32.

25. Martin, "Prehistoric Overkill, 396.

CHAPTER 10. BROKEN PARADIGM

1. Perego et al., "Distinctive Paleo-Indian Migration Routes," 2.

2. Bryson, "DNA Tracks Ancient Alaskan's Descendants."

3. Miotti and Salemme, "When Patagonia Was Colonized," 97–98.

4. Kenneth Beare, "Basic English Key Words List 1—Basic Verbs, Prepositions, Articles, etc.," About.com, English as 2nd Language, http://esl.about.com/library/vocabulary/bl850_basics.htm (accessed August 19, 2011).

5. Ibid.

6. Loeb, "Religious Organizations," 530.

7. Plato, cited by Davis, *First Sex,* 28.

8. Julia White, "The Yahgan," Looking Back, www.meyna.com/yahgan.html (accessed August 19, 2011).

9. Loeb, "Religious Organizations," 517–56.

10. Bryson, "DNA Tracks Ancient Alaskan's Descendants."

11. Huddlesten, *Origins of the American Indians,* 56.

12. Guthrie, "Mammals of the Mammoth Steppe," 65.

13. Watters and Stafford, "Redefining the Age of Clovis," 1122.

14. Nelson, "Evidence of the Earliest Americans," 28.

15. Scheinsohn, "Hunter-Gatherer Archaeology in South America," 344–45.

16. Plato, *Timaeus and Critias.*

17. Scheinsohn, "Hunter-Gatherer Archaeology in South America," 339.

18. Dillehay, *Monte Verde.*

CHAPTER 11. FINDING ATLANTIS

1. Laertius, *Lives of Eminent Philosophers,* vol. 1, 29.
2. Ibid., vol. 1, 37.
3. Vico, *New Science of Giambattista Vico,* 68.
4. Ibid., 57.
5. Ibid., 60.
6. Tylor, *Primitive Culture,* 255–56.
7. Freud, "Psychopathology of Everyday Life," 47–48.
8. Jung and Kerenyi, *Introduction to a Science of Mythology,* 102–3.
9. Lévi-Strauss, *Structural Anthropology,* 229.
10. Campbell, *Hero with a Thousand Faces,* 4.
11. Kuhn, *Essential Tension,* 322.
12. Strabo, *Geography of Strabo,* 154.
13. Proclus, *Commentaries of Proclus,* vol. 1, bk. 1, 164.
14. Donnelly, *Atlantis,* 1.
15. Ibid., 2.
16. West, *Mystery of the Sphinx.*
17. Time-Life Books, *Mystic Places,* 23.
18. Lyell, *Principles of Geology,* vol. I, 2–3.
19. Luce, *End of Atlantis.*
20. Reiche, "Language of Archaic Astronomy," 176.
21. *Epigraphic Society Occasional Papers,* vol. 24, 245–65.
22. Ibid., 257.
23. Davis, *The First Sex,* 3.
24. Ibid., 23.

CHAPTER 12. CITY OF ATLANTIS

1. Plato, *Timaeus and Critias,* 143.
2. Ibid., 144.
3. Ibid., 137.
4. Ibid., 283.
5. Flem-Ath and Wilson, *Atlantis Blueprint,* 318.
6. Ibid.

CHAPTER 13. WHY THE SKY FELL

1. Flem-Ath and Wilson, *The Atlantis Blueprint.*
2. Agassiz, *Geological Sketches,* 98.
3. Croll, in Imbrie and Imbrie, *Ice Ages,* 80.
4. Einstein, in Hapgood, *Earth's Shifting Crust,* Foreword.
5. Hays, Imbrie, and Schackleton, "Variations in the Earth's Orbit," 1121–32.
6. Wegener, *Entstehung der Kontinente und Ozeane.*
7. Ibid.
8. Freedman, "Solar Typhoons."
9. Ibid.
10. Woelfli and Baltensperger, "On the Change of Latitude."
11. Woelfli and Baltensperger, "Possible Explanation for Earth's Climatic Changes.
12. Ibid.

APPENDIX. A GLOBAL CLIMATE MODEL FOR THE ORIGINS OF AGRICULTURE AND THE SEQUENCE OF PRISTINE CIVILIZATIONS

1. Hapgood, *Earth's Shifting Crust;* and Hapgood, *Path of the Pole.*
2. Harris, "Alternative Pathways toward Agriculture," 179–244.
3. Cohen, *Food Crisis in Prehistory.*
4. Carter, "Hypothesis Suggesting a Single Origin of Agriculture," 89–134.
5. Vavilov, "Origin, Variation, Immunity, and Breeding of Cultivated Plants," 14–54; and Harlan, "Agricultural Origins," 468–74.
6. Boserup, *Conditions of Agricultural Growth.*
7. Harris, "Alternative Pathways toward Agriculture."
8. Vavilov, "The Origin, Variation, Immunity, and Breeding of Cultivated Plants."
9. Childe, *Man Makes Himself.*
10. Binford, "Post Pleistocene Adaptations," 313–41.
11. Cohen, *Food Crisis in Prehistory,* 8.
12. Einstein, in Hapgood, *Earth's Shifting Crust.*
13. Langway, Hansen, and Lyle, "Drilling through the Ice Cap," 202.
14. Vavilov, "Origin, Variation, Immunity, and Breeding of Cultivated Plants."

15. MacNeish, "Beginnings of Agriculture in Central Peru," 753–802.

16. Pickersgill and Heiser, "Origins and Distribution of Plants," 803–36.

17. Solheim, "Earlier Agricultural Revolution," 34–41.

18. Gorman, "A Priori Models and Thai Prehistory," 321–56.

19. Wendorf, "Late Palaeolithic Sites in Egyptian Nubia," 791–953.

20. Hapgood, *Path of the Pole*, ch. 10.

21. Kuhn, *Structure of Scientific Revolutions.*

22. Eddy, "Historical and Arboreal Evidence for a Changing Sun," 11–34.

23. Gribbon, *Strangest Star.*

BIBLIOGRAPHY

Agassiz, Louis. *Geological Sketches.* Boston: Tichnor & Fields, 1866.

Alexander, Hartley Burr. "Latin America." In *The Mythology of All Races,* edited by Louis Herbert Gray, George Foot Moore, and John Arnott MacCulloch. Boston: Marshall Jones Company, vol. XI, 1920.

———. "North America." In *The Mythology of All Races,* edited by Louis Herbert Gray, George Foot Moore, and John Arnott MacCulloch. Boston: Marshall Jones Company, vol. X, 1916.

Al-Nadim, Muhammad ibn Ishaq ibn. *The Fihrist of al-Nadim: A Tenth Century Survey of Muslim Culture.* Translated by Barnard Dodge. New York: Columbia University Press, 1970.

Anikouchine, William A., and Richard W. Sternberg. *The World Ocean: An Introduction to Oceanography.* Englewood Cliffs, N.J.: Prentice-Hall, 1973.

Aristotle. "On the Universe." In *Greek Geography,* edited by E. H. Warmington. London: J. M. Dent & Sons Ltd, 1934, 208.

Associated Press. "Bear-Bones Find Challenges Idea of When the Ice Age Began in Norway." August 23, 1993.

Baker, Paul E. *The Forgotten Kueteni.* Boise, Ida.: Mountain States Press, 1955.

Bancroft, Hubert Howe. *The Native Races.* San Francisco: The History Company, 1886.

Banelier, Adolf Frances Alphonse. *The Islands of Titicaca and Koati Illustrated.* New York: The Hispanic Society of America, 1910.

Barbeau, Marius. *Haida Myths: Illustrated in Argillite Carvings.* Bulletin no. 127, Anthropological Series no. 32, National Museum of Canada, Ottawa, 1953.

Barnes, John. "Ancient Purity and Polyglot Programs." *Sunday Times* (London), November 4, 1984, 13.

Bauval, Robert, and Adrian Gilbert. *The Orion Mystery: Are the Pyramids a Map of Heaven?* London: Atrium Press, 1994.

Bibby, George. *Looking for Dilmun.* New York: Knopf, 1969.

Binford, L. R. *New Perspectives in Archaeology.* Chicago: Aldine, 1968.

———. "Post Pleistocene Adaptations," in *New Perspectives in Archaeology.* Chicago: Aldine, 1968, 313–41.

Bingham, Hiram. *Lost City of the Incas.* New York: Sloan and Pearce, 1948.

———. "The Story of Machu Picchu." *National Geographic,* February 1915. 387–573.

Blacker, Carmen, and Michael Loewe, eds. *Ancient Cosmologies.* London: George Allen & Unwin, 1975.

Boas, Franz. *Kutenai Tales.* Smithsonian Institution: Bureau of American Ethnology, Bulletin 59. Washington, D.C.: U.S. Government Printing Office, 1918.

Boserup, E. *The Conditions of Agricultural Growth.* Chicago: Aldine, 1965.

Bourne, Edward Gaylord. *Spain in America.* New York: Harper & Brothers, 1904.

Brecher, Kenneth, and Michael Feirtag, eds. *Astronomy of the Ancients.* Cambridge, Mass.: The MIT Press, 1979.

Brinchurst, Robert. "Poem of the Elders." *A Story as Sharp as a Knife: The Classical Haida Mythtellers and their World.* Vancouver: Douglas & McIntyre, 1999.

British Columbia Department of Education. *Our People.* Vol. 8, *Kootney.* Victoria, B.C.: Department of Education, Division of Curriculum, series 1952–62, 1952.

Brundage, Burr Cartwright. *The Fifth Sun: Aztec Gods, Aztec World.* Austin, Tex.: University of Texas Press, 1979.

Bryson, George. "DNA Tracks Ancient Alaskan's Descendants." *Anchorage Daily News,* December 28, 2008.

Bunbury, E. H. *A History of Ancient Geography.* New York: Century Co., 1932.

Burland, C. A. *Montezuma: Lord of the Aztecs.* New York: G. P. Putnam's & Sons, 1973.

Burroughs, Captain Lorenzo W. "Letter to Charles Hapgood, August 14,

1961." In Charles H. Hapgood, *Maps of the Ancient Sea Kings: Evidence of Advanced Civilization in the Ice Age*. Philadelphia, Pa.: Chilton, 1966.

Cameron, Ian. *Lodestone and Evening Star: The Epic Voyages of Discovery 1493–1896 A.D.* New York: E. P. Dutton & Co., 1966.

Campbell, Joseph. *The Hero with a Thousand Faces*. Princeton, N.J.: Princeton University Press, 1968.

Canby, Thomas Y. "The Anasazi." *National Geographic,* November 1982, 580–81.

de Candolle, Alphonse. *Origin of Cultivated Plants*. New York: Hafner Publishing Co., 1886.

Carter, George F. "A Hypothesis Suggesting a Single Origin of Agriculture." In *The Origins of Agriculture* by Charles A. Reed. The Hague, the Netherlands: Mouton, 1977.

del Castillo, Bernal Diaz. *The Discovery and Conquest of Mexico 1517–1521.* Translated by Irving A. Leonard. New York: Farrar, Strauss and Co., 1956.

Childe, V. G. *Man Makes Himself.* New York: Mentor, 1951.

Clark, Ella E. *Indian Tales of the Pacific Northwest*. Berkeley and Los Angeles, Calif.: University of California Press, 1953.

Cohen, Mark N. *The Food Crisis in Prehistory: Overpopulation and the Origins of Agriculture*. New Haven, Conn., and London: Yale University Press, 1977.

Collins, Andrew. "Göbekli Tepe—Eden, Home of the Watchers?" *New Dawn,* special issue 8, Summer 2009.

Collins, Maurice. *Cortes and Montezuma*. London: Faber & Faber, 1954.

Concas, Captain V. M. "Report." In *World's Columbian Exposition: Report of the Committee on Awards, Special Reports upon Special Subjects or Groups*. Washington, D.C.: U.S. Government Printing Office, 1901.

Conor, S. J. Reilly. "Father Athanasius Kircher, S. J., Master of an Hundred Arts." *Studies: An Irish Quarterly Review* 44 (1955): 457–68.

Croll, James. *Climate and Time in Their Geological Relations; a Theory of Secular Changes of the Earth's Climate*. London: Daldy, Tsbister & Company, 1893.

Cuvier, Georges. "Revolutions and Catastrophes in the History of the Earth." In *A Source Book in Geology,* edited by Kirtley Mather. Cambridge, Mass.: Harvard University Press, 1939.

Davies, Gordon L. *The Earth in Decay: A History of British Geomorphology 1578–1878*. London: Macdonald Technical & Scientific, 1969.

Davis, Elizabeth Gould. *The First Sex*. Baltimore, Md.: Penguin Books, 1971.

De Camp, Lyon Sprague. *Lost Continents: The Atlantis Theme in History, Science, and Literature.* New York: Dover Publications, Inc., 1970.

de Leon, Pedro de Cieza. *The Incas of Pedro de Cieza de Leon.* Translated by Harriet de Onis. Norman, Okla.: University of Oklahoma Press, 1959.

Denham, Tim. "Envisaging Early Agriculture in the Highlands of New Guinea." In *Archaeology of Oceania: Australia and the Pacific Islands,* by Ian Lilley. Hoboken, N. J.: Wiley-Blackwell, 2006.

———. "Food for Thought," *Nature Australia* 28, no. 4 (2005).

Dictionary of Indian Tribes of the Americas. Newport Beach, Calif.: American Indian Publishers, 1980.

Dillehay, Tom D. *Monte Verde: A Late Pleistocene Settlement in Chile.* Washington, D.C., and London: Smithsonian Institution Press, 1989.

Dillehay, Tom D., Jack Rossen, Thomas C. Andres, and David E. Williams. "Preceramic Adoption of Peanut, Squash, and Cotton in Northern Peru." *Science* 316 (June 2007): 1890–93.

Dixon, Roland. "Achomawial Atsugewi Tales." *Journal of American Folk-Lore* 21 (1908).

———. "Ahasta Myths." *Journal of American Folk-Lore* 23 (1910).

Dockstader, Fredrick. "Pima." In *Dictionary of Indian Tribes of the Americas.* Newport Beach, Calif.: American Indian Publishers, 1980.

Donnelly, Ignatius. *Atlantis: the Antediluvian World.* New York: Harper, 1882.

Eddy, John A. "Historical and Arboreal Evidence for a Changing Sun." In *The New Solar Physics,* edited by John A. Eddy, 11–34. Boulder, Colo.: Westview, 1978.

Eddy, John A., ed. *The New Solar Physics.* Boulder, Colo.: Westview, 1978.

Einstein, Albert. "Letter to Charles H. Hapgood, 8 May, 1953." In *The Path of the Pole,* by Charles H. Hapgood. Philadelphia: Chilton Book Company, 1970.

———. "Report on Hapgood to the John Simon Guggenheim Memorial Foundation, 18 November 1954."

Encyclopedia Americana: International Edition. Danby, Conn.: Grolier Incorporated, 1986.

Epigraphic Society Occasional Papers, vol. 24 (2006).

Ernst-Martin, Ernst, Lemmel Feldkeller, and Anthony S. Russell. "Ankylosing Spondylitis in the Pharaohs of Ancient Egypt." *Rheumatology International* 23 (2003).

Evans, James. "Electronic Publications and the Narrowing of Science and Scholarship." *Science* 321 (July 18, 2008): 395–99.

Farmer, Penelope. *Beginnings: Creation Myths of the World*. London: Chatto & Windus, 1978.

Fedje, Daryl W., and Heiner Josenhans. "Drowned Forest and Archaeology on the Continental Shelf of British Columbia, Canada." *Geology* 28, no. 2 (2000).

Flem-Ath, Rand. "A Global Model for the Origins of Agriculture." *The Anthropological Journal of Canada* 19, no. 4 (1981): 2–7.

———. "The Piri Reis Map: 500 or 5000 years old?" *Duat,* 2002.

Flem-Ath, Rand, and Rose Flem-Ath. "A Knife that Shut Up." *Haida Laas,* 2009, 9–16. See: www.haidanation.ca/Pages/Haida_Laas/PDF/Journals/Smallpox_Journal.72.pdf (accessed November 9, 2011).

———. *When the Sky Fell: In Search of Atlantis*. Toronto: Stoddard/London: Weidenfeld & Nicolson/New York: St. Martins, 1995.

Flem-Ath, Rand, and Colin Wilson. *The Atlantis Blueprint*. London: Little Brown & Company, 2000; reprinted New York: Delacorte Press, 2001.

Freedman, Jared. "Solar Typhoons and Massive Earth Crust Displacement, www.solartyphoon.com/intro.htm (accessed January 26, 2011).

Freud, Sigmund. "Psychopathology of Everyday Life." In *The Standard Edition of the Complete Psychological Works of Sigmund Freud*. London: Hogarth Press, 1960.

Freund, Philip. *Myths of Creation*. New York: Washington Square Press, 1965.

Gorman, Chester. "A Priori Models and Thai Prehistory." In *The Origins of Agriculture,* edited by Charles A. Reed, 321–56. The Hague, the Neatherlands: Mouton, 1977.

Gould, Stephen Jay. "Is Uniformitarianism Necessary?" *American Journal of Science* 263, no. 3 (March 1965): 223–28.

Graves, Robert. "Introduction." *New Larouse Encyclopaedia of Mythology*. London: Prometheus Press, 1968.

Gray, Louis Herbert, George Foot Moore, and John Arnott MacCulloch. *The Mythology of All Races*. Boston: Marshall Jones Company, in 13 volumes, 1916–32.

Greenberg, Joseph, Christy Turner, and Stephen Zegura. "The Settlement of the Americas: A Comparison of the Linguistic, Dental, and Genetic Evidence." *Current Anthropology* 27, no. 5 (1986).

Gribbon, John. *The Strangest Star: A Scientific Account of the Life and Death of the Sun.* Glasgow: Fontana, 1980.

Gupta, Anil K. "Origin of Agriculture and Domestication of Plants and Animals Linked to Early Holocene Climate Amelioration." *Current Science* 87, no. 1 (2004).

Guthrie, Dale R. "Mammals of the Mammoth Steppe as Paleo-environmental Indicators." In *The Paleoecology of Beringia,* edited by David M. Hopkins, John V. Matthews Jr., Charles E. Schweger, and Steven B. Young. New York: Academic Press, 1982.

Hapgood, Charles. Letter to Arch C. Gerlach, the chief of the Map Division at Library of Congress, October 30, 1960. Hapgood's Archives, box 16. Yale University.

———. Personal letter to Rose and Rand Flem-Ath, August 3, 1977.

Hapgood, Charles H. *The Earth's Shifting Crust: A Key to Some Basic Problems of Earth Science.* New York: Pantheon Books, 1958.

———. *Maps of the Ancient Sea Kings: Evidence of Advanced Civilization in the Ice Age.* Philadelphia: Chilton, 1966.

———. Memorandum to President Eisenhower, August 3, 1960. President Eisenhower's Archives, Abilene, Kan.

———. *The Path of the Pole.* Philadelphia: Chilton Press, 1970.

Harlan, Jack R. "Agricultural Origins: Centers and Noncenters." *Science* 174 (1971): 468–74.

Harris, David R. "Alternative Pathways toward Agriculture." In *The Origins of Agriculture,* By Charles A. Reed. The Hague, the Neatherlands: Mouton, 1977.

Hays, J. D., J. Imbrie, and N. J. Schackleton. "Variations in the Earth's Orbit: Pacemaker of the Ice Ages." *Science* 194 (1976): 1121–32.

Hester, James J. "The Agency of Man in Animal Extinctions." In. *Pleistocene Extinctions: The Search for a Cause,* edited by P. S. Martin and H. E. Wright. New Haven, Conn.: Yale University Press, 1967.

Heyerdahl, Thor. *American Indians in the Pacific: The Theory Behind the Kon-Tiki Expedition.* London: George Allen and Unwin, 1952.

Holmberg, Uno. "Finno-Ugric, Siberian." In Gray, Moore, and MacCulloch. *The Mythology of All Races.* Edited by George Foot Moore, Louis Herbert Gray, and John Arnott MacCulloch.Boston: Marshall Jones Company, vol. IV, 1927.

————. "Finno-Ugric, Siberian." In *The Mythology of All Races, Volume IV*. Edited by George Foot Moore, Louis Herbert Gray, and John Arnott MacCulloch. New York: Cooper Square Publishers, Inc., 1964.

Hopkins, David M., John V. Matthews Jr., Charles E. Schweger, and Steven B. Young, eds. *The Paleoecology of Beringia*. New York: Academic Press, 1982.

Horgan, John. "Profile: Reluctant Revolutionary: Thomas S. Kuhn Unleashed 'Paradigm' on the World." *Scientific American* 264 (May 1991).

Huddlesten, Lee Eldridge. *Origins of the American Indians: European Concepts 1492–1729*. Austin, Tex.: University of Texas Press, 1967.

Hutton, James. "Theory of the Earth" in *Transactions of the Royal Society of Edinburgh*. Edinburgh, 1788.

Hutton, James. *Theory of the Earth with Proofs and Illustrations*. London: William Creech, Edinburgh and Cadell, Junior and Davies, 1795.

Illustrated London News. "A Columbus Controversy: America—And Two Atlantic Charts." February 27, 1932.

Imbrie, John, and Katherine Palmer Imbrie. *Ice Ages: Solving the Mystery*. Short Hills, N.J.: Enslow Publishers, 1979.

Inan, Professor Afet. *The Life and Works of the Turkish Admiral: Piri Reis*. Translated by Dr. Leman Yolac. Ankara, Turkey: Tuk Tarih Kurumu Basimei, 1954.

Jung, Carl G., and C. Kerenyi. *Introduction to a Science of Mythology*. London: Routledge & Kegan Paul Ltd., 1970.

Kircher, Athanasius. *Mundus Subterraneus*. 2nd ed. Amsterdam, 1678.

Kirk, G. S., and J. E. Raven. *The Presocratic Philosophers*. Cambridge: Cambridge University Press, 1957.

Kish, George, ed. *A Source Book in Geography*. Cambridge, Mass.: Harvard University Press, 1978.

Kuhn, Thomas S. *The Essential Tension*. Chicago: University of Chicago Press, 1977.

————. *The Structure of Scientific Revolutions*. 2nd ed. Chicago: University of Chicago Press, 1970.

La Berre, Weston. "The Aymara Indians of Lake Titicaca Plateau, Bolivia." *American Anthropologist* 50 (1948): 9.

Laertius, Diogenes. *Lives of Eminent Philosophers*. Translated by R. D. Hicks. Cambridge, Mass.: Harvard University Press, 1925.

Langway, C. C., Jr., J. R. Hansen, and B. Lyle. "Drilling through the Ice Cap:

Probing Climate for a Thousand Centuries." In *Frozen Future: A Prophetic Report from Antarctica,* by Richard S. Lewis and Philip M. Smith. New York: Quadrangle, 1973.

Lévi-Strauss, Claude. *Structural Anthropology.* Translated by Claire Jacobson and Brooke Grundfest Schoepf. New York: Basic Books/London: Allan Lane, 1963.

Lewis, Richard. *A Continent for Science.* New York: Viking Press, 1965.

Lewis, Richard S., and Philip M. Smith. *Frozen Future: A Prophetic Report from Antarctica.* New York: Quadrangle, 1973.

Lilley, Ian, ed. *Archaeology of Oceania: Australia and the Pacific Islands.* Hoboken, N. J.: Wiley-Blackwell, 2006.

Loeb, E. M. "The Religious Organizations of North Central California and Tierra Del Fuego." *American Anthropologist* 33, no. 4 (1931).

Londo, Jason P., Yu-Chung Chiang, Kuo-Hsiang Hung, Tzen-Yuh Chiang, and Barbara A. Schaal. "Phylogeography of Asian Wild Rice, *Oryza rufipogon,* Reveals Multiple Independent Domestications of Cultivated Rice, *Oryza sativa.*" *Proceedings of the National Academy of Sciences* 103, no. 25 (May 1, 2006): 9578–83.

Lowie, Robert H. *Anthropological Papers of the American Museum of Natural History.* New York: American Museum Press, 1924.

Luce, I. V. *The End of Atlantis: New Light on an Old Legend.* London: Thames and Hudson, 1969.

Lurie, Edward. *Louis Agassiz: A Life in Science.* Chicago: University of Chicago Press, 1960.

Lyell, Charles. *Principles of Geology: Being an Attempt to Explain the Former Changes of the Earth's Surface, by Reference to Causes Now in Operation.* 3 vols. London: John Murray, 1830 and 1832.

MacCulloch, John A., and Jan Machal. "Celtic, Slavic." In *The Mythology of All Races,* edited by Louis Herbert Gray, George Foot Moore, and John Arnott MacCulloch. Boston: Marshall Jones Company, 1918.

MacNeish, Richard S. "The Beginnings of Agriculture in Central Peru." In *The Origins of Agriculture,* edited by Charles A. Reed. The Hague, the Neatherlands: Mouton, 1977.

———. *Early Man in America.* San Francisco: W. H. Freeman, 1973.

Martin, Paul S. "Prehistoric Overkill: The Global Model." In *Quarternary Extinctions: A Prehistoric Revolution,* edited by Paul S. Martin and Richard G. Klein. Tucson, Ariz.: University of Arizona Press, 1984.

Martin, Paul S., and Richard G. Klein. *Quarternary Extinctions: A Prehistoric Revolution.* Tucson, Ariz.: University of Arizona Press, 1984.

Martin, P. S., and H. E. Wright, eds. *Pleistocene Extinctions: The Search for a Cause.* New Haven, Conn.: Yale University Press, 1967.

Mather, Kirtley, ed. *A Source Book in Geology.* Cambridge, Mass.: Harvard University Press, 1939.

Matsuoka, Yoshihiro, Yves Vigouroux, Major M. Goodman, G. Jesus Sanchez, Edward Buckler, and John Doebley. "A Single Domestication for Maize Shown by Multilocus Microsatellite Genotypying." *Proceedings of the National Academy of Sciences* 99, no. 9 (2002): 6080–84.

Miotti, L., and M. C. Salemme. "When Patagonia Was Colonized: People Mobility at High Latitudes during Pleistocene/Holocene Transition." *Quaternary International* 109–10 (2003).

The Mitchell Beazley Atlas of the Oceans. London: Mitchell Beazley, 1977.

Mooney, James. *Myths of the Cherokee.* American Bureau of Ethnology Annual Report, Part I. Washington, D.C.: U.S. Government Printing Press, 1900.

Moore, Andrew M. T. "A Pre-Neolithic Farmer's Village on the Euphrates." *Scientific America* 241 (August 1979): 62–70.

Moore, Ruth. *The Earth We Live On: The Story of Geological Discovery.* 2nd revised ed. New York: Knopf, 1971.

Morison, Samuel Eliot. *Admiral of the Ocean Sea.* Boston: Little Brown & Co, 1942.

Muke, John, Tim Denham, and Vagi Genorupa. "Nominating and Managing a World Heritage Site in the Highlands of Papua New Guinea." *World Archaeology* 3, no. 3 (September 2007): 324–38.

Müller, W. Max. "Egyptian." In *The Mythology of All Races.* Edited by Louis Herbert Gray, George Foot Moore, and John Arnott MacCulloch. Boston: Marshall Jones Company, vol. XII, 1918.

Mylrea, Paul. "Computer Helps Preserve Ancient Aymara Language." Reprint, *Nanaimo Free Press,* November 17, 1991, 8.

Nelson, Ray. "Evidence of the Earliest Americans," *Popular Science* (March 1994).

New Larouse Encyclopaedia of Mythology. London: Prometheus Press, 1968.

Olcott, William Tyler. *Sun Lore of All Ages.* New York: The Knickerbocker Press/London: G. P. Putnam's Sons, 1914.

Olymeyer, Lt. Col. Harold Z. Letter to Charles Hapgood, July 6, 1960. Part of the package sent to President Dwight D. Eisenhower.

Over, Raymond Van, ed. *Sun Songs: Creation Myths from around the World.* New York: A Mentor Book of the New American Library, 1980.

Ovid. *Metamorphoses.* Translated by Mary M. Innes. Middlesex, England: Penguin Books, 1955.

Palmer, Robin. *Dictionary of Mythical Places.* Reprint of the 1920 original. New York: Henry Z. Walck, Inc., 1975.

Perego, U. A., A. Achilli, N. Angerhofer, et al. "Distinctive Paleo-Indian Migration Routes from Beringia Marked by Two Rare mtDNA Haplogroups." *Current Biology* 19, no. 1 (2009): 1–8.

Pickersgill, Barbara, and Charles B. Heiser, Jr. "Origins and Distribution of Plants Domesticated in the New World Tropics." In *The Origins of Agriculture,* edited by Charles A. Reed. The Hague, the Neatherlands: Mouton, 1977.

Pitulko, V. V., P. A. Nikolsky, E. Y. Girya, et al. "The Yana RHS Site: Humans in the Arctic before the Last Glacial Maximum." *Science* 303, no. 5654 (2004): 52–56.

Plato. *Critias, Cletophon, Menexenus, Epistles.* Translated by R. G. Bury. Cambridge, Mass.: Harvard University Press, 1973.

———. *Laws.* Translated by R. G. Bury. Cambridge: Harvard University Press/ London: William Heinemann, Ltd., 1926.

———. *Timaeus and Critias.* Translated by Desmond Lee. Middlesex, England: Penguin Books, 1965.

———. *The Timaeus of Plato.* Translated by R. D. Archer-Hind. London: Macmillan & Co., 1888.

Plumley, J. M. "The Cosmology of Ancient Egypt." In *Ancient Cosmologies,* edited by Carmen Blacker and Michael Loewe. London: George Allen & Unwin, 1975.

Plutarch. *The Lives of the Noble Grecians and Romans.* Retitled *The Rise and Fall of Athens.* Translated by Ian Scott-Kilvert. Middlesex, England: Penguin Books, 1960.

Posnansky, Arthur. *Tihuanacu, the Cradle of American Man.* Translated by James F. Shearer. New York: J. J. Augustin, 1945.

Powell, Major J. W. "Mythological Philosophy." *Popular Science Monthly* 15 (1880): 795–808.

Prescott, W. H. *History of the Conquest of Mexico and History of the Conquest of Peru.* Reprint of the 1843 original. New York: Modern Library, 1936.

Proclus. *The Commentaries of Proclus on the Timaeus of Plato, in Five Books: Containing a Treasure of Pythagoric and Platonic Physiology.* Translated by Thomas Taylor. London: Thomas Taylor, 1820.

Reed, Charles A. *The Origins of Agriculture.* The Hague, the Neatherlands: Mouton, 1977.

Reiche, Harald A. T. "The Language of Archaic Astronomy: A Clue to the Atlantis Myth?" In *Astronomy of the Ancients,* edited by Kenneth Brecher and Michael Feirtag Cambridge, Mass.: The MIT Press, 1979.

Riley, Carroll L., J. Charles Kelly, Campbell W. Pennington, and Robert L. Rands, eds. *Man across the Sea: Problems of Pre-Columbian Contacts.* Austin, Tex.: University of Texas, 1971.

Roberts, Paul William. "Riddle of the Sphinx." *Saturday Night,* March 1993.

Rubin, M. J. "Antarctic Meteorology." In *Frozen Future: A Prophetic Report from Antarctica,* edited by Richard S. Lewis and Philip M. Smith. New York: Quadrangle, 1973.

Ruhlen, Merritt. "Voices from the Past." *Natural History,* March, 1987.

Rumney, G. R. *Climatology and the World's Climate.* New York: Macmillan, 1968.

Sanceau, Elaine. *Henry the Navigator.* New York: Archon Books, 1969.

Scham, Sandra. "The World's First Temple." *Archaeology* 61, no. 6 (November/December 2008).

Scheinsohn, Vivian. "Hunter-Gatherer Archaeology in South America." *Annual Review of Anthropology* 32 (2003).

Schoch, Robert. "Searching for the Dawn and Demise of Ancient Civilisation." *New Dawn,* special issue 8, Summer 2009.

Shirer, William L. *Gandhi: A Memoir.* New York: Washington Square Press, 1979.

Silverberg, Robert. *Mammoths, Mastodons and Man.* New York: McGraw-Hill Book Co., 1970.

Sobel, David. *Longitude: The True Story of the Genius Who Solved the Greatest Scientific Problem of His Time.* London: Penguin, 1996.

Sofaer, Anna. *The Sun Dagger.* Produced by the Solstice Project, Washington D.C. Directed by Albert Ihde, written by Anna Sofaer, and narrated by Robert Redford. Bullfrog Films, 1982.

Solheim, W. G. "An Earlier Agricultural Revolution." *Scientific American,* April 1972, 34–41.

Sorenson, John L. "The Significance of an Apparent Relationship between the Ancient Near East and Mesoamerica." In *Man Across the Sea: Problems of Pre-Columbian Contacts,* edited by Carroll L. Riley, J. Charles Kelly, Campbell W. Pennington, and Robert L. Rands. Austin, Tex.: University of Texas, 1971.

Strabo. *The Geography of Strabo.* Translated by H. C. Hamilton. London: G. Bell and Sons Limited, 1912.

Strahler, A. N. *Introduction to Physical Geography.* New York and London: John Wiley, 1973.

Stuart, Anthony. "Who (or What) Killed the Giant Armadillo?" *New Scientist,* July 17, 1986, 29–32.

Stykes, Bryan. *The Seven Daughters of Eve.* New York: W. W. Norton and Company, 2002.

Sutherland, Donald, and Michael J. C. Walker. "A Late Devonsian Ice-Free Area and Possible Interglacial Site on the Isle of Lewis, Scotland." *Nature* 309 (1984): 701–3.

Tilak, Bal Gangadhar. *The Arctic Home in the Vedas: Being Also a New Key to the Interpretation of Many Vedic Texts and Legends.* Poona City, India: Kesari, 1903.

Time-Life Books, ed.. *Mystic Places.* Alexandria, Va.: Time-Life Books, 1987.

Turney-High, Harry Robert. *Ethnology of the Kutenai.* Mildwood, New York: Draus Reprint Co., 1974.

Tylor, Edward B. *Primitive Culture: Researches into the Development of Mythology, Philosophy, Religion, Art and Custom.* London: John Murray, 1871.

U.S. Naval Support Force. *Introduction to Antarctica.* 4th ed. Washington, D.C.: U.S. Government Printing Office, 1969.

Vasiliev, A. A. *History of the Byzantine Empire: 324–1453.* Madison, Wis.: University of Wisconsin Press, 1952.

Vavilov, Nikolai Ivanovich. "The Origin, Variation, Immunity, and Breeding of Cultivated Plants." In "Selected Writing of Vavilov." Translated by K. Starr Chester. *Chronica Botanica* 13, no. 1–6 (1951).

Vereschain, N. K., and G. F. Baryshnikov. "Quaternary Mammal Extinctions in Northern Eurasia." In *Quaternary Extinctions: A Prehistoric Revolution,* edited by Paul S. Martin and Richard G. Klein. Tucson, Ariz.: University of Arizona Press, 1984.

Vico, Giambattista. *The New Science of Giambattista Vico.* Translated by Thomas Goddard Bergin and Max Harold Fisch. Ithaca, N.Y.: Cornell University Press, 1948.

Wallace, Alfred Russel. *The World of Life: A Manifestation of Creative Power, Directive Mind and Ultimate Purpose.* New York: Moffat, Yard, 1911.

Warmington, E. H. *Greek Geography.* London: J. M. Dent & Sons, Ltd., 1934.

Warren, William Fairfield. *Paradise Found: The Cradle of the Human Race at the North Pole: A Study of the Prehistoric World.* Boston: Houghton, Mifflin & Co., 1885.

Watters, Michael R., and Thomas W. Stafford Jr. "Redefining the Age of Clovis: Implications for the Peopling of the Americas." *Science* 315 (February 23, 2007).

Wegener, Alfred. *Die Entstehung der Kontinente und Ozeane* [The Origin of Continents and Oceans]. Braunschweig, Germany: Friedr., Vieweg & Sohn Akt.-Ges, 1915.

Wendorf, Fred. "Late Palaeolithic Sites in Egyptian Nubia." In *The Prehistory of Nubia,* edited by Fred Wendorf. Dallas. Tex.: Southern Methodist University Press, 1966.

Wendorf, Fred, ed. *The Prehistory of Nubia.* Dallas, Tex.: Southern Methodist University Press, 1966.

West, John Anthony. *Mystery of the Sphinx.* NBC television special hosted by Charlton Heston. Magic Eye/North Tower Films Production, 1993.

———. *Serpent in the Sky: The High Wisdom of Ancient Egypt.* Wheaton, Ill.: First Quest Edition, 1993.

Whitaker, Joseph. *Almanack for the Year of Our Lord 1992.* London: J. Whitaker and Sons, Ltd., 1992.

White, John. *Poleshift.* New York: Doubleday, 1980.

Woelfli, W., and W. Baltensperger. "Arctic East Siberia Had a Lower Latitude in the Pleistocene." Cornell University Library. http://arxiv.org/PS_cache/physics/pdf/0604/0604029v2.pdf (accessed March 30, 2006).

———. "On the Change of Latitude of Arctic East Siberia at the End of the Pleistocene." Cornell University Library. http://arxiv.org/abs/0704.2489.

———. "A Possible Explanation for Earth's Climatic Changes in the Past Few Million Years." Cornell University Library. http://arxiv.org/PS_cache/physics/pdf/9907/9907033v3.pdf.

Yule, Sir Henry. *The Book of Ser Marco Polo.* London: John Murray, 1870.

Yusuf, Akcura. "Turkish Interest in America in 1513: Piri Reis's Chart of the Atlantic." *The Illustrated London News*, July 23, 1932.

Zarte, Augustin de. *The Discovery and Conquest of Peru.* Middlesex, England: Penguin Books, 1968.

Zedar, Melinda A. "Domestication and Early Agriculture in the Mediterranean Basin: Origins, Diffusion, and Impact." *Proceedings of the National Academy of Sciences* 105, no. 33 (2008): 11597–604.

INDEX

Numbers in *italics* indicate illustrations.

239

BOOKS OF RELATED INTEREST

Atlantis in the Amazon
Lost Technologies and the Secrets of the Crespi Treasure
by Richard Wingate

Atlantis and 2012
The Science of the Lost Civilization and the Prophecies of the Maya
by Frank Joseph

Survivors of Atlantis
Their Impact on World Culture
by Frank Joseph

Atlantis and the Cycles of Time
Prophecies, Traditions, and Occult Revelations
by Joscelyn Godwin

Awakening the Planetary Mind
Beyond the Trauma of the Past to a New Era of Creativity
by Barbara Hand Clow

Lost Knowledge of the Ancients
A Graham Hancock Reader
Edited by Glenn Kreisberg

Forbidden History
Prehistoric Technologies, Extraterrestrial Intervention,
and the Suppressed Origins of Civilization
Edited by J. Douglas Kenyon

Suppressed History of America
The Murder of Meriwether Lewis and the Mysterious Discoveries
of the Lewis and Clark Expedition
by Paul Schrag and Xaviant Haze

INNER TRADITIONS • BEAR & COMPANY
P.O. Box 388
Rochester, VT 05767
1-800-246-8648
www.InnerTraditions.com

Or contact your local bookseller